METROPOLITAN MUSEUM OF ART

ATTIC RED-FIGURED VASES

A SURVEY

Revised Edition

BY GISELA M. A. RICHTER

NEW HAVEN

YALE UNIVERSITY PRESS

1958

TO

J. D. BEAZLEY

PREFACE TO THE FIRST EDITION

SINCE the publication in 1936 of the two-volume catalogue, *Red-figured Athenian Vases in the Metropolitan Museum of Art,* I have repeatedly been asked to republish part of the text in a smaller, less expensive volume. At last I have been able to carry out the suggestion. In preparing the book here offered I have freely borrowed from my catalogue, but I have also added much that is new. Our understanding of Attic vases has been enlarged and deepened during the last generation by increased knowledge of the painters who decorated them. To present a general survey of Athenian red-figure it was therefore necessary to give descriptions of at least the most prominent of these painters. As many of them were not represented in the Metropolitan Museum and had not been discussed in the catalogue, accounts of them had to be supplied. Naturally it was impossible in a short survey to discuss every known artist. Of the more than five hundred painters who have by now been recognized I have mentioned fewer than half—but enough, I hope, to give an idea of the manifold activity in the Attic potteries. In the descriptions of actual examples I have put the primary stress on the vases in New York, so that the book may also serve as a guide to that collection. It seemed a gain to view the New York vases as a part of a larger context. Though my chief theme is red-figure I have occasionally included short discussions of contemporary black-figured and white-ground vases, for the three techniques sometimes went on concurrently in the same potteries.

It would have been pleasant to give a wealth of illustrations. Descriptions of scenes and analyses of style without a picture ready to hand are tedious. As one of the primary motives, however, in writing the new book was to produce a low-priced volume, and as illustrations of course add to the cost of production, I have had to confine myself to relatively few pictures. I have in many cases chosen details instead of whole compositions, for large-scale single figures often bring out the style of a painter better than entire scenes on a small scale. In the selection preference has been given to examples in the Metropolitan

Museum. The majority of the pictures on the plates are reproduced from photographs; the line drawings in the text are by
Lindsley F. Hall, either drawn from the originals or redrawn
from other publications.

The notes give references to illustrations of all the published
vases mentioned, when possible in easily accessible books. I
have also in every case given a reference to Professor Beazley's
latest book, *Attic Red-figure Vase-painters,* 1942, where lists of
the works of each painter as well as full bibliographies of the
illustrations will be found. I have adopted throughout the
attributions given in that epoch-making book.

Vase inscriptions are transliterated into the Ionic alphabet
except when it was desirable for obvious reasons to show the
exact spelling of the original.

My text has been read by Miss Christine Alexander and
Miss Marjorie J. Milne, and I owe to them valuable suggestions
and corrections. Many of the notes on the inscriptions and
kalos names are by Miss Milne (often quoted with her signature). The section on Technique has been revised and greatly
improved by Miss Maude Robinson. Mr. A. Fieldman has helped
me with the preparation of the Index. I want also to thank
Professor H. R. W. Smith, whose encouragement induced me
finally to undertake the writing of this Survey. My debt to my
friend J. D. Beazley is greater than I can express in words. His
writings have revolutionized the study of Athenian vase painting and are an inspiration to us all. With his usual generosity
he has read my manuscript and has sent me many important
comments. I gratefully dedicate this book to him. Finally I
want to thank the Metropolitan Museum and the Yale University Press for making this publication possible.

PREFACE TO THE REVISED EDITION

In this new edition I have had to confine myself to the fewest
possible corrections. I have been able, however, to add short
descriptions of some new accessions to the New York collection
and to make a number of corrections, many of which I owe to
Sir John Beazley and Mr. D. von Bothmer. The numbers I give
for vases attributed to specific painters are no longer quite correct (see forthcoming 2nd ed. of Beazley's *ARV*). The part of the
Introduction that deals with the black glaze (pp. 27–30) has
had to be rewritten in view of recent discoveries.

ABBREVIATIONS AND BIBLIOGRAPHY

The list of abbreviations will serve as a general bibliography. The bibliographies on special subjects are given in notes to the relevant sections of the Introduction. For a more extended list cf. Beazley, *Attic Red-Figure Vase-Painters*, Oxford, 1942.

PERIODICALS, LEXICONS, CORPUSES, ETC.

AA—Archäologischer Anzeiger. Beiblatt zum Jahrbuch des deutschen archäologischen Instituts. Berlin, from 1889.

AJA—American Journal of Archaeology. Baltimore, Princeton, Norwood, Concord, from 1885.

AM—Mitteilungen des deutschen archäologischen Instituts, Athenische Abteilung. Athens, from 1876.

Annali—Annali dell' Instituto di Corrispondenza Archeologica. Rome, 1829–85.

Arch. Delt.—Archaiologikon Deltion. Athens, from 1915.

Arch. Ztg.—Archäologische Zeitung. Berlin, 1843–85.

Atti Soc. Magna Grecia—Atti e memorie della Società Magna Grecia. Rome, 1928–32.

BCH—Bulletin de correspondance hellénique. Paris, from 1877.

Br. Br.—Brunn and Bruckmann's Denkmäler griechischer und römischer Sculptur. Munich, from 1888.

BSA—Annual of the British School at Athens. London, from 1894.

BSR—Papers of the British School at Rome. London, from 1902.

*CIG—*Boeckh, August, *Corpus inscriptionum graecarum.* Berlin, 1828–1877.

CV—Corpus vasorum antiquorum. Paris and elsewhere, from 1922.

Daremberg-Saglio—Daremberg, C., Saglio, E., and others, *Dictionnaire des antiquités grecques et romaines.* Paris, 1877–1919.

Eph.—Ephemeris archaiologike. Athens, from 1883.

IG—Inscriptiones graecae. Berlin, from 1873; *ed. minor,* from 1913.

Jb.—Jahrbuch des deutschen archäologischen Instituts. Berlin, from 1886.

JHS—Journal of Hellenic Studies. London, from 1880.

Mél. d'arch.—Mélanges d'archéologie et d'histoire publiés par l'École française de Rome. Rome, from 1881.

MM Bulletin—Bulletin of the Metropolitan Museum of Art. New York, from 1905.

MM Studies—The Metropolitan Museum Studies. New York, 1928–36.

Mon. dell' Inst.—Monumenti inediti pubblicati dall'Instituto di Corrispondenza Archeologica. Rome and Paris, 1829–91.

Mon. Linc.—Monumenti antichi pubblicati per cura della Reale Accademia dei Lincei. Milan, from 1889.

Mon. Piot—Monuments et mémoires publiés par l'Académie des Inscriptions et Belles-Lettres (Fondation Eugène Piot). Paris, from 1894.

Museum Journal—The Museum Journal (The University Museum, University of Pennsylvania). Philadelphia, 1910–33.

NS—Notizie degli scavi di antichità, communicate alla Reale Accademia dei Lincei. Rome, from 1876.

Oest. Jh.—Jahreshefte des oesterreichischen archäologischen Institutes in Wien. Vienna, from 1898.

Pauly-Wissowa—*Paulys Real-Encyclopädie der classischen Altertumswissenschaft*, edited by G. Wissowa, W. Kroll and others. Stuttgart, from 1894.

Roscher's Lexikon—Ausführliches Lexikon der griechischen und römischen Mythologie, edited by W. H. Roscher. Leipzig, 1884–1937.

RM—Mitteilungen des deutschen archaeologischen Instituts, Roemische Abteilung. Rome, from 1886.

BOOKS

Albizzati—Albizzati, Carlo. *Vasi antichi dipinti del Vaticano*. Rome, from 1925.

Aurigemma, S¹, S²—Aurigemma, Salvatore. *Il R. Museo di Spina* (ed. 1 and 2). Ferrara, 1935, 1936.

Beazley—Beazley, J. D. *Attic Red-figure Vase-Painters*. Oxford, 1942.

Beazley, *ABS*—Beazley, J. D. *Attic Black-figure: a Sketch*. London, 1928.

Beazley, *ABV*—Beazley, J. D. *Attic Black-figure Vase-Painters*. Oxford, 1956.

Beazley, *Att. V.*—Beazley, J. D. *Attische Vasenmaler des rotfigurigen Stils. Tübingen, 1925.*

Beazley, *AWL*—Beazley, J. D. *Attic White Lekythoi*. London, 1938.

Beazley, *Berl.*—Beazley, J. D. *Der Berliner Maler*. Berlin, 1930.

Beazley, *CF*—Beazley, J. D. *Campana Fragments in Florence*. Oxford, 1933.

Beazley, *Kl.*—Beazley, J. D. *Der Kleophrades-Maler*. Berlin, 1933.

Beazley, *Panm.*—Beazley, J. D. *Der Pan-Maler*. Berlin, 1931.

Beazley, *Potter*—Beazley, J. D. *Potter and Painter in Ancient Athens.* Oxford, 1945.

Beazley, *VA*—Beazley, J. D. *Attic Red-figured Vases in American Museums.* Cambridge (Mass.), 1918.

Beazley, *V. Pol.*—Beazley, J. D. *Greek Vases in Poland.* Oxford, 1928. See also note on Sir John Beazley's publications at the end of this list.

Bechtel, *Personennamen*—Bechtel, Friedrich. *Die historischen Personennamen des Griechischen bis zur Kaiserzeit.* Halle, 1917.

Bieber, *HT*—Bieber, Margarete. *The History of the Greek and Roman Theater.* Princeton, 1939.

Bieber, *Th.*—Bieber, Margarete. *Die Denkmäler zum Theaterwesen im Altertum.* Berlin, 1920.

Buschor, *ALP*—Buschor, Ernst. "Attische Lekythen der Parthenonzeit," from *Münchner Jahrbuch* n. s. II, 1925.

Buschor, *Grab*—Buschor, Ernst. *Grab eines attischen Mädchens.* Munich, 1939.

Buschor, *Gr. V.*—Buschor, Ernst. *Griechische Vasen.* Munich, 1940.

Caskey and Beazley, *AVP*—Caskey, L. D. with the coöperation of Beazley, J. D., *Attic Vase Paintings in the Museum of Fine Arts, Boston.* London, I, 1931; II, 1954.

Diepolder, *P*—Diepolder, Hans. *Der Penthesilea-Maler.* Leipzig, 1936.

Ducati, *Midia*—Ducati, Pericle. "Vasi dipinti nello stile del ceramista Midia." *Memorie della R. Accademia dei Lincei,* 5th series, 14, fascicule ii. Rome, 1909.

Ducati, *Saggio*—Ducati, Pericle. "Saggio di studio sulla ceramica attica figurata del secolo iv av. Cr." *Memorie della R. Accademia dei Lincei,* 5th series, 15, fascicule iii. Rome, 1916.

Ducati, *Storia*—Ducati, Pericle. *Storia della ceramica greca.* Florence, 1922.

Dugas, *Aison*—Dugas, Charles. *Aison et la peinture céramique à Athènes à l'époque de Périclès.* Paris, 1930.

Enc. phot.—*Encyclopédie photographique de l'art: le Musée du Louvre.* Paris, 1937.

Fairbanks, *AWL*—Fairbanks, Arthur. *Athenian White Lekythoi,* vols. I and II. New York, 1907 and 1914.

Fick, *Personennamen*—Fick, August, and Bechtel, Fritz. *Die griechischen Personennamen nach ihrer Bildung erklärt und systematisch geordnet.* 2d ed. Göttingen, 1894.

FR—Furtwängler, Adolf, and Reichhold, Karl, and others.*Griechische Vasenmalerei: Auswahl hervorragender Vasenbilder.* 3 vols. Munich, 1904-32.

Gardiner, *Athl.*—Gardiner, E. Norman. *Athletics of the Ancient World.* Oxford, 1930.

Gerhard, *Trinkschalen*—Gerhard, Friedrich. *Trinkschalen und Gefässe des Königlichen Museums zu Berlin.* Berlin, 1848–50.

Graef and Langlotz, *Akropolis,* I and II—*Die antiken Vasen von der Akropolis zu Athen,* edited by Botho Graef (vol. I) and Botho Graef and Ernst Langlotz (vol. II), with the coöperation of Paul Hartwig, Paul Wolters, and Robert Zahn. Berlin, 1911–14, 1933.

Hahland, *M*—Hahland, Walter. *Vasen um Meidias.* Berlin, 1930.

Hahland, *Studien*—Hahland, Walter. *Studien zur attischen Vasenmalerei um 400 v. Chr.* (Inauguraldissertation, Philipps-Universität). Marburg, 1931.

Hartwig, *Gr. M.*—Hartwig, Paul. *Die griechischen Meisterchalen der Blüthezeit des strengen rothfiguren Stiles.* Stuttgart and Berlin, 1893.

Haspels, *Bf. Lekythoi*—Haspels, C. H. Emilie. *Attic Black-figured Lekythoi.* Paris, 1936.

Hoppin, I and II—Hoppin, Joseph Clark. *A Handbook of Attic Red-figured Vases, signed by or attributed to the various masters of the sixth and fifth century B.C.* 2 vols. Cambridge (Mass.), 1919.

Hoppin, *Bf.*—Hoppin, Joseph Clark. *A Handbook of Greek Black-figured Vases.* Paris, 1924.

Hoppin, *Euth. F.*—Hoppin, Joseph Clark. *Euthymides and His Fellows.* Cambridge (Mass.), 1917.

Klein, *Lieblingsinschriften*—Klein, Wilhelm. *Die griechischen Vasen mit Lieblingsinschriften.* 2d ed. Leipzig, 1898.

Kretschmer, *Vaseninschriften*—Kretschmer, P. *Die griechischen Vaseninschriften, ihrer Sprache nach untersucht.* Gütersloh, 1894.

Langlotz, *Würzburg*—Langlotz, Ernst. *Griechische Vasen in Würzburg.* Munich, 1932.

Langlotz, *Zeitbestimmung*—Langlotz, Ernst. *Zur Zeitbestimmung der strengrotfigurigen Vasenmalerei und der gleichzeitigen Plastik.* Leipzig, 1920.

Licht, *Sittengeschichte*—Licht, Hans. *Sittengeschichte Griechenlands.* Dresden, 1925–28.

Löwy, *Polygnot*—Löwy, Emanuel. *Polygnot: ein Buch von griechischer Malerei.* 2 vols. Vienna, 1929.

von Lücken, *GV*—von Lücken, Gottfried. *Greek Vase Paintings.* The Hague, 1921.

Meisterhans, *Grammatik*—Meisterhans, K. *Grammatik der attischen Inschriften.* 3d ed., revised by Eduard Schwyzer. Berlin, 1900.

Metzger, *Repr. du IV siècle*—Metzger, H. *Les représentations dans la céramique attique du IV siècle.* Paris, 1951.

Mus. Greg.—*Museum Etruscum Gregorianum.* Rome, 1842.

Neugebauer, *Führer*, II—Neugebauer, K. A. *Staatliche Museen zu Berlin. Führer durch das Antiquarium II, Vasen*. Berlin, 1932.

Nicole, *Meid.*—Nicole, Georges. *Meidias et le style fleuri*. Geneva, 1908.

Panofka, *Pourt.*—Panofka, Theodor Sigismund. *Antiques du Cabinet du Comte de Pourtalès-Gorgier*. Paris, 1834.

Pellegrini, *VPU*—Pellegrini, Giuseppe. *Catalogo dei vasi antichi dipinti delle collezioni Palagi ed Universitaria*. Bologna, 1900.

Pfuhl—Pfuhl, Ernst. *Malerei und Zeichnung der Griechen*. 3 vols. Munich, 1923.

Pfuhl, *Masterpieces*—Pfuhl, Ernst. *Masterpieces of Greek Drawing and Painting* (translated by J. D. Beazley). New ed. London, 1950.

Philippart, *CAB*—Philippart, Hubert. *Les coupes attiques à fond blanc*. Brussels, 1936.

Pottier—Pottier, Edmond. *Vases antiques du Louvre*, 1903. Paris, 1897–1922.

Richter, *Craft*—Richter, Gisela M. A. *The Craft of Athenian Pottery*. New Haven, 1923.

Richter, *Greek Painting* [4]—Richter, Gisela M. A. *Greek Painting: The Development of Pictorial Representation from Archaic to Graeco-Roman Times*. New York, 1952.

Richter, *Kouroi*—Richter, Gisela M. A., with the coöperation of Irma A. Richter. Two hundred and eight photographs by Gerard M. Young. *Kouroi. A Study of the Development of the Greek Kouros from the Late Seventh to the Early Fifth Century B.C.* New York, 1942.

Richter, *MM Handbook* [6]—Richter, Gisela M. A. *Handbook of the Classical Collection* (The Metropolitan Museum of Art). 6th ed. New York, 1930.

Richter, *Sc. Sc.*—Richter, Gisela M. A. *The Sculpture and Sculptors of the Greeks*, 2d ed. New Haven, 1930; new, revised ed., 1950.

Richter and Hall—Richter, G. M. A., and Hall, L. F. *Red-figured Athenian Vases in the Metropolitan Museum of Art*. New Haven, 1936.

Richter and Milne—Richter, Gisela M. A., and Milne, Marjorie J. *Shapes and Names of Athenian Vases*. New York, 1935.

Riezler, *WAL*—Riezler, Walter. *Weissgrundige attische Lekythen*. 2 vols. Munich, 1914.

Robinson and Harcum, *Catalogue*—Robinson, D. M., and Harcum, C. G. *A Catalogue of the Greek Vases in the Royal Ontario Museum of Archaeology, Toronto*, edited by J. H. Iliffe. 2 vols. Toronto, 1930.

Rumpf, *M.u.Z.*—Rumpf, A. *Malerei und Zeichnung, Handbuch der Archäologie*, IV, 1. Munich, 1953.

Schefold, *KV*—Schefold, Karl. *Kertscher Vasen*. Berlin-Wilmersdorf, 1930.

Schefold, *U*—Schefold, Karl. *Untersuchungen zu den Kertscher Vasen*. Berlin and Leipzig, 1934.

Seltman, *AV*—Seltman, Charles T. *Attic Vase-Painting* (Martin Classical Lectures, III). Cambridge (Mass.), 1933.

Smith, *L*—Smith, H. R. W. *Der Lewismaler*. Leipzig, 1939.

Smith, *Menon Painter*—Smith, H. R. W. *"New Aspects of the Menon Painter." University of California Publications in Classical Archaeology*, I, no. 1. Berkeley, 1929.

Strena—*Strena Helbigiana*. Leipzig, 1900.

Swindler, *AP*—Swindler, Mary Hamilton. *Ancient Painting, from the Earliest Times to the Period of Christian Art*. New Haven, 1929.

Webster, *N*—Webster, Thomas Bertrand Lonsdale. *Der Niobidenmaler*. Leipzig, 1935.

ARTICLES ON RED-FIGURE BY J. D. BEAZLEY

In Richter and Hall, pp. 225 f., a list was given of Beazley's articles and reviews on red-figure published up to 1936. In 1951 the Clarendon Press published a complete list of Beazley's publications.

CONTENTS

PREFACE   v

ABBREVIATIONS AND BIBLIOGRAPHY   vii

LIST OF ILLUSTRATIONS   xix

INTRODUCTION

General

Importance of Greek vase paintings, 1; Period of Athenian red-figure, 1; Attraction for potters, archaeologists, painters, and historians of art, 2; General development, 2; Style of individual painters, 2; Assigned names, 3; Salient characteristics, 3; Relation to mural and panel paintings, 4; Our knowledge of the artists, 5.

Subjects

Subjects taken from mythology and daily life, occasionally from contemporary events, 7; Interest added by furnishings, utensils, and attire, 8; Comparison with subjects in later paintings, 8; Difference between Greek and later outlook, 9.

Ornaments

Function, 10; Repertoire, 10; Many variations on a few standard motives, 10.

Shapes

Reminiscent of architecture, 10; Was there an underlying principle of design?, 11; A few standard shapes with many variations, 11; Names of shapes, 14.

Inscriptions

Referring to figures represented, 14; Addressed to the beholder, 15; *Kalos* names, 15; Signatures, 16; Meaningless inscriptions, 19; Dipinti and graffiti, 19; Faulty spelling, 21; Attic, Doric, and Ionic forms of letters, 21.

Chronology

Absolute chronology based on dated events, relative chronology on the degree of naturalism attained, 22.

Technique

I. PREPARATION OF THE CLAY   24

II. FASHIONING OF THE VASE   24
(1) Wheel work
    a. Throwing   24
    b. Turning   25
(2) Molding   26
(3) Building   26
(4) Attachment of handles   26

III. DECORATION OF THE VASE   27
(1) The black glaze   27
(2) The treatment of the
    surface   28
(3) The painting   29
    a. Red-figure   29
    b. White ground   31

IV. THE FIRING   31
    Greek kilns   33

V. ACCIDENTS   34

VI. ATHENIAN POTTERIES   35

CHAPTER I. EARLY STYLE, ABOUT 530–500 B.C.

Historical background, 36; Technical and stylistic analysis, 36; Comparisons with painting and sculpture, 42; Chronological data, 43; Shapes, 45; The painters, 45.

(1) *The Andokides Painter, Psiax, and the Goluchow Painter* 46
Andokides Painter 46
Psiax 46
Goluchow Painter 48

(2) *Oltos, Epiktetos, and other cup painters* 48
Oltos 48
Epiktetos 49
Pheidippos 50
Hischylos Painter 50
Thaliarchos Painter 51
Euergides Painter 51
Pasiades 51
Apollodoros (= Epidromos Painter and Kleomelos Painter?) 51

Peithinos 52
Skythes 52
Hegesiboulos Painter 52
Kiss Painter 52
Ambrosios Painter 53
Hermaios Painter 53
Chelis Painter 53
Bowdoin-Eye Painter 53
Nikosthenes Painter 53
Epeleios Painter 53
Painter of Berlin 2268 53

(3) *Euphronios, Euthymides, Phintias, and their followers* 53
Euphronios 53
Euthymides 55
Phintias 56
Smikros 56
Sosias Painter 57
Vienna Painter 57
Dikaios Painter 57
Hypsis 57
Gales Painter 58

CHAPTER II. RIPE ARCHAIC STYLE, ABOUT 500–475 B.C.

Historical background, 59; Stylistic analysis, 59; Technique, 63; Comparisons with sculpture, 64; Chronological data, 64; Shapes, 65; The Painters, 66.

(1) *The Kleophrades Painter, the Berlin Painter, and other painters of large pots* 66
Kleophrades Painter (Epiktetos) 66
Berlin Painter 68
Nikoxenos Painter 70
Eucharides Painter 71
Myson 71
Geras Painter 72
Harrow Painter 72
Syleus Painter 72

Copenhagen Painter 72
Syriskos Painter 72
Gallatin Painter 73
Diogenes Painter 73
Tyszkiewicz Painter 73
Troilos Painter 73

(2) *Painters of small pots* 73
a. In Red-figure 73
Dutuit Painter 73
Tithonos Painter 73
Providence Painter 74
Bowdoin Painter 74
b. In Black-figure 75
Diosphos Painter 75
Sappho Painter 75
Athena Painter 75
Haimon Painter 75

CONTENTS

Theseus Painter 75

(3) *The Panaitios Painter, the
Brygos Painter, Makron,
Douris, and other cup
painters* 76
Panaitios Painter 76
Eleusis Painter 77
Brygos Painter 78
Makron 81
Douris 83
Triptolemos Painter 83

Cartellino Painter 83
Onesimos 85
Colmar Painter 85
Antiphon Painter 85
Thorvaldsen Group 86
Magnoncourt Painter 86
Foundry Painter 87
Briseis Painter 87
Painter of the Paris Gigan-
tomachy 87
Dokimasia Painter 88

CHAPTER III. EARLY FREE STYLE,
ABOUT 475–450 B.C.

Historical background, 89; Stylistic
analysis, 90; Technique, 92; Comparisons with sculpture, 93; Chronological data, 93; Shapes, 93; The
Painters, 94.

(1) *The Pan Painter and other
mannerists* 94
Pan Painter 94
Pig Painter 96
Leningrad Painter 96
Agrigento Painter 96
Nausikaa Painter (Polygno-
tos) 97

(2) *The Penthesileia Painter
and his associates* 97
Penthesileia Painter 97
Pistoxenos Painter 99
Splanchnopt Painter 100
Painter of Bologna 417 100
Wedding Painter 100
Painter of Brussels R 330 100

(3) *The Niobid Painter and his
associates* 100
Niobid Painter 100
Altamura Painter 101
Painter of the Woolly Silens 101
Painter of the Berlin Hydria 102
Painter of Bologna 279 102
Geneva Painter 102

(4) *The Villa Giulia Painter
and his associates; "fol-
lowers of Douris"* 104

Villa Giulia Painter 104
Chicago Painter 105
Methyse Painter 106
Akestorides Painter 106
Painter of Munich 2660 107
Euaion Painter 107
Painter of Louvre C A 1694 107
'Euaichme Painter 107

(5) *Other Painters* 107
Telephos Painter 107
Clinic Painter 108
Amymone Painter 108
Hermonax 108
Oionokles Painter 109
Nikon Painter 109
Painter of the Yale Oino-
choe 109
Painter of the Yale Lekythos 109
Painter of London E 342 109
Syracuse Painter 109
Cleveland Painter 109
Painter of London E 100 110
Aigisthos Painter 110
Orchard Painter 110
Painter of Bologna 228 110
Alkimachos Painter 110
Deepdene Painter 110
Sotades Painter 111
Lewis Painter (Polygnotos) 112
Zephyros Painter 112
Sabouroff Painter 112
Painter of Munich 2363 113
Ethiop Painter 113

Vouni Painter   114
Inscription Painter   114
Aischines Painter   114

Tymbos Painter   114
Carlsruhe Painter   114
Ikaros Painter   114

CHAPTER IV. FREE STYLE, ABOUT 450–420 B.C.

Historical background, 115; Stylistic analysis, 115; Technique, 116; Comparisons with sculpture, 117; Chronological data, 117; Shapes, 117; The painters, 117.

(1) *The Achilles Painter and his followers*   118
    Achilles Painter   118
    Bosanquet Painter   121
    Thanatos Painter   121
    Painter of Munich 2335   121
    Phiale Painter   122
    Persephone Painter   123
    Dwarf Painter   124

(2) *The Mannheim Painter and others*   124
    Mannheim Painter   124
    Danae Painter   125
    Painter of London E 497   125
    Menelaos Painter   126
    Kleio Painter   126
    Eupolis Painter   126
    Painter of Athens 1943   126
    Cassel Painter   126
    Polydektes Painter   127
    Richmond Painter   127

(3) *Polygnotos and his circle*   127
    Polygnotos   127
    Lykaon Painter   128

Orpheus Painter   129
Christie Painter   130
Hektor Painter   130
Peleus Painter   130
Coghill Painter   130

(4) *Other Painters of Pots*   130
    Naples Painter   130
    Painter of the Louvre Centauromachy   130
    Nekyia Painter   130
    Trophy Painter   131
    Athanasia Painter   131
    Penelope Painter   132
    Marlay Painter   132

(5) *The Eretria Painter and other painters of cups and small vases*   132
    Eretria Painter   132
    Kalliope Painter   135
    Kodros Painter   135
    Painter of London D 14   136
    Kraipale Painter   136
    Washing Painter   136
    Shuvalov Painter   137
    Disney Painter   137
    Painter of the Edinburgh Oinochoe   137
    Klügmann Painter   137
    Xenotimos Painter   138

CHAPTER V. LATE FIFTH-CENTURY STYLE, ABOUT 420–390 B.C.

Historical background, 139; Stylistic analysis, 139; Technique, 141; Comparisons with sculpture, 141; Chronological data, 141; The painters, 142.

(1) *The Kleophon Painter, the Dinos Painter, and Others. Late followers of Polygnotos*   143

Kleophon Painter   143
Dinos Painter   143
Chrysis Painter   144
Polion   144
Aison   146
Kadmos Painter   146
Pothos Painter   146

(2) *The Meidias Painter and his school* 146
    Meidias Painter 146
    Aristophanes 149
    Mikion Painter (Euemporos?) 149
    Nikias Painter 150
(3) *The Talos Painter, the Pronomos Painter, and the Suessula Painter* 150
    Talos Painter 150
    Pronomos Painter 150
    Suessula Painter 151

(4) *Painters of cups and small vases* 151
    Painter of London 106 152
    Mouret Painter 152
    Straggly Painter 152
    Mina Painter 152
    Worst Painter 152
    Gaurion (potter) 152

(5) *White-ground vases* 152
    Manner of Woman Painter 153
    Reed Painter 153
    Triglyph Painter 153

CHAPTER VI. THE FOURTH CENTURY

Historical background, 154; Stylistic analysis, 154; Technique, 155; Comparisons with sculpture, 155; Chronological data, 156; Shapes, 156.

(1) FIRST THIRD OF THE CENTURY 157
  a. *The ornate style: The painter of the New York Centauromachy and other pot painters* 157
    Painter of the New York Centauromachy 157
    Meleager Painter 157
    Xenophantos Painter 157
    Painter of the Oxford Grypomachy 158
    Retorted Painter 158
    Black-Thyrsos Painter 158

    Oinomaos Painter 158
  b. *The plainer style: The Erbach Painter, the Jena Painter, and others* 158
    Erbach Painter 158
    Painter of London F 64 158
    Painter of London F 1 158
    Jena Painter 158
    Q Painter 159
    Painter of Vienna 155 159
    Painter of Vienna 202 159
    Painter of Vienna 116 159
    Fat Boy Group 159
    Brown-Egg Painter 159
(2) THE KERCH STYLE, ABOUT 370–320 B.C. 159
(3) VASES WITH RELIEFS 162

NOTES 165
INDEX 201

ILLUSTRATIONS

Figures 1 through 33 are in the text and figures 34 through 125 are grouped following page 164.

The figures in the text are by Lindsley F. Hall, either drawn from the originals or redrawn from other publications.

Figure   *Page*

1. Shapes of Athenian red-figured vases   12
2. Shapes of Athenian red-figured vases   13
3. From the psykter 10.210.18 by Oltos in New York   38
4. From the fragmentary kylix 07.286.50 by the Kiss Painter in New York   38
5. From the amphora by the Andokides Painter in Munich (Redrawn from FR, pl. 4)   39
6. From the kylix by Skythes in the Villa Giulia Museum, Rome (Redrawn from *Mon. Piot*, XX [1913], pl. VII, 1).   39
7. From the hydria 10.210.19 by the Berlin Painter in New York   40
8. From the kylix by Oltos in Tarquinia (Redrawn from Pfuhl, fig. 360)   40
9. From the kylix by Psiax in Munich (Redrawn from *Jb.*, X [1895], pl. 4).   41
10. From the kylix 14.146.1 by Psiax in New York   41
11. From the kylix 41.162.112, perhaps by Epiktetos, in New York   42
12. From the kylix 10.212 by Epiktetos in Boston (Redrawn from Caskey and Beazley, *AVP*, pl. III, 6)   43
13. From an amphora by the Andokides Painter in the Louvre (Redrawn from FR, pl. 111)   43
14. From the psykter 10.210.10 by Oltos in New York   44
15, 16. From the kylix 14.146.1 by Psiax in New York   44, 45
17. From the hydria 10.210.19 by the Berlin Painter in New York   60
18. From the kantharos 12.234.5 by the Brygos Painter in New York   61
19. From the pelike G R 578 by the Geras Painter in New York   61
20. From the kylix 12.231.1 by Makron in New York   62

Figure   *Page*

21. From the kylix 30.1 by the Panaitios Painter in Bow-
    doin College, Brunswick, Maine (Redrawn from
    Beazley, *VA*, p. 86, fig. 54)   62

22. From the amphora by the Berlin Painter in Berlin
    (Redrawn from von Lücken, *GV*, pl. 52)   63

23. From the lekythos 25.189.1 by the Brygos Painter in
    New York   63

24. Eyes on vases of the ripe archaic style in New York   63
    a, b. From the hydria 10.210.19 by the Berlin
          Painter
       c. From the lekythos 28.57.12 by the Brygos
          Painter
       d. From the lekythos 13.227.16 by the Dutuit
          Painter
    e, f. From the kylix 20.246 by Makron
    g, h. From the amphora 13.233 by the Kleophrades
          Painter
       i. From the hydria 11.212.7 by the Syleus
          Painter

25. From the lekythos 07.286.67 by the Providence
    Painter in New York   64

26. From the hydria 10.210.19 by the Berlin Painter in
    New York   64

27. From the kylix G R 1120 by Makron in New York   64

28. From the lekythos 07.286.67 by the Providence
    Painter in New York   65

29. From the lekythos 13.227.16 by the Dutuit Painter
    in New York   65

30. From the lekythos 25.78.2 by the Tithonos Painter
    in New York   65

31. From the calyx krater 07.286.86 by the Painter of the
    Berlin Hydria in New York   91

32. Eyes on vases of the Early Free Style in New York   92
    a. From the lekythos 26.60.77 by Hermonax
    b. From the stamnos 17.230.37 by the Deepdene
       Painter
    c. From the column krater no. 29.131.7 by the
       Painter of Bologna 228
    d. From the neck of a loutrophoros 07.286.70 by
       the Painter of Bologna 228
    e. From the skyphos 06.1079 by the Penthesileia
       Painter

f. From the double disk 28.167 by the Penthesileia Painter

g. From the column krater 34.11.7 by the Orchard Painter

h. From the hydria 06.1021.190 by the Chicago Painter

i, j. From the bell krater 23.160.80 by the Danae Painter

k. From the oinochoe 06.1021.189 by the Mannheim Painter

l. From the bell krater 24.97.96 by the Villa Giulia Painter

m. From the bell krater 07.286.85 by the Methyse Painter

33. Eyes on vases of the Free Style in New York　　116

a. From the lekythos 08.258.18 by the Achilles Painter

b. From the bell krater 28.57.23 by the Persephone Painter

c, d. From the amphora 06.1021.116 by the Lykaon Painter

e. From the lekythos 17.230.35 by the Phiale Painter

f. From the bell krater 28.57.23 by the Persephone Painter

34. Herakles and Kerberos, by the Andokides Painter. From the amphora F 204 in the Louvre.

35. Victorious young athlete being crowned, by Oltos. From the psykter 10.210.18 in the Metropolitan Museum. Photograph by E. Milla.

36. Man dancing to the music of the flute, by Psiax. From a plate in the collection of Monsieur Jameson Paris.

37. Youth riding a cock, by Epiktetos. From a plate in Castle Ashby. Photograph by Marie Beazley.

38. Man walking with his dog, by the Hegesiboulos Painter. From the kylix 07.286.47 in the Metropolitan Museum. Photograph by E. Milla.

39, 40. Athletes, by Pheidippos. From the kylix 41.162.8 in the Metropolitan Museum. Photograph by E. Milla.

41. Cow led to sacrifice, by the Gales Painter. From the lekythos 13.195 in the Museum of Fine Arts, Boston.

42. Boxer, by the Hischylos Painter. Fragment of a kylix, 22.139.81, in the Metropolitan Museum. Photograph by E. Milla.

43. Herakles and Antaios, by Euphronios. From the amphora G 103 in the Louvre. Drawing by Reichhold, FR., pl. 92.

44. Revelers, by Euthymides. From the amphora 2307 in the Museum antiker Kleinkunst, Munich. Drawing by Reichhold, FR, pl. 14.

45. Achilles bandaging the wounded arm of Patroklos, by Sosias. From the kylix 2278 in the Staatliche Museen, Berlin. Drawing by Reichhold, FR, pl. 123.

46. Satyr and Maenad, by Phintias. From the amphora R C 6843 in the Museum of Tarquinia. Drawing by Reichhold, FR, pl. 91.

47. Warrior, by the Kleophrades Painter. From the calyx krater 08.258.58 in the Metropolitan Museum. Photograph by E. Milla.

48. Youth playing the kithara, by the Berlin Painter. From the amphora 56.171.38 in the Metropolitan Museum. Photograph by T. McAdams.

49. Dionysos, by Myson. From the column krater 07.286.-73 in the Metropolitan Museum. Photograph by E. Milla.

50. Satyr, by the Geras Painter. From the pelike G R 578 in the Metropolitan Museum. Photograph by E. Milla.

51. Theseus and Skiron, by the Gallatin Painter. From the amphora 41.162.101 in the Metropolitan Museum. Photograph by E. Milla.

52. Nike, by the Dutuit Painter. From the lekythos 13.227.16 in the Metropolitan Museum. Photograph by E. Milla.

53. Thetis and Hephaistos, by the Dutuit Painter. From the amphora 13.188 in the Museum of Fine Arts, Boston.

54. Artemis, by the Providence Painter. From the lekythos 41.162.18 in the Metropolitan Museum. Photograph by E. Milla.

55. Hermes, by the Tithonos Painter. From the lekythos 25.78.2 in the Metropolitan Museum. Photograph by E. Milla.

56. Woman working wool, by the Bowdoin Painter. From the lekythos 06.1021.90 in the Metropolitan Museum. Photograph by E. Milla.

57. Youth reading aloud to listeners, by the Panaitios Painter. From the kyathos 2322 in the Staatliche Museen, Berlin.

58. Warrior, by an artist of the Thorvaldsen Group. From the kylix 41.162.1 in the Metropolitan Museum. Photograph by E. Milla.

59. Herakles, by the Panaitios Painter. From the kylix 12.231.2 in the Metropolitan Museum. Photograph by E. Milla.

60. Athena, by the Brygos Painter. From the lekythos 25.189.1 in the Metropolitan Museum. Photograph by E. Milla.

61. Athena, by the Brygos Painter. From the lekythos 09.221.43 in the Metropolitan Museum. Photograph by E. Milla.

62. Theseus welcomed by Athena, by the Briseis Painter. From the kylix 53.11.4 in the Metropolitan Museum. Photograph by T. McAdams.

63. Maenad and Satyr, by Makron. From the kylix 06.1152 in the Metropolitan Museum. Photograph by E. Milla.

64. Satyr, by Douris. From the psykter E 786 in the British Museum. Drawing by Reichhold, FR, pl. 48.

65. Woman putting away her clothes, by Douris. From the kylix 23.160.54 in the Metropolitan Museum. Photograph by E. Milla.

66. Artemis, by the Pan Painter. From the lekythos 670 in the Hermitage. *Oest. Jh.,* XVI (1913), pl. II.

67. Pan, by the Pan Painter. From the bell krater 10.185 in the Museum of Fine Arts, Boston.

68. Ganymede, by the Pan Painter. From the oinochoe 23.160.55 in the Metropolitan Museum. Photograph by E. Milla.

69. Nike crowning a victorious youth, by the Penthesileia Painter. Double disk 28.167 in the Metropolitan Museum. Photograph by E. Milla.

70. Man and boar, by the Penthesileia Painter. From the kylix 41.162.9 in the Metropolitan Museum. Photograph by E. Milla.

71. Perseus and Medusa, by the Diosphos Painter. From

the lekythos 06.1070 in the Metropolitan Museum. Photograph by E. Milla.

72. Eros and Aphrodite, by the Wedding Painter. From the pyxis 39.11.8 in the Metropolitan Museum. Photograph by E. Milla.

73. Paris, by the Penthesileia Painter. From the pyxis 07.286.36 in the Metropolitan Museum. Photograph by E. Milla.

74. Battles of Lapiths and Centaurs and of Greeks and Amazons, by the Painter of the Woolly Silens. Volute krater 07.286.84 in the Metropolitan Museum. Photograph by E. Milla.

75. Triptolemos, by the Niobid Painter. From the hydria 41.162.98 in the Metropolitan Museum. Photograph by E. Milla.

76. Dionysos, by the Oionokles Painter. From the amphora 41.162.21 in the Metropolitan Museum. Photograph by E. Milla.

77. Maenad, by Hermonax. From the lekythos 41.162.19 in the Metropolitan Museum. Photograph by E. Milla.

78. Maenad, by the Methyse Painter. From the bell krater 07.286.85 in the Metropolitan Museum. Photograph by E. Milla.

79. Flying figures, by the Sotades Painter, on a vase in the form of a knucklebone (astragalos) E 804 in the British Museum. Drawing by Reichhold, FR, pl. 136, 2.

80. Herdsman, by a follower of the Brygos Painter, on a cup in the form of a hoof 38.11.2 in the Metropolitan Museum. Photograph by E. Milla.

81. Charon's boat, by the Sabouroff Painter. From the lekythos 21.88.17 in the Metropolitan Museum. Photograph by E. Milla.

82. Prothesis, the lying in state of the dead, by the Sabouroff Painter. From the lekythos 07.286.40 in the Metropolitan Museum. Photograph by E. Milla.

83. Mourners at two graves, by the Vouni Painter. From the lekythos 35.11.5 in the Metropolitan Museum. Photograph by E. Milla.

84. Hermes and the infant Dionysos, by the Villa Giulia Painter. From the bell krater E 492 in the British Museum.

85. Seated man, by the Euaichme Painter. From the sky-

phos 41.162.5 in the Metropolitan Museum. Photograph by E. Milla.

86. Boy playing the lyre, by the Akestorides Painter. From the kylix 22.139.72 in the Metropolitan Museum. Photograph by E. Milla.

87. Satyr, by the Euaion Painter. From the kylix 06.1021.-177 in the Metropolitan Museum. Photograph by E. Milla.

88. Amazon, by the Mannheim Painter. From the oinochoe 06.1021.189 in the Metropolitan Museum. Photograph by E. Milla.

89. Muse on Mount Helikon, by the Achilles Painter. From a lekythos in the collection of Baron von Schoen, Munich.

90. Girls listening to music, by the Danae Painter. From the bell krater 23.160.80 in the Metropolitan Museum. Photograph by E. Milla.

91. Amymone, by the Phiale Painter. From the lekythos 17.230.35 in the Metropolitan Museum. Photograph by E. Milla.

92. Persephone, Hermes, and Hekate, by the Persephone Painter. From the bell krater 28.57.23 in the Metropolitan Museum. Photograph by E. Milla.

93. Orpheus and the Thracians, by the Painter of London E 497. From the bell krater in the Metropolitan Museum. Photograph by E. Milla.

94, 95. The shade of Elpenor and Odysseus, by the Lykaon Painter. From the pelike 34.79 in the Museum of Fine Arts, Boston.

96. Perseus and Medusa, by Polygnotos. From the pelike 45.11.1 in the Metropolitan Museum. Photograph by E. Milla.

97. A trainer (?). From the fragment of a kylix, 07.156.8, by the Foundry Painter. In the Metropolitan Museum. Photograph by E. Milla.

98. The wounded Philoktetes on the island of Lemnos. From the lekythos 56.171.58 in the Metropolitan Museum. Photograph by T. McAdams.

99. Woman. From the fragment of a krater, 17.230.23, by the Chicago Painter. In the Metropolitan Museum. Photograph by E. Milla.

100. Athanasia and Tydeus. Fragment of a bell krater, 12.229.14, in the Metropolitan Museum. Photograph by E. Milla.

101. Preparations for the wedding of Thetis, by the Eretria Painter. From the onos 1629 in the National Museum, Athens. Photograph by Marie Beazley.
102. Woman putting on her chiton, by the Eretria Painter. From the squat lekythos 30.11.8 in the Metropolitan Museum. Photograph by E. Milla.
103. Thetis, by the Eretria Painter. From the lekythos 31.11.13 in the Metropolitan Museum. Photograph by E. Milla.
104. Nereid, by the Painter of London D 14. From the pyxis 40.11.2 in the Metropolitan Museum. Photograph by E. Milla.
105. Maenads and Satyr (Kraipale, Ephymnia, Sikinnos) by the Kraipale Painter. From the oinochoe 00.352 in the Museum of Fine Arts, Boston.
106. Youths at an incense burner, by the Shuvalov Painter. From the oinochoe 08.258.24 in the Metropolitan Museum. Photograph by E. Milla.
107. Satyr, by or near the Coghill Painter. From the volute krater 24.97.25 in the Metropolitan Museum. Photograph by E. Milla.
108. Female head, in the manner of the Kleophon Painter. From the pelike 1951.9–9.1 in the British Museum.
109. Male head, by the Talos Painter. From the stand 12.229.15 in the Metropolitan Museum. Photograph by E. Milla.
110. Warrior leaving home, by Aison from the head-kantharos 27.122.9 in the Metropolitan Museum. Photograph by E. Milla.
111. Youth reclining, by the Dinos Painter. Fragment of a bell krater, 24.97.38, in the Metropolitan Museum. Photograph by E. Milla.
112. Boxers, by Polion. From the volute krater 27.122.8 in the Metropolitan Museum. Photograph by E. Milla.
113. Pelops, by an artist near the Meidias Painter. From the amphora 1460 in the Municipal Museum, Arezzo.
114. Aphrodite, by the Meidias Painter. From the pelike 37.11.23 in the Metropolitan Museum. Photograph by E. Milla.
115. Chariot with Erotes, by the Meidias Painter. From the hydria 81947 in the Archaeological Museum, Florence.
116. Youth sitting at his grave, in the manner of the

Woman Painter. From the white lekythos 06.1169 in the Metropolitan Museum. Photograph by E. Milla.

117. Youth sitting at his grave. From the white lekythos 41.162.12 in the Metropolitan Museum. Photograph by E. Milla.

118, 119. Mourners at a grave. From the white lekythos 07.-286.45 in the Metropolitan Museum. Photograph by E. Milla.

120. The flute player Pronomos, by the Pronomos Painter. From the amphora 2340 in the National Museum, Naples. Drawing by Reichhold, FR, pls. 143–144.

121. Poseidon. From the hydria 21.88.162 in the Metropolitan Museum. Photograph by E. Milla.

122. Greeks and Amazons, by the Suessula Painter. From the amphora 44.11.12 in the Metropolitan Museum. Photograph by E. Milla.

123. Pompe, Dionysos, and Eros. From the oinochoe 25.190 in the Metropolitan Musuem. Photograph by E. Milla.

124. Herakles and a Hesperid. From the hydria 22.139.26 in the Metropolitan Museum. Photograph by E. Milla.

125. Woman and her maid. From the skyphos 06.1021.181 in the Metropolitan Museum. Photograph by E. Milla.

INTRODUCTION

GENERAL

W HEN we speak of the art of the Greeks most of us think of their sculpture and architecture—the statues, friezes, and temples that have withstood two or three thousand years of destruction. We seldom think of Greek painting, for the simple reason that practically all the murals and panels that have survived to our day belong to a later age, not to the creative early periods when the foundations of European painting were laid. This great gap is filled, to some extent at least, by the wealth of painted scenes on Greek pottery that have come down to us. Through them we may in some measure visualize the lost monumental pictures, which were praised in such enthusiastic terms by Greek and Roman writers, and follow the development of ancient painting step by step—just as we might glean something of the evolution of modern painting from the graphic arts of to-day. Greek vase decorations therefore assume an importance even over and above their own intrinsic worth.

The pottery discussed in this book is the so-called Athenian red-figure, in which the decoration is "reserved" in red against a black-glazed background. It was produced in Athens during her greatest political and economic prosperity, when painting developed from a decorative to a representational art. The beginnings of this ware can be placed in the last third of the sixth century B.C., when Athens, thanks to the beneficent reforms of Solon and the brilliant rule of Peisistratos, had risen from a comparatively small though enterprising community to a powerful city-state. Before that time, in the middle of the sixth century, Athenian black-figured pottery—with the decoration in black glaze on the red background of the terracotta—had already conquered foreign markets, as the graves of Etruria, South Italy, and the Eastern Mediterranean testify. The reversal of the color scheme from the time-honored dark on light to the new light on dark opened up fresh possibilities to an already flourishing craft. During the whole of the fifth century Athenian red-figured vases retained their ascendancy but the long-drawn-out

Peloponnesian War and Athens' final defeat by Sparta at Aigospotamoi in 405 B.C. seriously crippled her once far-flung commerce. Athenian red-figure still enjoyed a limited popularity
until about 320 B.C. and then was finally ousted by the more
popular relief ware. The history of Attic red-figured pottery,
therefore—its rise, acme, and decline—took up approximately
two centuries—from the later archaic period, that is, the time
of the Siphnian frieze, to that of Praxiteles, Skopas, and Lysippos,
or from the time of Simonides, Pindar, and Aeschylus to that of
Menander.

The attraction of this pottery is manifold and its study should
appeal to a wide public. The precision of the shapes and the
thin, satiny black glaze are an inspiration to the potter. The fine
line drawing and the adaptation of the figures to allotted spaces
of varying shapes and curving surfaces afford pleasure to the
painter. The scenes supply invaluable material to the archaeolo-
gist for the understanding of Greek life and thought, for Greek
myths and Athenian life are here illustrated in a series of "contemporary" pictures. To the historian of art a rich feast is likewise presented. He finds here a wealth of paintings, ranging in
date from the archaic to the fully developed style, in which the
many problems of representation are gradually solved. It is one
of the great achievements of the Greeks to have emancipated the
art of drawing from a conventional system of two-dimensional
formulas and to have shown the way to represent on a flat surface three-dimensional figures as they appear to the eye. The
vase paintings alone have survived to tell this captivating tale.
Here we can trace the gradual evolution of representational
drawing. The rendering of the human figure was the subject
which above all others interested the Greek artist. Slowly he
gained a knowledge of the complex mechanism of the human
frame, was able to represent the folds of thin and heavy draperies,
solved one by one the problems of foreshortening, imparted volume to his figures, and introduced spatial relations into his compositions.[1] Moreover in this slow unfolding of the history of
Greek painting we can trace more than a general development.
Individual personalities stand out as clearly as in Renaissance
painting, and they are distinguishable in the same ways. Each
artist reveals himself by the general effect of his picture and by
his own particular rendering of individual forms; only the dif-

SUBJECTS

As in the earlier, black-figured vases the subjects in red-figure are at first taken largely from mythology.⁹ The time-honored legends of the Olympian gods, of Herakles and Theseus, of the Trojan War, supply a large proportion of the themes. Records of contemporary life are comparatively few. As time progressed, however, the artist drew his inspiration increasingly from the life around him. He watched the youths in the gymnasiums and depicted them at their exercises—running, jumping, throwing the javelin and the discus, and being crowned for victory; he represented them riding, arming, departing for battle, and fighting; he watched them in their homes and painted the gay banquets, or symposia, with men reclining on their couches, eating and drinking, and flute girls and hetairai ministering to their pleasures; he delighted in the riotous antics of the revelers; he depicted the women busy with their household and other occupations—carding wool, spinning, weaving, bathing, dressing, dancing, making music, and performing religious rites—the children at play with their balls and little carts, their tops, hoops, dogs, and pet birds; he represented men and women making love, getting married, and being buried; and he showed mourners at biers and graves. Everything that the artist saw around him he drew with the same frank and eager interest; even subjects which the modern artist avoids he unhesitatingly brings before us as part of life and nature. There was no censorship in Greek art.¹⁰

But side by side with these pictures from everyday life the mythological scenes remain. The myths were too much part of Greek thought to be discarded. And so the exploits of Herakles and of the other heroes against monsters and wicked men are not forgotten, nor the gay adventures of the Olympians, nor Dionysos with his merry retinue of satyrs and maenads, nor the Amazons and centaurs. But even here there is more variety in the representations than before. The stories are no longer rendered so closely according to traditional forms; the individual artist gives more scope to his imagination. Occasionally he even represents historical events, for instance contests of Greeks and Persians or the sojourn of the poet Anakreon in Athens.

In all these scenes, everyday, mythological, or historical, great interest is added by the paraphernalia—the furnishings, utensils, and attire.¹¹ We learn from them of many things which time has destroyed and which often survive only in these representations —the forms of the Greek chairs and tables; of the couches with their mattresses, covers, and pillows; of the baskets and chests; the sticks of the young men; the flute cases and sword sheaths; the dresses, shoes, and headgear. Without these representations our knowledge of the details of Greek life would be meager indeed.

As the subjects of red-figured vase paintings are much the same as those of the contemporary monumental Greek paintings— judging at least from descriptions of these in ancient literature —they can help us to visualize the scope and the limitations of Greek painting in general. When we compare them with those current in art to-day we note two great gaps in the ancient repertoire—landscape and portraiture. Landscape in classical Greek art is always subsidiary; it is confined to an occasional tree or shrub or rock suggesting an outdoor scene and serving merely as the setting in which human figures enact their parts. It does not form a separate study for its own sake. The same is true of still life and animals.¹² Though furnishings play an important role as accessories, and animals are popular companions, they rarely appear by themselves. The interest centers in the human figures. Likewise, portraiture in our sense of the word is practically nonexistent in Athenian vase painting. Even when a figure is given the name of a specific contemporary person—Anakreon, for instance—there is no attempt to make him look different from his companions (see p. 58). It is true that occasionally what have been called individualized figures appear in the midst of the more generalized types—an old Oriental walking with his dog, a father or mother grieving for a dead son, an old man or an old woman. But, though these are deviations from the typical young men and women favored in Greek art, they too are really types rather than individuals—types of an Oriental, an old man, a sorrowing woman. Interest in individual character per se does not appear in Greek painting until a later period.

Except for these important omissions the repertoire of the early Greek artist is not unlike that of later times. He too chose his topics from legend, from everyday life, and occasionally from history. Naturally his myths and events are purely Greek, whereas in our time artists can choose from the stories of many nations; but the general idea is the same. In other words, the Greek artist's chief interest is in story-telling, in depicting the events of life, heroic or humble, sacred or profane. This theme, though rather despised by some modern critics as being merely illustrative, also inspired the majority of mediaeval and later European artists. They too chose for their subjects illustrations from the life of Christ, the deeds of saints, and the happenings of daily life. Though the content of religion and some aspects of life had changed, the artist's method of translating these into pictorial form remained the same. Nevertheless there is a great difference between the Greek and the later outlook. The subject may be similar or even identical—a mighty deed, a báttle, a farewell, a woman dancing—but the treatment of it is unlike. In a pregnant phrase George Santayana sums up this fundamental difference between the ancient and modern outlook: ". . . The ancients poetized the actual surroundings and destiny of man rather than the travesty of these facts in human fancy and the consequent dramas within the spirit." [18] It is "the actual surroundings and destiny of man" that formed the chief preoccupation of the Greek artist and constituted the subjects he preferably treated; whereas later artists were more interested in the human reaction to these surroundings, in the "dramas within the spirit," which these events produce. When Schongauer portrays a saint, Rembrandt an old man, and Forain a dancer, it is the character and personality of the individual, shaped by the circumstances of his life, that are brought out. In Greek representations, on the other hand, it is not the individual but the action that is of primary interest. The expressions of Theseus and Herakles hardly vary in their many adventures, but the action in each scene differs according to the circumstance. And it is this action that the Greek artist poetized by his imaginative conception. Though from our modern viewpoint the Greek conception may not seem sufficiently individualized, it is after all this very detachment which gives Greek art its peculiar value. By not stressing the accidental, by lifting their representations into the impersonal sphere, the Greeks achieved a quality of greatness that remains potent today. The pattern that underlies their works has given them permanence.

ORNAMENTS

Ornamental bands and designs were used on Athenian vases to frame the figured scenes and to decorate the portions of the vase not occupied by these scenes—the mouth, the neck, the shoulder, the spaces round the handles, the base of the body. They stand out against the plain black portions, lending richness to the effect of the whole. Sometimes they were used sparingly, at other times profusely; but always, though subsidiary, they play an important part in the composition, helping to link the figured scenes to the shape of the vase. They are drawn free hand without stencils or other guiding instrument. The repertoire is not large—meanders, palmettes, tongues, eggs, the lotos, the ivy, the laurel, scrolls, rays, spirals, crosses, checkers, dots, and simple lines practically make up the list.[14] Each motive is infinitely varied. There are single, double, triple, quadruple, and interlocking meanders; meanders alternating with saltires, crosses, and checkers; single, double, and slanting palmettes; palmettes interlaced with scrolls; and a rich assortment of ivy and lotos patterns. Different patterns are favored at different times; their composition varies from period to period; each motive, while current for a considerable time, has a certain chronological development. And even during one period the ornament is often drawn and composed in so individual a manner that we can either assign it definitely to the artist of the picture or, in rare instances, conclude that it was added by another painter (see p. 69).

SHAPES

The sense for symmetry and proportion conspicuous in the decorations of Greek vases is equally apparent in their shapes. Compared to the vases of other countries with their softly undulating contours, Greek pottery gives the impression of sturdy architecture. The strongly articulated forms, often derived from metalwork, appear as three-dimensional designs; the various parts—mouth, neck, body, foot, handles—are nicely related to one another and to the whole. As our eye glides up and down the satisfying curves we feel that even a slight variation in the widths or the heights of the various parts, a little change in the position of the handles, would affect us unpleasantly. We are reminded of the Greek definition of beauty as an interrelation of parts to the whole and to one another.[15] Was such perfect proportion obtained by instinct? Or was it the result of an underlying principle of design? The question is a moot one. An obvious arithmetical proportion does not seem to hold; but many vases, when carefully measured and analyzed, have been shown to correspond to certain simple geometrical proportions and to circle geometry.[16] It does not seem farfetched to suppose, considering the known Greek interest in geometry, that the designers of this architectural pottery felt the same need that the architects did in their temples of having the given areas proportionately interrelated. And perhaps this underlying scheme gradually became instinctive and was not worked out in every instance. Be that as it may, the modern potter anxious to improve his sense of form can learn much from the study of Greek vases—however different in composition from his own.

Broadly speaking, there are only a few standard shapes in Athenian pottery, for the Greek potter, like the early Greek sculptor, was content to adhere to a few prescribed types, with changes in details. By such variations, however, the number of the shapes is greatly increased. We have, for instance, as mixing bowls the volute krater, the calyx krater, the bell krater, the column krater, the lebes; at least two chief varieties of water jar; several forms of amphora, including the neck amphora, the pointed, and the Panathenaic; numerous forms of wine, oil, and perfume jugs and many types of cups.[17] Each shape is expressive of the function it has to perform. In the course of time we can note a certain development in these shapes. The sturdy early forms tend gradually to become slenderer. And as each potter makes his pot he creates an individual design, slightly changing the size, the curves, the proportions. There is no mass production in Attic red-figure; there are no dinner sets with dozens of identical dishes; only occasionally instances occur of vases made in pairs or groups.[18] To become intimately acquainted with these Greek forms, to appreciate their subtle distinctions, and to watch their slow development is to obtain an insight into the mind of the Greeks and their approach to art.

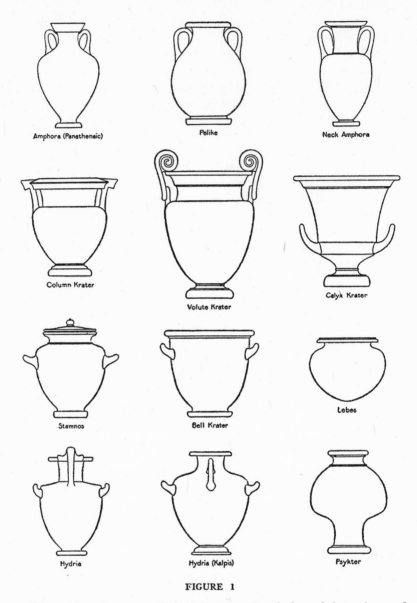

FIGURE 1

The various kraters and the lebes were bowls for mixing wine and water, the psykter was a wine cooler, the hydria a water jar, the amphora a storage jar, the stamnos a wine container, the pelike a container.

Oinochoe

Oinochoe

Oinochoe (Chous)

Loutrophoros

Kylix

Kylix

Skyphos

Stemless Kylix

Skyphos

Kyathos

Kantharos

Squat Lekythos

Lekythos

Pyxis

Pyxis

Pyxis

Lekanis

Aryballos

Alabastron

Lebes Gamikos

FIGURE 2

The lebes gamikos was a wedding vase, the loutrophoros both a wedding and a sepulchral vase. The lekythos and the aryballos were oil bottles, the alabastron a perfume bottle, the oinochoe a wine jug, the kantharos, kylix, and skyphos were drinking cups, the kyathos may have been a dipper. The pyxis or kylichnis was a box for toilet articles, the lekanis a covered dish often used as a wedding present.

The original Greek names of some of the shapes are known; for others names have had to be invented. The subject of the names of Athenian vases and the development of each shape are discussed in Miss Milne's and my *Shapes and Names of Athenian Vases* (1935), and a list of all the various shapes in use during red-figure is given by Beazley in his recently published *Athenian Red-figure Vase-Painters,* pp. VIII f. It is unnecessary, therefore, to go over the field again here; but for the convenience of the reader we include line drawings [19] of the principal shapes with the names which have been generally assigned to them (figs. 1, 2).

The vases were for use, not merely for ornament, and are well adapted for their various functions, as practical experiments show.[20] They served as utensils of rich and poor in the days before glass came into general use.

INSCRIPTIONS

The inscriptions on Athenian vases form an important study which opens up many avenues of research.[21] They are of various kinds:

(1) Many of the extant inscriptions refer to the figures represented, supplying their names and thus making the task of identification easy, especially in mythological scenes. The names are generally in the nominative, occasionally in the genitive (with εἰκών,[22] "likeness," understood): Αἴας, "Ajax"; 'Αφροδίτης, "of Aphrodite." Sometimes an animal is named: "Xanthos," for a horse; or an object is described: θᾶκος, "a seat," ὑδρία, "a water jar," κρήνη, "a fountain." The names given to deities and heroes are generally those known from Greek literature—mostly in the forms current in the Attic dialect, e.g., Perreus (Perseus), Olytteus (Odysseus), Perrephatta and Pherrephatta (Persephone); but for Nereids, Muses, Amazons, maenads, satyrs, etc., vase painters often invented names—at least the names they use do not always tally with those in the literary works preserved to us. Since names of heroes and deities were not as a rule given to individuals in classical times,[23] especially in the period preceding the fourth century, we can take it for granted that when they occur on the vases the scene is intended for a mythological one. Thus what appears to be an ordinary household is trans-

ferred to Olympos or the bottom of the sea by the names given to the individual figures.

(2) Occasionally the action of a figure is described: ἁλούμενος εἰσι, "he is going to jump," is written next to a youth swinging his jumping weights.[24] Or a person is making a remark, the words generally issuing from his mouth: οὐ δύναμ' οὔ, "I cannot (sing), no I cannot," says a man reclining on a couch, one hand to his head, in the other his cup;[25] ἔλα, ἔλα, "get up," shouts a driver to his horses,[26] the very words used in Greece to-day to urge on a horse; ἤδη μὲν ἤδη πλέο[ν]· παραβέβακεν, "it is as full as it can be, it is spilling over," declares an oil merchant to his customer about an amphora standing between them;[27] and ὦ Ζεῦ πάτερ αἴθε πλούσιος γεν[οίμαν], "Zeus, would that I might get rich," says an oil merchant under his breath in another oil-selling scene.[28] A toast to Euthymides and one to Leagros appear on vases by Phintias and Euphronios,[29] apparently spoken by the hetairai represented on the vases. Rarely a whole dialogue is given: ἰδοὺ χελιδών, "look, a swallow," says a youth looking at a flying bird; νὴ τὸν Ἡρακλέα, "by Herakles, you are right," rejoins a man; αὐτηί, "there it is," says a boy, pointing to the bird; by his side is the title of the picture, ἔαρ ἤδη, "spring is here."[30]

(3) Sometimes the inscription is not explanatory of the scene depicted but is addressed to the person using or looking at the vase: προσαγορεύω, "I greet you" (see p. 51); ὡς οὐδέποτε Εὐφρόνιος, "Euphronios never did anything like this," on a scene by Euthymides (see p. 55).

(4) The custom among vase painters of naming a favorite youth or girl is of particular interest. The formulas employed are: so and so καλός, so and so καλή (the former much more frequently);[31] or merely the words ὁ παῖς καλός, "the boy is handsome," without the mention of a name; sometimes ναίχι, "yes," or κάρτα, "very," are added for emphasis; or, often, just καλός is used. These inscriptions need not have any relation to the subject represented, but occasionally the boy or girl depicted appears to be the favorite named.

We know from literature the admiration of the Greeks for the beauty of boys. Boys rather than women formed the center of attraction. We have many radiant descriptions of these boys in Plato's Dialogues.[32] We may suppose that the boy called "handsome" by the vase painter was a favorite of the client or of the artist or was a universally acknowledged "beauty." Kritias, for instance, tells Sokrates—after an absence at the siege of Poteidaia —of the new "beauties"—περὶ τῶν καλῶν.³³ The same kalos name is apt to occur on a number of vases by one artist and is employed also by others, but only by contemporaries (except when different boys with the same name are meant); for the bloom of youth fades after a few years and one does not remain a fair boy for long.³⁴ This law of nature has provided archaeologists with clues for the dating of vases, for pots with the same kalos names must be contemporary and occasionally a fair boy became a promi-nent man. Thus Miltiades, the victor of Marathon in 490, per-haps had his praises sung on a vase twenty to thirty years earlier than that event, that is, about 520–510. Leagros and his son Glaukon, distinguished Athenian generals, give landmarks for the vases of about 510–505 and 470. And so on. These chronologi-cal data will be discussed in detail in the introductory chapters of the different sections.

(5) Most precious of all are the signatures of artists. Consid-ering the large number of vases preserved, such signatures are rare. Only about fifty names of artists (including potters and painters) are preserved on red-figured vases, most of them occur-ring several times. Not only the best work was signed. In fact most of the finest vases have no signature and some poor ones do. Some distinguished artists signed a few of their works (not necessarily their best) but left many unsigned; other equally great or perhaps greater artists never signed, at least their names are not recorded on the vases stylistically identified as theirs. To mention a few instances: Myson's name is known from a single signature on a second-rate column krater found on the Akropo-lis, but he did not sign his extant masterpieces—the amphora with Croesus in the Louvre and the krater with Aithra in the British Museum (see p. 71). Makron's name occurs once, on his masterpiece in Boston, and perhaps a second time, on a pyxis in Athens (see p. 81). On the many works attributed to the Panaitios Painter, the Berlin Painter, the Brygos Painter, the Achilles Painter not a single painter's signature appears.

The formula employed by the artist is either, so and so "made it" (ἐποίησεν, ἐποίει) or, so and so "painted it" (ἔγραψεν, ἔγραφε). Rarely he uses both, "painted and made it" (ἔγραψεν κἀποίησεν). A few times a double signature occurs: "so and so made it and so and so painted it." "Made it" is the commonest form. Now and then the same name occurs on different vases, sometimes with "made it," sometimes with "painted it." In two instances—on black-figured little-master cups—two men sign with epoiesen.[35]

Such is the evidence. It has sometimes been interpreted to indicate that the name which appears with *epoiesen* is that of the owner of the pottery, the employer of the "factory hands." [36] But if this were true, if "so and so made it" were the mark of an atelier, would not this trademark occur on all the better pieces, rather than on a few? [37] Furthermore epoiesen means "made it." It is the word regularly used by the sculptor when he signs, and it would be the natural term for the potter, that is, the maker, to employ. The beauty of the Greek shapes, their harmonious proportions, the achievement implied in such products as a kylix with a bowl twelve inches or more in diameter or a large stamnos with overhanging shoulder, make it only natural that the potter should be considered at least on a par with the decorator.[38]

Egrapsen,[39] "painted it," of course refers to the decorator. It is the term regularly employed by a painter. But when a man signs only with epoiesen, is he only the potter or the painter as well? We know definitely that in some cases he is not the painter. The vases signed by Hieron as potter (epoiesen) cannot have been also painted by him, since in one case Makron signed as painter (egrapsen) jointly with Hieron as potter, and the majority of the vases signed only by Hieron are painted in the same style as the specimen he signed with Makron (see p. 81). Occasionally the verb epoiesen may refer also to the painting, but we can never be sure. Of course when a man signs *egrapsen kapoiesen,* "painted and made it," he is the potter as well as the painter. The feeling for form and for decoration are often allied. One individual may have both gifts—the ability to fashion vases and the ability to ornament them; but not necessarily, as we know from present experience. As a matter of fact, however, there are very few certain instances in Athenian red-figure of the same men having both potted and painted; the double signature egrapsen kapoiesen is only preserved of Douris, Myson, and perhaps Epiktetos. And though the names of Euphronios, Phintias, and Pasiades occur on some vases with epoiesen and on others with egrapsen, the decorators of the epoiesen vases are not identical with those of the egrapsen ones (see pp. 51, 53 f., 56).

In a few cases the same name, with the verb egrapsen, occurs on vases which are different in style. For instance, a pelike in Berlin is signed *Epiktetos egrapsen,* but the decoration is not in the style of the well-known vase painter Epiktetos, but in that of the artist who has been called the Kleophrades Painter, since he decorated a cup potted by Kleophrades (see p. 66). The name Polygnotos occurs with the verb egrapsen on vases by at least three different artists—the man whom we have called Polygnotos for some time (see p. 127), the so-called Lewis Painter (see p. 112), and the so-called Nausikaa Painter (see p. 97). The name Douris occurs with egrapsen not only on the many vases by the painter who has long been familiar by that name, but on a vase by the so-called Triptolemos Painter (see p. 83). In these cases the most reasonable explanation is that more than one vase painter bore the name in question.

Most signatures are painted in the fields of the vases, before firing, but they also occur on handles or feet or rims; and sometimes they are incised instead of painted, before or after firing. Thus Hieron generally incised his name on the handle,[40] occasionally on the foot; Andokides on the foot.[41] The fact that most signatures, including those with epoiesen, are painted, presumably by the decorator of the vase, has been advanced as an argument against the theory that epoiesen refers to the potter. But surely the potter even when he did not paint the decoration could nevertheless sign his work with the brush or could let someone else do it for him.[42] We know too little of ancient practice in these matters to have definite opinions.

It is tempting to speculate regarding the why's and wherefore's of signatures. If a signature did not signify an artist's pride in his handiwork—as presumably it did not, since so much first-rate work is unsigned and there are a number of signed inferior vases —why did the artist sign? Hardly to advertise his work, for in that case he would have made a practice of signing his best products. Hardly to autograph gifts to friends, for most signatures were affixed before firing. Not, as was sometimes the case in the Renaissance, for identification away from home, for many vases found in Italy have no signatures and many examples discovered in Athens have. On the present evidence, the only answer is that we do not know. It looks as if a signature were due merely to the whim of the maker.

Most of the extant signatures on red-figured vases belong to the late sixth and early fifth centuries. The great names of Andokides, Epiktetos, Euphronios, Euthymides, Phintias, Sosias, Smikros, Onesimos, Kleophrades, Brygos, Hieron, Makron, Douris, all date from that time. But the custom continued through the fifth century (Sotades, Hermonax, Polygnotos, Epigenes, Xenotimos) to its closing years (Meidias, Aristophanes, Mikion) and into the early fourth century (Xenophantos). The only Athenian signatures of the later fourth century so far known are on Panathenaic amphorae.

(6) There are many meaningless inscriptions. Apparently the painter began to give names to his figures or to supply a kalos name and then added letters that made no sense. Since inscriptions generally have a decorative value and play their part in the design, the artist may sometimes have felt it necessary to supply them regardless of whether they had any meaning.[43]

(7) On the under side of the feet of Greek vases (rarely elsewhere) there sometimes appear inscriptions, *dipinti* (painted) or *graffiti* (scratched in the clay). They consist of marks, one or more letters, ligatures, names of vases (often abbreviated), descriptions of vases ("large" or "small"), numerals (sometimes with τιμή, "price," added), kalos names, and so on. One might expect, therefore, to learn from them many things, for instance, the correct ancient names of some of the vases. A detailed study, however, by Hackl and others [44] has shown that this is not the case; that many of the price graffiti are apparently memoranda of transactions, often with no relation to the vase on which they have been scratched. Nevertheless one can glean from them a number of interesting facts.

(a) Ionic forms of letters, though they do not occur in other inscriptions on vases until about 490–480, appear earlier in the graffiti. Occasionally on the same vase there are an inscription in pure Attic and a graffito with Ionic forms. Hackl, therefore, surmised that the writers of the graffiti were the traders who scratched memoranda of their orders on sample vases, and that these middlemen, who formed the link between the Athenian Kerameikos and the Etruscan market, were Ionians, at least up to about 480. After that date the Ionian script was used increasingly in Athens and is therefore no longer a distinguishing mark. We must remember, however, that the Ionian alphabet was the book script even before 480; [45] so that any trader might have used it as an international handwriting.[46]

(b) Before about 480 the numerals employed in the graffiti belong to the so-called Milesian or alphabet system, after that time to the Attic decimal (acrophonic) system.[47] The change from the convenient Milesian system to the more clumsy Attic has been explained by the theory that Athenian traders stepped in at that time.

(c) The nature of the memoranda affords a glimpse of how the negotiations were made. The letters, marks, ligatures, abbreviations probably stood for the name of the buyer, the names and descriptions of vases for the order given, and the numerals for the quantity of vases ordered or for their price (in drachmas and obols).

(d) The prices mentioned are particularly interesting.[48] There are not many certain instances, but enough to give us an idea. Six kraters cost 4 drachmas; twenty bathea 1 drachma and 1 obol; twenty oxides 3 obols.[49] This information tallies with that derived from Aristophanes, *Frogs* 1236, that a lekythion cost an obol. Large vases were of course more expensive than small ones, and decorated ones than plain ones—as is shown by the graffiti which refer to ὑδ(ρίαι) ποι(κίλαι) costing fully 3 and 2 drachmas apiece.[50] Considering that a drachma was a good day's wage in the fifth century, the prices are on the whole what one would expect.

(e) By far the majority of the graffiti of the kind described above occur on vases found in Italy. This supposedly favors the theory that Ionian traders carried on the overseas trade.[51]

(f) Recently a number of vases with graffiti have been found in the Athenian Agora.[52] These consist chiefly of names on *ostraka* (sherds used in ostracism), kalos names, or two or three letters (perhaps indications of ownership), or a ligature of *de*, presumably for *demosia* = state property, for occasionally the entire word is written out.

(g) The few Etruscan graffiti [53] which occur on Athenian vases are mostly owners' names and such words as *suthina*, "tomb article." They were therefore probably inscribed in Etruria. We may call attention in this connection to the inscription metru menece on a red-figured fragment from Populonia [54] which has been tentatively read as "Metru made it" or "Metru gave it." [55] The inscription is painted on the glaze and fired and must therefore have been added when the vase was made. This would seem to indicate that this vase, and presumably some other Attic vases, were actually made in Italy—unless we assume that the Etruscan inscription on the vase from Populonia was added in Athens for the benefit of an Etruscan client.

(h) Some graffiti in the Cypriot syllabary occur on Attic vases.[56] They usually consist of a dedication or an owner's name; but two on a red-figured bell krater have been interpreted as price memoranda.[57] This would point to lively traveling by traders.

The technique of the inscriptions varies. The majority, as we saw in the case of the signatures, are painted in a dark red pigment either on the black glaze or on the red terracotta; a few are incised before firing (and occasionally glazed over [58] or filled with white paint); [59] some, like the graffiti, are incised, generally after firing; in rare instances they are in relief.[60] Athenian vase painters were often faulty spellers; and since many apparently spelled by sound, their inscriptions throw light on the way a word was pronounced by the populace.[61] For instance, on a little stand in New York [62] the name of the well-known vase painter is spelt with an ε—Kletias—showing for the first time that his name was really Kleitias, not Klitias as spelt on the François and other vases, and that the pronunciation of the "e" sound in this word as "ι" is, in certain circles at least, as old as the sixth century B.C. Occasionally, but not often, non-Attic forms appear—chiefly Doric ones, once in a while Ionic ones.[63] Up to about 490 the letters are written in Attic script (except the graffiti, see p. 19); after 480, Ionic letters begin to appear: [64] first Ξ and ν ; then ʌ for lambda, Γ for gamma, and Ω ; finally H for η instead of for the rough breathing.[65] The early appearance of these Ionic letters on the vases, as compared with official stone inscriptions, is of course explained by the fact that pots are not official documents; the Ionic forms were in general use long before they were adopted by the state.[66] After about 450 we often find A for ʌ and ε for ϛ; but even on vases by the same artist varying forms occur.[67]

CHRONOLOGY

The chronology of red-figured Athenian vases—both relative and absolute—has by now become reliably established. The absolute dating is based on landmarks similar to those used for the sculptures of that period. These landmarks are dated events—the Samian attack on Siphnos before 524 B.C., which supplies a date for the reliefs of the Siphnian Treasury and the vases related to them (see p. 43); the sojourn of Anakreon in Athens in the late sixth century, which gives a date to the vases with representations of him (see p. 58); the battle of Marathon in 490, which dates the mound in which the fallen Athenians and some vases were buried (see p. 64); the sack of Athens by the Persians in 480 and 479 with the consequent stowing away of the broken statues and vases in pits on the Akropolis (see p. 65); the battles of Samos and Corcyra in 441–440 and 433–432 under the general Glaukon, who was probably the fair youth named on vases of the "Early Free" period (see p. 93); the erection of the Periklean and post-Periklean buildings to whose sculptures the vase paintings of the second half of the fifth century are stylistically related (see p. 117); the purification of the island of Delos in 425 when the contents of certain graves—including vases—were transferred to Rheneia (see p. 141); the death of Dexileos in the battle of Corinth in 394 B.C. which gives an approximate date for the vases found in his burial-plot (see p. 142); the visit to Athens of the Theban musician Pronomos, who is mentioned by Aristophanes and in an inscription, and is named on a volute krater in Naples (see p. 142); the burial of Lacedaemonians in 403 B.C. in the Athenian Kerameikos which dates the vase fragments found in their grave (see p. 142); the occurrence of names of Athenian archons on late Panathenaic vases (see p. 156); and so on.

With this framework of absolute dates it has been possible to establish a general chronology for red-figured vases. A more precise dating of individual vases is based on relative chronology. Since the absolute landmarks show that, just as in sculpture, the change from stylization to naturalism was steadily progressive, we can date vase paintings in relation to one another, according to the degree of naturalism attained in the renderings of the figures and of the draperies. Of course in these relative dates a certain leeway must be allowed when we connect them with absolute dates; for, as we pointed out in *Kouroi*,[68] there must have been progressives and conservatives among ancient artists, just as there are to-day. In spite of the undoubted fact that, stylistically, throughout the period we are discussing there was a constant progression from conventionalized to naturalistic painting, it is quite possible that some people lagged behind and during their maturity painted in the style current in their youth. We must date their works in the period in which their style was generally practised; for it is the artist's style not his individual propensities that concerns us here.

We have recorded in our various sections the specific evidence, both absolute and relative, which has supplied the dates of our periods and of the works of individual artists. The wealth of vases at our command has made it possible in many cases to be more precise in the assignment of dates than is possible in contemporary sculptures.

TECHNIQUE

In every form of art it is important to understand the technique involved. Only by realizing the possibilities and limitations inherent in tools and materials can we estimate the value of the achievement.

Our information on the technique of Athenian pottery is from two sources, firstly from a few statements by ancient writers and from representations of potters at work on Greek vases and plaques, and secondly from the vases themselves.[69] Neither kind of data can usefully be interpreted except in the light of the modern potter's experience, for any potter, whether ancient or modern, works within the limits of his material—clay. Much of what is said below about the preparation of the clay and the fashioning of the vase is drawn from modern practice. The Athenian black glaze and the practice of making line drawings with it has no exact modern analogy.

I. PREPARATION OF THE CLAY [70]

There are two classes of clay—sedimentary and residual. Sedimentary clay has been moved about on the earth's surface by rains, floods, and so forth and in its journeys has picked up and incorporated various ingredients or "sediments." Consequently when fired it is buff, or pink, or red according to the amount of iron in it. A sedimentary clay is often in its natural state a satisfactory pottery body or base without the addition of other ingredients, and answers the three requirements of the potter—plasticity (to enable it to hold its form), porosity (to enable it to dry properly and the water to escape), and vitrification (to enable the clay to be fired without cracking or too great shrinkage). A residual clay has remained or "resided" in its original pocket. It is the purest form of clay, fires white, and is nonplastic.

Athenian pottery was made of sedimentary clay. It had a high percentage of iron in its composition and fired pinkish red. The shapes testify to an unusual degree of plasticity. The white residual clay was used by the Athenians only for a coating or engobe on the white-ground vases (see p. 31).

To prepare the clay for the potter, it has to be mined, washed, sieved, mixed, and blunged; excess water must be pressed out to obtain the right consistency; and the clay must be wedged or beaten to remove air and to even the texture. In modern Greece the wedging is done by treading the clay with bare feet; in an American studio pottery the procedure is to cut a ball of clay in two on a taut wire, throwing the two parts vigorously one on top of the other on a plaster or hardwood stationary board, lift the whole lump, cut it in two again, and repeat the process until the air is beaten out and the texture is even.

II. FASHIONING OF THE VASE

(1) WHEEL WORK

(a) *Throwing.* The potter places a ball of wedged clay on the wheel head, centers it as the wheel rotates by the firm grip of his moist hands, and then forms the desired shape, constantly adding water.[71] The smaller Greek vases were thrown in one piece, the larger ones in sections. The joins of the latter were generally made at structural points; for instance, at the junction of neck and body or of body and foot. On the inside, the joins are often clearly visible; to conceal them on the outside, and to add strength, coils of soft clay, or slip (liquid clay), were sometimes added.[72]

Many potters to-day carefully design and draw their shapes on paper first, and it is possible that Athenian potters did the same (see pp. 10 f.). The required proportions could easily be obtained while throwing by checking with rule and calipers.[73] Complete accuracy is not required at this stage; for minor changes can be made during the subsequent process of "turning" (see below).

The extant representations of the potter's wheel on Greek vases indicate that it was of the type propelled by a helper.[74] Though there is literary evidence for the employment of the kick wheel from the second century B.C.,[75] there is no information regarding its use earlier; but it may, of course, have been known,[76] for the mechanics involved are simple enough. The only wheel heads which have survived are Aegean or Roman and of terracotta. Nowadays plaster, metal, and wood are used for the purpose.

(b) *Turning*. After having been left to dry until firm, or leather-hard, the vase is turned, that is, it is recentered and refined with metal cutting-tools while it revolves on the wheel.[77] By this continued trimming off of shavings of clay the walls can be thinned, if necessary, the moldings sharpened and refined, and any adjustments made in width and height. Judging from modern experience, all the intricate, delicate details of foot, shoulder, and mouth in Athenian vases could be obtained by tools of a few standard shapes in various sizes.[78] When more clay was needed it could be added in slip (liquid) form. Thus the vase could be made to correspond exactly to a planned design. If the vase is made in sections, each is separately turned, the sections are assembled and set together with slip in between the sections, and the whole is turned once more.[79] In the narrow-mouthed Athenian vases, like the amphora and hydria, the insides were not turned, but left as thrown. We can often see the ridges caused by the fingers of the potter as he lifted the clay in throwing the shape. But wide-mouthed vases, where the inside is as conspicuous as the outside, were carefully turned throughout.

For the smoothing of the surface and the removal of the turning marks, metal scrapers and soft sponges are found useful now
and doubtless were employed in ancient times; for, though the
marks of the turning tools can often be detected here and there
on Athenian vases,[80] the better-worked examples are generally
beautifully smooth.

(2) MOLDING

The process which enables the potter to produce a number
of identical vases by pouring or pressing clay into a mold was
used in red-figure only for plastic vases where the work de-
manded it. The molds were not made of plaster as nowadays but
of terracotta, and generally in two parts. The clay was pressed
(not poured) into each part separately, left to harden, and re-
leased itself upon shrinkage. Finally the parts were joined with
slip and the seams effaced. Often the lip was thrown separately
on the wheel and attached. On the insides of the vases the several
joins are often clearly visible; also the marks of the fingers where
they had pressed the clay. The majority of the extant examples
are in the shape of human and animal heads; [81] some in that of
single figures or groups.[82] Only in a few cases has chance preserved several replicas of the same vase. Occasionally a plastic
head was added to a vase.[83]

(3) BUILDING

The art of building—that is, fashioning a vase by building it
up with coils or slabs of clay—was practised in Greece during
the Early Bronze Age. Many examples of that period from Crete,
Cyprus, and elsewhere have survived. However, when once the
art of throwing on the wheel was invented, the slower process of
building was abandoned—except for the plain, coarse "household" pots and pitchers used for storing and cooking.[83a] There
are no built Attic black- or red-figured vases. Nowadays, on the
other hand, the two processes of building and throwing are practised side by side in studio potteries.

(4) ATTACHMENT OF HANDLES

Handles are attached in leather-hard condition, the joins being made with slip. Their general shape is obtained while the
clay is soft, then, when leather-hard, they can be refined with

modeling tools. Athenian handles were handmade, not molded. Only those parts which showed were carefully smoothed; the parts which were hidden (for instance the under parts of column-krater handles) were left rough [84]—just as were the insides of narrow-mouthed vases. The Greek potter's attitude was evidently the same as that of the Greek sculptor, who was apt to leave unfinished those parts of his statue which were not visible. It was no use spending time on unnecessary toil. Better to bestow infinite care on what was important—the shapes and proportions and the finish of the parts which showed.

III. DECORATION OF THE VASE

(1) THE BLACK GLAZE

Instead of attempting the brilliant color effects of the Egyptians, Persians, and Chinese, the Greek potters confined themselves to a single variety of black, which was made to contrast with the vivid orange-red of fired clay. The consistency of this black medium was long a puzzle, until it was successfully reproduced by Theodor Schumann in experiments made during the last war at Heisterholz, Westphalia.[85] He demonstrated that the black is not a glaze in the modern sense, for it contains insufficient alkali to render it fusible at a given temperature; it is simply liquid, iron-containing clay, similar to that out of which the Attic pottery was made, but peptized—that is, with the heavier particles eliminated by means of protective colloid. By using the fluid made of the lighter particles of the clay, he obtained a "glaze" of remarkable thinness and smoothness, and yet which had sufficient body to make single lines stand out in relief.

Charles F. Binns had in 1929 [86] put forward the theory that the Greek black was not produced by the addition of a separate substance but by the action of the fire; that is, the pottery was fired first under oxidizing, then under reducing, and finally under reoxidizing conditions (not in three separate firings, but in three stages of the same fire). Dr. Schumann's experiments proved this surmise to be correct. In the first, oxidizing fire, when there is an excess of air and oxygen, the carbon of the fuel combines with the two atoms of oxygen in the air to form carbon dioxide (CO_2); whereas in the subsequent reducing fire, when the air is shut off and smoke introduced, the carbon monoxide (CO)—which is very hungry for oxygen—extracts oxygen from the red ferric oxide (Fe_2O_3) present in the clay and converts it into black magnetic oxide of iron (Fe_3O_4) or ferrous oxide (Fe_2O); [87] then in the third, reoxidizing fire, in which air is again introduced, the clay (which together with the glaze turned black during the reducing fire) becomes again red, since it is sufficiently porous to readmit the oxygen, whereas the denser glaze remains black.[88] The red spots that frequently occur on what were intended to be black areas can be explained as caused either by the fact that the glaze was applied too thinly and so was porous enough to reabsorb the oxygen during the third stage of the firing, or by the clay having been protected from reduction in the kiln through stacking or contact with a jet of air.[89] The relatively few cases where red-glazed areas were intentionally, not accidentally, produced—that is, when they occur in precisely defined areas, consciously contrasted with the black—may be explained as due either to a second, purely oxidizing firing for those parts that were to come out red, or to the addition of red ocher to the glaze for the parts that were to become red. That the second, simpler method is possible has been demonstrated by Dr. Marie Farnsworth.[90]

Since the white slip of the white-ground vases (cf. p. 31) contained only a small quantity of iron, it was much less affected by the reducing fire than was the black glaze (made of the red-burning clay) and so only assumed occasionally an ivory hue in the reoxidizing fire. The red ocher applications (cf. below) and the red accessory colors were, like the terra-cotta body, sufficiently porous to reabsorb the oxygen.[92]

The black glaze of Athenian pottery was essentially the same as that used centuries before on the geometric and other early vases.[93] But it had gradually improved in quality until it had developed into the rich, satiny black of the sixth and fifth centuries B.C.; then, in the later, South Italian wares, it again deteriorated, indicating that it required delicate manipulation.

(2) TREATMENT OF SURFACE

The first process in the decoration of a red-figured vase was, it seems, to cover the surface with a thin, protective wash made of diluted peptized clay (Lasur), which imparted a slightly glossy, reddish hue after firing (since it was applied thinly it reoxidized in the third stage of the firing). The red was further intensified by the application of red ocher over the surface; only in a few instances is it well enough preserved to convey an idea of the original effect.[94]

(3) THE PAINTING

(a) *Red-figure.* An examination of the paintings on red-figured Athenian vases suggests the procedure to have been somewhat as follows:

A preliminary sketch for the decoration was made, probably with a wooden tool.[95] The smooth, shallow lines of this sketch are plainly visible on most vases, at least in certain lights. Sometimes the final design in glaze differs from the preliminary sketch.[96] Doubtless as to-day the painter drew his decoration directly on the vase and frequently changed his design as he painted it in permanently; for the application of an elaborate decoration to a curving vase is something difficult to anticipate in the flat surface of a cartoon.[97] In painting the decoration in glaze the outlines of the figures were drawn outside the spaces intended for them, first by a narrow line of glaze, then by a broader stripe. Then perhaps the background was filled in. Bands and plain uninterrupted glaze surfaces were applied as the vase revolved on the wheel or in the hand.[98] All this work was done with the brush, various sizes being used as required. Finally the details within the red silhouette were painted, flat or in relief. The relief lines for the contours and inner markings of the figures were perhaps drawn with a special tool (see below). Also lines and washes were added in thinned glaze where they were intended to appear brown (see pp. 38 f., 63).

Of course the procedure was doubtless not always the same, depending largely on the whim of the artist. For instance, in an unfinished scene on a krater in New York [99] the outlines of the figures have been indicated by contour stripes, the background has been filled in, and certain details (hair, features, folds) have been painted in flat lines; but the relief lines are lacking throughout. On the other hand on various fragments of unfinished vases [100] the background has not been filled in, whereas the interior markings are completed.

The tool used to produce the famous black relief line—a glaze line which stands out in relief—has been much discussed, and numerous suggestions have been made—a fine brush, a single bristle, a reed, a feather, a pen, a quill. The chief requirement is a tool pliant yet offering a certain amount of resistance, which holds enough glaze to produce the long-drawn-out unbroken lines so frequent in red-figure. The groove which often runs down the middle of the relief line is not a clue, as some have thought; for actual experiments indicate that a slight pressure of any instrument produces such a result. Moreover, some relief lines have no groove but a ridge, and occasionally a line with a ridge continues into one with a groove.[101] The whole question can now be viewed in a new light since the discovery of the consistency of the black medium.

The vase painters on the Caputi hydria [102] grasp their brushes in their fists, the bristles downward—in Japanese fashion; likewise the youth painting a krater, on a bell krater in Oxford.[103] The youth decorating a kylix, on a kylix in Boston,[104] and the painter on a fragment in Athens [105] hold their brushes between thumb and forefinger. Both methods were therefore in use.

Either before or after the figured scenes the ornamental motives were painted with the brush, freehand without the aid of stencils, as their irregularities conclusively show (see p. 10).

When the decoration in black and diluted black glaze was completed the accessory colors [106] were added. Their choice and the extent to which they were used differed somewhat in the various periods. The commonest was red, which was employed for such details as fillets, wreaths, flowers, etc. White appears occasionally for details in the early period,[107] rarely in the ripe archaic and early free periods, more profusely later. Over it we often find—in the late period—yellow lines in thinned glaze. That these colors were fired is shown by the discoloration of the black glaze beneath them; often their former presence can be determined only by this discoloration. As the taste for polychromy grew we find red, blue, green, and pink applied in tempera technique after firing (cf. pp. 141, 155). The colors were often applied over a (fired) white undercoating, which gave them a lighter, more luminous tone.[108] The coloring is in fact identical with that used in the terra-cotta statuettes. Gold leaf was used rarely at first, increasingly in the later periods, to indicate jewelry, weapons, and other gleaming objects, occasionally even for whole figures (see p. 163). It was generally laid over applied buff clay, sometimes with a white undercoating—of course after firing, for gold leaf could not have stood burning.

Applied clay was employed occasionally for objects which were meant to stand out in relief, such as fillets, spear shafts, shields, etc.[109] Sometimes, especially in the late period, it was used for entire figures (see p. 163), and whole scenes (see pp. 163 f.); it was often gilded or painted various colors.

While the vase was being decorated it was no doubt kept in leather-hard condition by being placed in a special room or closet where a damp atmosphere was induced to prevent the ware from drying. Thereby plenty of time could be spent on the decoration if necessary, and the work need not be hurried. Before being fired the vase was thoroughly dried.

(b) *White-ground*. Concurrently with red-figure another technique was in use in the later sixth and in the fifth century— the white-ground, in which a white slip (liquid clay) coating was applied on the body of the vase. Over this the figures were painted in solid black in silhouette (with details incised as in black-figure), or in outline (with merely minor areas, for instance the hair, in solid black); or the two methods were employed together on the same vase. The outline technique, inherited from the seventh century, had persisted "as a thin trickle, side by side with the broad stream of black-figure, throughout the sixth century." [110] It gradually gained in favor on white-ground vases and presently ousted the black silhouettes. At first the whole drawing was in black-glaze lines, then partly in black partly in diluted glaze lines, then the whole design was drawn in diluted glaze lines, and lastly in matt black or reddish lines (see pp. 41, 64, 75, 93, 119–122, 141); moreover solid washes in tempera colors were applied on draperies and on other large areas, first red and yellow, then also blue, purple, green, mauve, and pink. A similar technique was occasionally used directly on the black glaze.[110a]

IV. THE FIRING

The temperature at which Athenian vases were fired was rather lower than is usual to-day. It seems to have been about 950°–960° C.[111] (corresponding to about cone 08–07); at least

any considerable increase over this temperature causes a change
in the pinkish buff of the clay and the rich black of the glaze, as
well as an additional contraction. As 950 C. is approximately
the melting point of silver, the ingenious suggestion has been
made that silver was used by the Greeks for regulating the heat,[112]
in the same way that modern potters use the Seger cones. But
previous to the invention of these heat-recording cones firings
were judged by the color of the burn through a spy hole, and
it is perhaps more likely that the Greeks used this simple method.

The evidence favors the theory that Greek pottery was once-
fired, like most ancient wares, not twice-fired—that is, before and
after glazing—like most modern pottery: [113] (1) The incised lines
on black-figured Athenian vases must have been made on the
black glaze while the clay was leather-hard; their delicacy, swing,
and smoothness could not have been attained by incision into
hard, fired clay or even into dry clay; and if black-figured ware
was once-fired, surely the red-figured vases—many of them contemporary with the black-figured ones—were also. (2) The light
incisions on the glaze used for the indication of the ground and
other details on late red-figured vases (see p. 141) must have
been made before firing. (3) The numerous dents on Athenian
vases could only have occurred before the pots were fired; [114]
since the marks left by the objects which caused the dents go over
the glaze,[115] it follows that the ware must have been decorated
before firing. (4) The applied clay, used to make certain details
of the decoration stand out in relief (see pp. 31, 64, 163), would
never have adhered to already fired clay. It must have been added
to the vase while the latter was still leather-hard.[116]

The only serious objection against a single fire—that the vase
painters represented on the Caputi hydria [117] and the Boston
kylix [118] handle their pots in what would seem a precarious way
for green ware—can be met by the theory that the ancient Greek
clay was as tough as is the modern Greek clay. At least actual
experiments with Athenian clay to-day have shown that there
would be no risk connected with holding a cup by its stem or
tipping a vase on its foot while leather-hard.[119] The clay not
only is unusually plastic, and so stands up better while it is being thrown than most of our clays, but is not nearly so vulnerable
when leather-hard or bone-dry. That this was also a characteristic
of the ancient clay is suggested by the shapes of Athenian pottery

—the wide-spreading kylikes, the stamnoi with their incurving shoulders, and other forms with overhanging rims and projecting handles. Though there are occasional instances of sagging (probably due to uneven turning), the fact that such shapes were current indicates that the clay must have been appropriate for them. It should be noted, moreover, that in the Caputi hydria one of the vases (and perhaps also the other) is placed on a support, evidently to prevent the strain from being borne by the edge of the foot. If the vase had been fired this precaution would not have been necessary.

As was pointed out above (see pp. 27 f.), the Athenian potters fired their ware partly under oxidizing, partly under reducing conditions. The fuel seems to have been wood or charcoal.

Like modern potters the ancients doubtless packed their kilns as full as possible, placing as many vases together as practicable; for firing is a long and expensive process. About twelve hours or more are allowed to-day for firing an earthenware kiln of average size, and about three times as long for cooling. The under parts of the feet on which Athenian pots stand are almost always unglazed, for the obvious reason that the vases were fired resting on their feet.[120] But to conserve space, at least some vases were evidently stacked one inside another. The marks left on the glaze by such stacking can often be seen, especially on the insides and outsides of kylikes [121] and occasionally the glaze of the covered area has fired a different color from the rest of the vase.[122] An additional advantage of such stacking in the case of a kylix would be that the slender stem did not have to carry the weight of the bowl. That such stacking of glazed ware was possible shows the nonadhesive quality of the Greek glaze.

GREEK KILNS

Our chief information regarding Greek kilns is derived from representations on Corinthian and Attic pottery.[123] Most of the actual kilns found are of the Roman period; [124] but several of prehistoric Greek times have recently come to light,[125] and a few of the classical period.[126]

From this evidence—assuming the same general type to have been in use throughout antiquity—we learn that the Greek kiln was divided horizontally into two parts—an upper, domed chamber for the placing of the pots and a lower one for the fuel; [127] and that there were three openings, one at the bottom to admit the fuel, one at the side to receive the ware and to serve as a spy hole, and one at the top to let out the smoke and to permit the regulation of the draught.

Mr. Binns made the plausible suggestion that the sides and domed top of the Greek kiln were made of brushwood (interlaced boughs and osiers) plastered over with clay.[128] We have evidence that this practice obtained in neolithic [129] as well as Roman times; [130] and baking ovens are still so made in modern Greece.[131] If the walls of ancient Greek kilns were of a temporary nature and only the bottoms were of stone, this would explain why more Greek kilns have not been found or at least recognized.[132] Moreover, in such a kiln the process of firing under both reducing and oxidizing conditions—known to have been in use by the Greeks—would come about of its own accord. The burning of the branches and the resultant smoke would cause reduction; but after the branches had been burned there would be no more smoke and the fire would automatically turn into an oxidizing one.

V. ACCIDENTS

The test of a pot comes in the fire. Defects in the preparation of the clay, in the construction, in the glazing, in the firing, all are revealed when the vase emerges from the kiln. That there were plenty of mistakes and mishaps in Greek vases as in modern ones becomes evident when we examine even museum pieces. We see many cases of warped lips [133] and sagged shoulders,[134] of dents [135] and cracks,[136] and of red spots in the black glaze.[137] Spalls —that is, chips produced by particles of limestone which became embedded in the clay and then exploded in the fire—are not infrequent,[138] likewise rifts in the glaze, caused by a more rapid shrinkage of the glaze than of the clay.[139] Occasionally the different sections in which the larger vases were made were not put together successfully. For instance, the body of a column krater in New York [140] was not set straight on the foot; it leans slightly to one side; consequently neck and handles had to be shaped irregularly so as to produce a level top.

Sometimes the body is not the usual pinkish buff but has

turned gray, owing to a reducing fire.[141] Occasionally the different fragments of a vase differ in color (from pink to gray), the vase having evidently been broken at the funeral pyre and its various parts subjected to different conditions.[142]

Some injuries of course have happened since the burial of the vase. In this class belong the frequent cases in which the glaze has become disintegrated and has exposed what may be a red ocher application underneath,[143] and the vases in which the surface has deteriorated.[144]

When a Greek pot was broken that was not the end of it. There are many instances of broken vases repaired with rivets in antiquity. Generally only the holes are preserved, occasionally parts of the bronze rivets also. The repairs sometimes go right through the decoration, even when this could have been avoided.[145] Pots were obviously prized for their use as well as their beauty.[146]

VI. ATHENIAN POTTERIES

We may gain a picture of what an Athenian pottery was like from the representations on Greek vases of potters at work.[147] It was probably not very different from the potteries of modern Athens—open-air places for the preparation of the clay and for the kiln, closed rooms for the making of the vases and the glazing. That a number of people worked in one establishment is shown by the vase representations, and stands to reason. The keen rivalry between the various potteries is indicated by Aristotle's [148] remark: "We like those who resemble us and have the same tastes, provided their interests do not clash with ours and that they do not gain their living in the same way; for then it becomes a case of 'Potter [being jealous] of potter.' " [149]

I. EARLY STYLE, ABOUT 530—500 B.C.

THE momentous change from the black-figured to the red-figured technique took place about 530–525 B.C., that is perhaps in the concluding years of the reign of Peisistratos († 527). The historical background of the Early Style is, therefore, first the rule of the Peisistratids, then—after the death of Hipparchos (514 B.C.) and the fall of Hippias (510 B.C.)—the introduction of Kleisthenes' constitution (508–507) and the beginning of the Athenian democracy.

The change from the black-figured to the red-figured technique involved important innovations. The figures instead of being painted in black silhouettes on a red ground were "reserved" in red against a black-glaze background, and interior lines instead of being incised were drawn in black glaze—full strength for the salient parts, diluted, to appear yellowish brown, for details. To sharpen the outlines of the figure or parts of it a contour line in relief was often added (see p. 29). The red and the white accessory colors so popular in black-figure were now used only sparingly. White was abandoned for the flesh of female figures and its use was confined to details, such as the white hair of an old man. Red appears more frequently than white—for inscriptions, wreaths, branches, fillets. In addition, applied clay was occasionally used (see p. 31). In other words, the variegated effect of black-figure was toned down considerably.

Naturally the new technique was evolved only gradually. Black-figure and red-figure went on concurrently for some time, a few painters using both techniques, occasionally on the same pot,[1] and confirmed red-figure artists like Euthymides continuing to use effectively ornamental designs in black against red around their red-figure compositions. Moreover black-figure as an independent style continued at least until the second quarter of the fifth century, and long after for the Panathenaic amphorae. In fact the majority of black-figured vases now extant date from the last third of the sixth century, when the red-figured style was already in vogue. The outstanding artists of black-figure, however—Kleitias, Nearchos, Lydos, Exekias, Amasis—all date from about 560 to 530. After 530 there are some first-class artists who produced—as far as we know—only black-figured vases, for instance the Acheloos Painter and the Antimenes Painter, but not many. The great talent of the time had evidently gone over to red-figure.[2]

In the drawing of the figures the artists of red-figure at first adhered to the conventions which had prevailed in black-figure. They did not draw the human form direct from nature but conceived it in their minds as it could be most readily apprehended, using a set of formulas similar to that of the Egyptians. The head was shown in profile (rarely in front view), the eye in front view, the trunk in either front or profile view, the legs were drawn in profile. The various parts are distinct and easily recognizable, although the figures thus pieced together often appear strangely distorted (see figs. 9–11). The motion of these figures over the black ground made a lively surface pattern in which the laws of symmetry and balance were observed. The figures were all ranged along one line as if they all moved in the front plane. The action was carried across the stage but not into or out of it. There was as yet no feeling for depth; or next to none, for, however flattened out the figures were made to appear, the third dimension could not be entirely ignored. It made itself felt when figures were made to overlap or when one form was drawn across another or partly covering another, as was the case with the two profile thighs and with the arms placed in action. The rendering of profile views suggested a certain amount of plasticity; for instance, the profile of the head suggested the bulge of the skull, and the lines of the drapery, though straight and shadowless, suggested depth in folds. Thus the third dimension insinuated itself somewhat incongruously into an otherwise two-dimensional design; and when the artist became aware of it he was faced with the problem of representing form and space on a flat surface. Henceforth, with true Greek inquisitiveness he set out in search of a solution, and we find him experimenting and slowly groping his way.

And so into the time-honored conventionalized scheme there were gradually introduced important innovations. The transition between a full-front trunk and profile legs was made less forced by placing the rectus abdominis on one side (see fig. 3), sometimes at an angle (see fig. 4), below a full-front chest. Sometimes one leg was shown in front or back view, with the other in profile (see figs. 9, 10). The collarbone on the farther side was occasionally made shorter than the nearer one to suggest the slanting away (see fig. 5),[3] or it was omitted (see fig. 14). In the

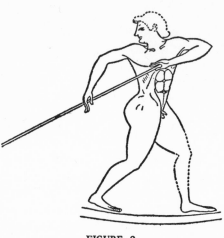

male chest the farther side was sometimes drawn in contracted form alongside the median line (see fig. 6).[4] Female breasts when in front view were represented by two profiles turned right and left (see fig. 7); when in profile view two profile breasts were sometimes drawn in the same direction and placed widely apart (see fig. 41), but generally only one profile breast was indicated (see figs. 8, 46). Occasionally the foreshorten-

FIGURE 3

ing of a limb was attempted (see figs. 9, 12). A fairly convincing way of rendering a turn of the torso was attained by drawing the nearer shoulder across the front view of the chest (see fig. 45). The back view of a figure was occasionally indicated (see figs. 9–11), but as yet with little attempt at foreshortening, the farther shoulder blade being drawn without contraction; the only indication of the turn of the trunk was given by the direction of the spine.[5] At the end of the century, however, a fairly successful three-quarter back view was sometimes attained (see fig. 44).

The indication of bones and muscles varied with individual artists; some gave much, others little, anatomical detail. A regular scheme was developed, the most

FIGURE 4

prominent divisions being generally marked in black, the rest in thinned glaze (see figs. 3, 6, 9, 17). Thus the clavicles, shoulder blades, pectorals, hips, spine, and ankles were generally drawn in black, whereas the serratus magnus, the rectus abdominis, and the bones and muscles of the arms (deltoid, biceps, triceps, the extensors of the forearm) and legs (the hollow near the great trochanter, the thigh muscles, the two vasti, the kneecap, the calf, and the peroneal muscles) when shown were generally indicated in diluted glaze.[6]

FIGURE 5

The forms were simplified: the ribs were indicated by a series of straight lines (see figs. 3, 9, 10); the serratus magnus by a set of single curves (see fig. 4); the rectus abdominis was at first marked by adjacent ovals (see figs. 10, 12), then loops were added above to show the connection with the thorax (see fig. 4).

The eye, which is one of the most important criteria in the stylistic development of Greek vases, was represented in this early period in full-front view—by two shallow curves, generally meeting at both corners, and a black dot or a circle and dot in the center (see figs. 4, 6, 8, 10, 13). As time progressed the curves became asymmetrical, to show the difference between the outer corner and the tear duct (see fig. 14). The distinction observed in black-figure between male and female eyes—the former round, the latter elongated—was discarded; all were made elongated, except, occasionally, Herakles' "fiercely gleaming eyes." [7]

FIGURE 6

A simple scheme sufficed for the hair. The mass was painted black, with a row of short curls or strands along the brow, temples, and neck, sometimes with longer curls at the sides. In order to show up this black mass against the black background the upper contour was indicated at first by an incised, then by a reserved line.

Just before the introduction of red-figure an important change had taken place in the fashion of women's dress—the heavy woolen peplos was superseded by the thin linen chiton.[8] This change is clearly reflected in the vase paintings. In the black-figured vases before about 540 the regular woman's costume is the heavy peplos, represented as foldless and ornamented with decorative designs. In the decade 540–530 both peplos and chiton occur, side by side. In the early red-figured vases the Ionic chiton has already become the prevailing

FIGURE 7

fashion. The folds are represented by parallel or radiating, curved or straight lines with zigzags at the edges, at first running in one direction only, presently in two opposite directions, up and down from a central pleat (figs. 8, 16).[9] At the end of the period under discussion (the last decade or so of the sixth century) the central pleat is generally drawn considerably higher than the lowest one, is broader than the others, and each group of pleats is divided from the next by a smooth, unpleated portion sometimes diversified by curving lines (see fig. 45). The same schemes were used for chitons of men (see figs. 10, 15), and similar ones for mantles but in larger formation, to suggest the heavier material (see figs. 4, 16). The lower edge of the garment on the farther side of the legs was indicated not by zigzags, like the nearer edge, but by a curving, often wavy, line (fig. 16).

In the earliest red-figured scenes we sometimes note survivals of the black-figured technique. Incisions appear for a few details—regularly for the contour of the hair, occasionally elsewhere, for instance for spear heads, anatomical markings, and folds of garments. Red is used as an accessory color for such things as manes and tails of horses (see p. 48). White appears now and then as a wash on the figures

FIGURE 8

(see p. 46). The full possibilities of red-figure were realized only after some time. However, the greater swing with which the interior lines could be drawn in glaze instead of by incisions was bound to effect the general outlook of the vase painter. The new technique was a welcome help in his quest to portray what increasingly interested him—the complicated mechanism of the human figure in its manifold movements and gestures. Moreover, the change from black-figure to red-figure entailed an instructive lesson in the art of spacing; for, after having been accustomed to draw his figures as patterns of dark upon light, he now had to reverse the process. He had to outline carefully with his brush and to cover with black the empty spaces of the ground, reserving light shapes for the figures. In so doing his attention was forcibly drawn to the pattern made by the background which sustained the movement of his figures. The importance of these "intervals," which contribute much to the unity of the design, was well understood by the Greeks. We may quote from Xenophon's *Oeconomica:* [10] "Yes, no serious man will smile

FIGURE 9

when I claim that there is beauty in the order even of pots and pans set out in neat array. . . . There is nothing, in short,

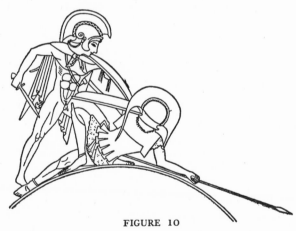

FIGURE 10

that does not gain in beauty when set out in order. For each set looks like a troop of utensils, and the space between the sets is beautiful to see, when each set is kept clear of it, just as a troop of dancers about the altar is a beautiful spectacle in itself, and even the free space looks beautiful and unencumbered."

Side by side with red-figure white-ground vases were produced in Attic potteries at this time. At first the old technique of black-

figure was retained, that is, the figures were drawn in black silhouette on the white ground with inner markings and some of the contours incised. Occasionally, however, some of the figures were drawn in outline in black glaze, as in red-figure (see p. 51).

The innovations we have described were of course not confined to vase painting; they must have been introduced also into the lost murals and panels of the time. The few paintings on marble stelai and on ter-

FIGURE 11

racotta slabs [11] that have survived show the same evolution; and among the scanty literary records on the subject [12] there is an interesting tradition of epoch-making changes in the art of panel painting parallel to those we have noted on the vases. As usual, the innovations are credited to one individual. Pliny [13] tells us that a certain Kimon of Kleonai, whom he names as a successor of the Athenian Eumaros, "devised *catagrapha,* and represented the features in different postures, looking backward or upward or downward. He marked the attachments of the limbs, gave prominence to the veins, and also discovered the wrinkles and the folds of drapery." A Eumares is mentioned as the father of Antenor on an inscribed base from the Akropolis dated perhaps about 530–520 B.C.[14] If Eumaros and Eumares are identical, Kimon, Eumaros' "successor," must have been either contemporary with Antenor or immediately posterior to him. He probably lived, therefore, at the very period of early red-figure.

Furthermore contemporary reliefs and statues show the same new interest in foreshortening and in the rendering of muscles and folds, and similar devices for their representation. Thus on the figures of the Ephesos drums (550 B.C. and later) [15] and on the Siphnian frieze (probably 530–525),[16] the draperies are no longer stiff and practically foldless, as in the earlier sculptures.

They have the same radiating folds on the mantles which we noted in early red-figure, the same wavy lines for the chitons, the same zigzag edges running mostly in one direction, occasionally in two opposite ones but then in asymmetrical formation. The stacking toward a central pleat appears first in tentative form on sculptures of the second quarter and the middle of the sixth century, for instance on the Lyons kore, here and there during the second half of the sixth century,

FIGURE 12

and in fully developed, symmetrical form in the sculptures datable about 525–500 B.C., for instance, on the pediments of the temple of Apollo at Delphi and on the stele of Aristion.[17] On the reliefs of one of the statue bases in Athens (about 510) there are attempts at foreshortening similar to those on the vases; for instance, the rectus abdominis is placed at an angle below a full-front breast, and the trunk and one leg are placed in front view, the other leg in profile.

FIGURE 13

Besides such parallels on dated sculptures we have other clues for the dating of early red-figure in the kalos names, that is, the names of the young "beauties" of the time (see pp. 15 f.). They are important evidence, for, as we have said, some of these fair boys became prominent men later and their dates are known. Nevertheless, the information is often inconclusive and we must be careful not to draw undue inferences. Let us therefore carefully examine the evidence.[18]

On a black-figured vase signed by Timagoras,[19] dated stylistically about 540, is the inscription Ἀνδοκίδης καλὸς δοκεῖ Τιμαγόραι.

If this Andokides was the well-known potter, as has been thought, we should obtain support for dating the vases signed by him about 525–520. But, as we have records of a distinguished Athenian family from about the middle of the sixth century on in which this rare name also occurs,[20] it seems more likely that the Andokides praised as kalos was a young scion of that family than that he was the potter.

On a plate in Oxford,[21] with a rider by the Cerberus Painter, dated stylistically about 520–510, a Miltiades is praised as kalos. If this Miltiades was the victor of Marathon, we should obtain support for dating the plate considerably before 490. But we also know that the great Miltiades was made tyrant of the Chersonese after 524–523 and before 514–513 and that in 493 his eldest son was old enough to command

FIGURE 14

a ship. Therefore in the decade 520–510 Miltiades was probably in his thirties, which is perhaps rather old for being called kalos.

On cups by Epiktetos and others the beauty of a Hipparchos is extolled.[22] If—as may well be—he is identical with the distinguished Hipparchos, συγγενής of Peisistratos,[23] who was elected archon in 496–495 and was ostracized in 487,[24] he would help to date the work of Epiktetos as contemporary with his youth.

Memnon is called fair on cups by the vase painter Oltos; [25] on one of these,[26] as well as on a lekythos signed by the potter Gales [27] and on a fragment of a calyx krater by the early Kleophrades Painter [28] are pictures of the poet Anakreon. The last was entertained in Athens by Hipparchos, the son of Peisistratos, and may have stayed on in Athens after the fall of the tyranny.[29] By this evidence the youth of Memnon

FIGURE 15

and the productive period of Oltos, Gales, and the early Kleophrades Painter are dated not earlier than the last quarter of the sixth century.

Leagros is mentioned as kalos on vases by Euphronios, Euthymides, the early Panaitios Painter, the Kiss Painter, the Eleusis Painter, the Colmar Painter, and the potter Kachrylion.[30] On vases of the style of a generation later Glaukon, "the son of Leagros," is so praised.[31] There was a general Leagros, son of Glaukon, who was killed in battle in 465.[32] As boys in Greece were apt to be named after their grandfathers, the general and the fair boy of Euphronios may well have been identical. The decade 510–500 is therefore a possible date for Leagros' youth. We thus obtain additional support for the dates assigned on stylistic grounds to the painters and the potter above mentioned.[33]

FIGURE 16

On vases by Phintias and Euthymides a Megakles is praised as fair.[34] This same name was found partially erased on a votive plaque from the Akropolis,[35] and it might refer either to Megakles the son of Hippokrates, who was ostracized in 486, or to his first cousin Megakles son of Kleisthenes, who was ostracized at an unknown date. If either is identical with the Megakles of the vases we obtain additional support for the dates assigned to Phintias and Euthymides.

From the foregoing analysis it is clear that the kalos names occasionally fortify dates obtained on stylistic grounds.

Further evidence for dating early, as well as later, red-figure has been supplied by the broken vases that were dumped into unused wells and recently unearthed in the Athenian Agora, Corinth, and elsewhere.[35a] Though such dumping in the same well was not restricted to the same year, it was nevertheless confined to a limited period, and vases found together form an approximately contemporary group.

The favorite shapes of this early period were the amphora, the neck amphora, the hydria, the volute and column kraters, and especially the kylix in a variety of forms. Several new shapes now made their appearance—the stamnos, the pelike, the kalpis, and the psykter.[36] The calyx krater, already used by Exekias in his late period,[37] now became prevalent. The eye kylix gradually superseded the little-master cup.[37a]

We can distinguish a number of prominent painters who worked in this period—some at the very beginning of the new technique, others during the last two decades of the century.

(1) THE ANDOKIDES PAINTER, PSIAX, AND THE GOLUCHOW PAINTER

The foremost artists of the beginning of red-figure were the Andokides Painter and Psiax. They may well be credited with the invention of the new technique—unless there were other painters of whom no work has survived.

Of the seven vases signed by the potter Andokides, with epoiesen, four were painted by one artist: the amphora with a combat and a kitharist in the Louvre,[38] the amphora with Amazons and women bathing, also in the Louvre; [39] the kylix with archers and a trumpeter in Palermo; [40] and the amphora with wrestlers and the struggle for the tripod, in Berlin.[41] As the real name of this artist is not known he has been called the ANDOKIDES PAINTER. Twenty-six other works have been attributed to him, mostly on large vases—amphorae and hydriai, a few on kylikes.[42] He painted in both black-figure and red-figure, sometimes in both techniques on the same vase. On the amphora in the Louvre with women bathing, he used the new light-on-dark scheme, but with a white slip on his figures. As he worked at the beginning of a new technique he was naturally an experimenter. Lysippides,[43] Pordax, and Mnesilla occur as kalos and kale names on his black-figured amphorae in London and Munich.

His figures, often dressed in elaborately decorated and carefully pleated garments and posed in rather affected attitudes, bring before us the luxurious Peisistratid days; they are the painted counterparts of some of the sculptured Maidens from the Akropolis. His work has strength as well as delicacy. The wrestlers, for instance, on the Berlin amphora, and the Herakles driving an ox to sacrifice, on an amphora in Boston,[44] stand out by their clean contours and lively designs. And he was able to dramatize his pictures. Herakles, on an amphora in the Louvre,[45] placating the three-headed Kerberos while he holds the chain in readiness (see fig. 34), is vividly characterized, and so are the gay, wild-eyed satyrs on an amphora in Orvieto.[46]

The artist who decorated the amphora in Philadelphia [47] signed by the potter Menon used to be called the Menon Painter, but he has recently been identified with PSIAX,[48] who signed, with egrapsen, the two alabastra in Carlsruhe [49] and Odessa [50]

potted by Hilinos. Besides these three vases twenty-eight others
have been attributed to him, black-figured and red-figured, large
and small.[51] Among them is an amphora in Madrid [52] signed by
the potter Andokides and decorated with Apollo, Artemis, Leto,
and Ares in red-figure on one side, and a Dionysiac scene in
black-figure on the other. Another amphora in Munich [53] has
a red-figured scene of Dionysos reclining and a black-figured
chariot of Herakles. Such "bilinguals" are of great interest, for
they supply contemporary pictures by the same artist in the two
different techniques. A red-figured kylix in New York [54] is one
of Psiax's best works. On the interior is an archer in Oriental
costume—pointed cap with long lappets and long-sleeved jacket
—holding a horse by a long lead. The exterior is decorated with
a (fragmentary) chariot scene and a battle. On the left of the
latter a youth is blowing a trumpet, the signal for attack. Then
comes a group of three warriors; the one in the middle, attacked
from front and back, is sinking, blood streaming from a wound
in his leg. To the right a warrior is standing over his fallen
opponent, ready to kill him with the sword. The turmoil is
vividly conveyed by the attack and fall of the contestants, the
long spears going in different directions, and the asymmetrical
composition.

Other lively combats comparable to the New York one appear on an aryballos once in Bologna,[55] a kylix in Munich,[56] and
a fragment of a kylix in Leningrad.[57] A kyathos in Milan,[58] with
Dionysos, Satyrs, and Maenads, has a head, exquisitely modeled
in relief, inside, near the base of the handle. Among the black-
figured vases we may mention especially a kylix in Odessa [59] with
Diomede, Perseus, and Hermes, four plates in London and Berlin [60] with single figures, and a plate in a private collection [61]
with a group of a man dancing and a woman playing the flute,
on a white ground (fig. 36)—all highly finished works.

The name Psiax appears without a verb on two bilingual eye
kylikes in Munich [62] and New York.[63] The decorations on them
may or may not be by the artist himself. Besides the kalos name
Menon those of Hippokrates, Karystios, and Smikrion occur on
Psiax's vases.

Psiax's paintings are distinguished for their dainty grace and
meticulous execution, the delicate, slightly hesitant line, and the
wealth of detail. His style is distinctive and easily recognized.

Similar renderings occur again and again, for instance, the farther edge of the chiton sleeve drawn as an arc of slightly wavy outline, with a little circle for the button, and the small, boneless hands with thumbs turned back at the tips.

Like the Andokides Painter, Psiax was an experimenter. He worked in different techniques—black-figure, red-figure, black on white, white on red, and red-figure with added colors—he employed unusual technical devices, for instance applied red clay for such things as spear shafts,[64] and he placed some of his figures in surprisingly bold attitudes. Though as a rule he still pieced his figures together from separately conceived parts (see fig. 9) he occasionally attempted three-quarter views; for instance, in the New York attacking warrior (see fig. 10), where the abdominal muscle and the patella of the right knee are shifted to one side and the shield is foreshortened.[65] We have here one of the earliest extant attempts of such renderings.

THE GOLUCHOW PAINTER [66] also belongs to the beginning of red-figure. Only four works have so far been attributed to him, among them two oinochoai in Goluchow,[67] one with a discus thrower, the other with an akontist. In these vigorous figures all the anatomical markings are drawn in full-strength glaze, the importance of subordinating some details by painting them in diluted glaze not having yet been understood. As a result the general effect is somewhat confused.

(2) OLTOS, EPIKTETOS, AND OTHER CUP PAINTERS

The rimless kylix with deep, strongly curving bowl, which in the last third of the sixth century took the place of the little-master cup, was evidently a challenge to the artists of the time and many specialized in its decoration. Sometimes, like Pheidippos, they subdivided the larger space now available by inserting large eyes on each side; at other times they utilized the whole zone for their figured scenes.

The signature of OLTOS,[68] with egrapsen, has been preserved on two kylikes—one with Homeric heroes, in Berlin,[69] another, very large one, with deities, in Tarquinia.[70] His style has been recognized in over a hundred vases, some signed by the potters

Pamphaios, Kachrylion, Chelis, Euxitheos, and perhaps Tleson. The interiors of his kylikes are occasionally black-figured, but his art is essentially in red-figure. Whereas the Andokides Painter, Psiax, and the Goluchow Painter were still in an experimental stage, Oltos was at home in the new technique. He had mastered the use of the relief line and had learned to confine himself to a sober color scheme.

His extant works are chiefly on cups, but some of his best paintings are on the more monumental shapes—Achilles and Briseis on an amphora in London,[71] Herakles and Acheloos on a stamnos, also in London,[72] and the satyrs and maenads on an amphora with ribbon handles in Paris.[73] The scene on a psykter in New York [74] is an outstanding work. Athletes with their trainers are practising in the palaestra to the music of a flutist. One is swinging his jumping weights; "he is going to jump," the inscription informs us. A discus thrower is ready for the backward swing. A youth is preparing to throw the javelin. A boy, laden with branches, is being crowned for his victory by the manager of the games (see fig. 35). We are reminded of Pindar's description of the runner Alexidamos: "Many leaves did they fling upon him, and many a wreath, and many plumes of victory had he received before." [75]

Oltos' thickset figures, drawn with strong, incisive lines, have a virile simplicity. Each stands out as a separate design, skilfully adjusted to the curving space. We may note as characteristic renderings the downward curving line for the mouth, the often angular lobe of the ear, the hands either clenched or held loosely with thumb and fingers forming a broad loop, the well-developed thighs, the long, flat feet. There is much repetition in Oltos' work; figures in similar attitudes occur again and again; but he too was interested in the new conception of drawing, and we find him experimenting with foreshortening by shifting the abdominal muscle to one side and thereby suggesting the torsion of the figure (see fig. 3). He frequently used the kalos name Memnon—which practically occurs only on his vases.

EPIKTETOS [76] signed, with egrapsen, several cups and plates, as well as a calyx krater in Rome.[77] He also signed, with epoiesen (perhaps also with egrapsen), a fragmentary plate in Athens: [78] *[E]piktetos epo[iesen Epiktetos egr]apsen.* He was, therefore, both painter and potter. Most of his eighty-odd extant works are on cups and plates. In the early kylikes the interior is black-figured, the exterior red-figured. He worked with several potters —Hischylos, Nikosthenes, Andokides, Pamphaios, Python, Pistoxenos—and, in his later works, he repeatedly used the kalos name Hipparchos.[79]

Epiktetos was one of the greatest masters of his time. He combined grace and elegance with strength. His neat, spruce figures, drawn in flowing lines, generally with few anatomical markings, have a living quality and are masterpieces of design. The action in each case is intimately studied, yet every line and spot of color —including the inscriptions—play their part in the rhythmical compositions. "You cannot draw better, you can only draw differently," is Sir John Beazley's apt comment.[80] It would be difficult indeed to excel some of his later pictures—the satyr holding a wineskin, on a kylix in the British Museum,[81] the satyr drinking wine, on a kylix in Baltimore,[82] and the lovely single figures and groups on his plates,[83] for instance, the boy riding a cock, in Castle Ashby (fig. 37).[84] The running warrior on a kylix in New York [85] is a more modest, less highly finished work (see fig. 11). The figure is drawn with the trunk in back view, the head and legs in profile; the device on the profile shield, a satyr's head, is shown entire, but narrowed to suggest foreshortening.

PHEIDIPPOS,[86] an early contemporary of Epiktetos, signed, with *egraphe,* a cup in London,[87] which also has the signature of the potter Hischylos. His ten extant works are all on eye cups, and consist mostly of single figures of athletes and warriors. He uses bold, thick lines, gives little anatomical detail, and is apt to draw the profile chest of his figures in one sweeping curve. His facial type, with narrow eye, long nose, and short line for the mouth is easily recognized. A kylix in New York [88] is an excellent example. On the inside is a running Dionysos in black-figure; on the outside are a runner, with arms held close by his sides, and a warrior, bending down to pick up his spear (figs. 39, 40).

THE HISCHYLOS PAINTER,[89] who decorated a kylix in Munich [90] signed by Hischylos as potter, was one of the earliest red-figure cup painters. Only a few works have been attributed to him, among them a boxer on the fragment of a cup in New York (fig. 42).[91] The rendering of the boxer's abdominal muscle (drawn in full-strength glaze lines) is noteworthy. It is still rep-

resented with three transverse divisions above the navel whereas
in Psiax's pictures the later rendering with two divisions is already used. Though drawn in full front it is shifted a little to
the far side, and the bulge of the external oblique over the iliac
crest is marked only on the near side to suggest the torsion. We
have here one of the earliest attempts at foreshortening (see
pp. 37, 48).

THE THALIARCHOS PAINTER,[92] called after a kalos name he
used, is related in style to Epiktetos. Four dainty little boxes,
including one in New York, have been attributed to him.

THE EUERGIDES PAINTER [93] decorated over a hundred cups, several signed by Euergides as potter. Nimble youths in attitudes of
movement are his favorite subjects. His best and most interesting product is a fragmentary kylix in Athens [94] with a vase
painter and the goddess Athena, among other groups. As a rule,
however, he was content to draw rapidly with a strong, flowing
line, but without delicacy or precision. A typical example, in
New York,[95] has athletes practising—a youth preparing to jump,
his weights swung forward; another about to throw the javelin;
a third, also a jumper, swinging his weights; two runners about
to start; and a youth preparing to throw the discus.

A group of alabastra painted in the Euergides Painter's manner are inscribed *prosagoreuo,* "I greet you"; [96] one in the
Louvre [97] is signed *Paidikos epoiesen;* three, on white ground
with the figures drawn partly in black-glaze lines, are signed
Pasiades epoiesen.[98] The signature *Pasiades egrapsen* occurs on a
fragmentary white lekythos in Athens,[99] but the figures on it
are different in style from those on the vases signed by Pasiades
as potter. To judge from this evidence, either the same PASIADES
sometimes potted and sometimes painted, or there were two
artists named Pasiades, a potter and a painter. The white-ground
vases with outline drawing just mentioned are among the earliest extant in this technique (see p. 31).

The signature of APOLLODOROS,[100] with egrapsen, is preserved
on two kylikes, one in the Louvre [101] with a symposion, another,
fragmentary, with combats, in Rome and Castle Ashby.[102] Eighteen other kylikes have been attributed to him, including one
in New York [103] with a youth standing before an altar. Like
Apollodoros' other work it is delicately drawn with a flowing
line; the long, stacked folds of the mantle and the nervous hand

with slender, cushioned fingers are characteristic renderings. The style is already ripe archaic, but Beazley thinks that we may have early works by this artist on the cups now attributed to THE EPIDROMOS AND KLEOMELOS PAINTERS [104] (so called after their favorite kalos names).

PEITHINOS signed with egrapsen the magnificent kylix in Berlin [105] with Peleus and Thetis. It is the only work by him so far recognized; but the masterly rendering of the drapery with its many stacked folds and the delicate drawing of every detail show that he was outstanding.

SKYTHES,[106] whose signature with egrapsen is preserved on several cups—in Rome, Paris, and Berlin—and who frequently used the kalos name Epilykos, has drawn a number of finely individualized figures, for instance, the boy singing to the lyre on a kylix in Rome (fig. 6),[107] and the gesticulating youths on a fragmentary kylix in Berlin.[108] Twenty-six works have been attributed to him, all on kylikes, except one on a small stand. It is not certain whether he is the same man as the Skythes who signed, with egrapsen, two black-figured plaques in Athens.[109] On a third black-figured plaque in Athens [110] the name Skythes appears as dedicator: Skythes man[etheken] "Skythes dedicated me." Again we do not know whether this Skythes is the same as the vase painter.

Of THE HEGESIBOULOS PAINTER only one certain work remains —the kylix in New York [111] signed Hegesiboulos epoiesen. He too was an individualist. The bearded old man going for a walk with his dog (fig. 38), on the interior of the kylix, is well characterized. The large, hooked nose and long skull suggest that he was an Oriental (a Syrian, a Phoenician, or a Jew). Another kylix signed by the potter Hegesiboulos is in Brussels; [112] but the white-ground picture on it—a woman spinning a top—was not painted by the same artist as the New York cup and is much later.

THE KISS PAINTER,[113] to whom the pictures on five kylikes have been assigned, painted one in New York [114] with a youth and a girl kissing (fig. 4). She has placed her arms round his neck and is putting her face up to his. The torsion of his body is rendered in the piecemeal manner of the day. The chest is in full front, the legs in profile; the abdominal muscle, though in full front, is placed obliquely, to suggest foreshortening. Another kissing scene appears on a kylix in Berlin.[115] On a cup in Baltimore [116] the kalos names Leagros and Epidromos are inscribed.

Other prominent artists who specialized in decorating cups are THE AMBROSIOS PAINTER,[117] called after the name he gave a youth on a kylix in Orvieto; [118] THE HERMAIOS PAINTER,[119] who decorated several cups signed by the potter Hermaios; and THE CHELIS PAINTER,[120] who painted cups signed by the potter Chelis, one perhaps together with Oltos.

Besides these able artists there were others, of more average ability, who painted in a cursory, rather coarse, but often vivid style. Such are THE BOWDOIN-EYE PAINTER,[121] who decorated a number of cups, including an eye kylix with jumpers at Bowdoin; THE NIKOSTHENES PAINTER,[122] who painted cups and other vases, several of which are signed by the potters Nikosthenes and Pamphaios; THE EPELEIOS PAINTER,[123] called after the kalos name Epeleios which he used on his kylikes in Munich, New York, and Bryn Mawr; and THE PAINTER OF BERLIN 2268, [124] who decorated cups, jugs, and other small vases. The favorite subjects are revelers, athletes, warriors, and satyrs—themes which gave opportunity for depicting lively figures in rapid motion.

(3) EUPHRONIOS, EUTHYMIDES, PHINTIAS, AND THEIR FOLLOWERS

In the last decade of the sixth century three distinguished painters were active—Euphronios, Euthymides, and Phintias. They form the transition, so to speak, from the more restricted style of early red-figure to the broader ripe archaic; for they introduced an ampler type of drawing which soon became common property.

The vases signed by EUPHRONIOS present an interesting problem. The evidence is as follows: [125] The name occurs on sixteen vases. On four (perhaps five) it is followed by egrapsen, "decorated it," on ten by epoiesen, "made it"; on one the verb is missing; on another it was never added. The pictures on the vases signed with egrapsen and therefore certainly painted by Euphronios are: the contest of Herakles and Antaios (see fig. 43) and the flute player on a calyx krater in the Louvre; [126] the reclining hetairai on a psykter in Leningrad; [127] the horseman and the story of Herakles and Geryon on a kylix in Munich; [128] the wedding of Peleus on a fragmentary kylix in Athens and Chicago; [129] and the Herakles and youths on a fragmentary calyx krater in the Louvre.[130] These pictures are not in the same style as those signed *Euphronios epoiesen* and are somewhat earlier. We know that the painter Euphronios collaborated with the potters Kachrylion and [Euxi]theos and that Euphronios the potter collaborated with several painters: one of his cups is signed *Onesimos egrapsen* (see p. 85), six have been attributed to the Panaitios Painter (see p. 76), two, possibly three, to the Pistoxenos Painter, who was active in the next generation (see p. 99).

To judge by this evidence there are three possibilities: Euphronios may have started as a painter and later specialized in potting; or he may have done both concurrently, but his early signed pots and his later paintings have not survived; or there were two artists named Euphronios—one a painter who worked in the late sixth century, the other a potter who was active in the first half of the fifth century.

The painter Euphronios was an artist of great power. Besides the five signed vases, a number of others have been attributed to him. He favored large vases, such as kraters and amphorae, for which his massive style was specially suited. His often copious anatomical markings show his preoccupation with current problems. In his signed group of Herakles and Antaios (fig. 43) the muscular structure of the two nude figures is drawn in great detail (with no foreshortening to speak of, however). The contracted face of Antaios, with open mouth and teeth showing, is a remarkable early representation of physical pain, comparable to that of the approximately contemporary giant on a metope from Selinus.[131] In the signed picture of Peleus and Thetis, in Athens, the nails and the joints of the fingers are marked, and the folds of draperies are drawn in rich, variegated patterns. Euphronios did not, however, lose himself in detail. The aristocratic young horseman on the cup in Munich, and the hetairai in Leningrad, with their undulating contours, are masterpieces of design. The eleven revelers, on the neck of a volute krater in Arezzo,[132] form a lively composition in which each figure is an independent unit but all are interrelated.

Several kalos names appear on Euphronios' vases: Leagros

(several times), Melas, Philiades, Xenon, Smikythos. Most of them do not occur elsewhere.[133]

The signature of EUTHYMIDES,[134] with egrapsen or egraphe, has survived on six vases: two amphorae in Munich, one with Hektor arming and revelers,[135] the other with Thorykion arming and athletes;[136] a kalpis in Bonn[137] with a symposion; a psykter in Turin[138] with athletes; a fragmentary plate in Adria[139] with a warrior; and a fragmentary kylix in Florence[140] with deities. On three of these he calls himself ὁ Πολίου, "the son of Pollias."[141] A fragmentary cylinder, recently found in the Athenian Agora,[142] with the letters Polio still preserved, doubtless also originally had his full signature.

The best work by Euthymides, however, is on his unsigned vases: the statuesque group of Theseus carrying off Korone, on an amphora in Munich;[143] the two richly draped, fleeing women on the same vase; and the beautifully poised, single figures of a satyr and a youth pouring wine, on a neck amphora in Goluchow.[144] They are drawn with an ease and a sureness of touch which only a great master can achieve.

The kalos name Megakles occurs on the signed hydria in Bonn,[145] and the name Leagros, without kalos, on fragments of a pelike in the Louvre.[146]

On the signed amphora in Munich 2307, with revelers and Hektor arming, Euthymides has proudly put "Euphronios never did anything like this": ὡς οὐδέποτε Εὐφρονιος. The boast has been interpreted as a general challenge to a rival—friendly or hostile. But if we compare the paintings on this vase, and especially the revelers near whom the inscription is written (see fig. 44), with some of Euphronios' masterpieces—the Herakles and Antaios for instance (see fig. 43), or the young horseman—Euthymides' claim seems hardly justified. In one respect, however, these two revelers excel all Euphronios' extant work and are indeed among the most successful of their time—in the foreshortening. They are drawn in three-quarter front and three-quarter back views with the farther side of the chest, abdomen, back, clavicle, shoulder foreshortened with remarkable understanding. By way of contrast the other figures on the same vase and in fact in most of Euthymides' other paintings are still more or less pieced together from full front and profile views; and this applies also to Euphronios' work, including his Antaios. We may surmise, therefore, that it was the foreshortening in this picture on which Euthymides prided himself. If this supposition is correct the interest of the inscription is greatly enhanced. It voices the rivalry among vase painters in the new manner of drawing that was being evolved and that gradually changed Greek painting from two-dimensional designs to three-dimensional pictures, and it shows that the vase painters were taking an active part in this problem, not merely copying the mural and panel painters of the day.

The signature of PHINTIAS [147] appears on four vases with egrapsen, on three with epoiesen. One of those with epoiesen—the kylix in Athens [148] with a warrior—was not decorated by the painter Phintias, and the two others are aryballoi without figure decoration. [149] We do not know for certain, therefore, that Phintias the painter and Phintias the potter were the same man, though, of course they may well have been; for they are contemporary and we know definitely—in the case of Douris—that a painter-potter collaborated with other potters (see p. 83). The four vases which Phintias signed as decorator are an amphora in Tarquinia [150] with the struggle for the tripod and a Dionysiac scene (see fig. 46); a hydria in London [151] with youths fetching water at a fountain; a kylix in Baltimore [152] with a youth selecting a vase in a potter's shop, purse in hand; and a kylix in Munich [153] with Herakles and Alkyoneus and the struggle for the tripod. The latter, his earliest extant work, also bears the signature of the potter Deiniades.

The name Phintias is variously spelt in these signatures—Phintias, Philtias, Phintis, Phitias. A toast to Euthymides, σοι τηνδι Εὐθυμιδει [λατασσω], appears on an unsigned hydria in Munich [154] with women reclining and a music lesson. The two artists were evidently friends. The kalos names Megakles, Sostratos, and Chairias occur on Phintias' vases.

Phintias' work resembles that of Euthymides and of Euphronios in a certain monumental quality; but his figures are more winsome, and move with more grace and lightness of step. The idyllic scene in London of youths at the fountain and the Munich music lesson are among the most sensitive pictures of their time.

Great artists like Euphronios and Euthymides naturally had imitators. SMIKROS, [155] a follower of Euphronios, was one of the most gifted. His signature, with egrapsen, survives on two stamnoi, a ruined one in London [156] and a well-preserved one in Brussels.[157] Four other vases have been attributed to him. His best work is the signed symposion in Brussels, with youths and women reclining on decorated couches while two servants fill a large wine bowl for the feast. The scene is remarkably lifelike and the rich, crowded composition on the one side makes a good contrast with the sparser grouping on the other. The kalos names Antias, Pheidiades, and Eualkides occur on Smikros' vases.

THE SOSIAS PAINTER [158] decorated a kylix in Berlin [159] signed by the potter Sosias. On the outside Herakles is represented entering Olympos in the presence of deities, on the inside Achilles is seen tending the wounded Patroklos (see fig. 45). The latter is one of the most famous pictures in Greek vase painting and is notable for its expressive attitudes. The preoccupation of Achilles as he bandages his friend's arm and the pain of Patroklos sitting on his round shield with averted face are admirably conveyed. Armor, drapery, hair, anatomy are drawn in fluid lines with a wealth of detail. The picture of Herakles entering Olympos on a fragmentary kantharos in Athens [160] is the only other work definitely attributed to the Sosias Painter. The inscription *Sosias epoiesen* occurs on a small stand in Berlin; [161] but the vigorously drawn crouching Satyr on it can hardly be by the meticulous, sensitive artist who painted Sosias' kylix. On the foot of a bowl recently found in the Athenian Agora [162] is the inscription Σωσιας καταπυγων E[. . . . .]ιος φησιν ὁ γραψας, "Sosias is a lewd fellow, says E[. . . . .]ios." The fragmentary name may have been Euphronios, for the letters would fit the space.

THE VIENNA PAINTER,[163] called after his picture of Aigisthos on a pelike in Vienna,[164] THE DIKAIOS PAINTER [165] named after the kalos name he used on an amphora with youths and warriors in the Louvre,[166] and HYPSIS [167] belong to the Euthymidean circle. Only two works of Hypsis remain—the Amazons and the chariot scene on a hydria in Munich,[168] on which the full signature *Hypsis egrapsen* appears, and the two girls at a fountain on a kalpis in Rome,[169] which has only the name Hypsis. The latter picture especially has great charm. It is not composed in the old, conventional way with a row of women carrying water jars, but is freshly observed. Two girls have come to a fountain. One has placed her jar under a lion-headed spout and is stepping aside, lifting her skirt so as not to get wet; the other has filled her jar from a satyr-headed spout and is supporting it on her knee, before lifting it to her head. Both have little cushions for protection of their heads. The fountain house is inscribed *krene Dionysia,* "fountain of Dionysos." A well preserved hydria in New York [170] with two armed youths performing a pyrrhic dance is also by some companion of Euthymides.

THE GALES PAINTER [171] also belongs here. He decorated two lekythoi signed *Gales epoiesen*—one in Boston [172] with cows being led to sacrifice (see fig. 41), the other in Syracuse [173] with three revelers. The latter is a famous vase, for one of the revelers is inscribed Anakreon, and is evidently the well-known poet, who was also represented on other vases of this time, for instance, on a kylix by Oltos in London and on a fragment of a calyx krater by the early-Kleophrades Painter in private possession (see p. 44).

II. RIPE ARCHAIC STYLE, ABOUT
500–475 B.C.

THE next period of Athenian red-figure is concurrent with the Persian wars. At the end of the sixth century Athens had changed from a tyranny to a democracy. Hippias fell in 510, and in 508–507 the constitution of Kleisthenes was introduced. Soon afterwards the Persian danger threatened and all energies had to be spent in the defense which culminated in the victories of Marathon (490), Salamis (480), and Plataiai (479).

It is noteworthy that during these times of stress Athenian vase painting excelled. The finest work in red-figure was done in and just before this period. We may surmise several reasons for this: pottery as a flourishing industry must have attracted the artistic talent of the time; perhaps because of the national danger there were fewer commissions for large paintings and sculpture; and, most important of all, the time was ripe for a flowering of the craft.

We know as little of the Greek panel and mural paintings of this period as of the preceding one, for they have all disappeared and our literary records are scanty. But it stands to reason that the art of the Sikyon panels and of the Gordion murals (see p. 165, note 2) continued; and the late archaic Etruscan tomb paintings, which show strong Greek influence, perhaps suggest that mural painting was also practised in Greece.

The style of this period is a continuation and expansion of that of the earlier one, but the outlook has changed. Though much the same scheme is adhered to for the rendering of muscles and bones, of eye, hair, and drapery, we note an unmistakable quickening of spirit. The bodies have developed, they bend, turn, twist more easily and naturally; the draperies have become more expressive of the action of the figures; the attitudes are more varied. In other words, the scope of the artist has become enlarged. And yet the feeling for design is still a determining factor.

It is indeed in this period that we can enjoy to the full the stylization of archaic Greek painting. Though interest in nature had by now been fully aroused and the artists were eagerly watching the great spectacle of life around them, the stylizing traditions were still potent and they translated even their innovations into conventionalized schemes. The muscles still form linear decorations, the draperies rich designs, and the compositions rhythmical patterns whose effectiveness is as yet little disturbed by attempts at plastic renderings.

The increased interest in nature is shown first by a more detailed study of the human body. The individual parts are more

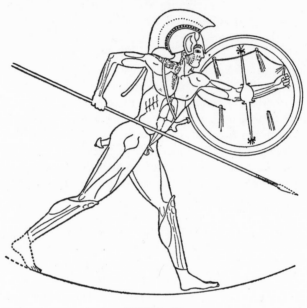

FIGURE 17

carefully observed than before (contrast figs. 3 and 17). Thus the serratus magnus is marked by a set of curves, either in a single row as before (see fig. 18) or in a double one to show the interlacement with the digitations of the external oblique muscle arising from the ribs (see fig. 17). The rectus abdominis is no longer rendered by adjacent ovals; its shape is more developed and its connection with the thorax is now commonly indicated (see fig. 17). The shape of the obliquus externus abdominis bulging over the iliac crest is shown by curved lines (see figs. 17, 18).

Great progress has also been made in the understanding of foreshortening. The set of formulas which served the preceding generation is enriched and enlarged. The artist gradually learned

to indicate the three-quarter view by contracting the farther side
of the chest, clavicle, abdominal muscle, shoulder blade. The
full profile view becomes rarer. In male figures the farther side
of the chest is often indicated by an additional curve (see fig. 19)
and part of the farther shoulder is drawn. In female figures the
breasts are drawn side by side in profile
pointing in one direction (see fig. 20), or
one breast is drawn full-front, the other in
profile (see fig. 21). The placing of one leg
in full-front (or full-back) view and the
other in profile is common. Occasionally a
leg in three-quarter view is attempted, with
the line of the shinbone and kneecap placed
nearer to the inner side and the patella also
shifted (see fig. 22); and gradually a fore-

FIGURE 18

shortened hand or foot is achieved (see figs. 22, 23). But side by
side with these innovations the old renderings persist, especially
in the earlier years of the period.

The eye is now generally unsymmetrical; the iris (a large dot
or circle and dot) is gradually moved toward the inner end, and

FIGURE 19

that end is often open to suggest the profile view (see fig.
24). Simple though the means
were, the artist could distinguish the rolling eye of a
Herakles carrying off the tripod from that of a pursuing
Apollo (fig. 24, g–h), or the
eye of an attacking Achilles
from that of a dying Amazon
(fig. 24, a–b), or could suggest the eagerness of two lov-
ers (fig. 24, e–f). These are
among the first attempts at
the rendering of emotion.

Another slight but signifi-
cant change is noticeable in the rendering of the chin. Here-
tofore the line of the profile chin generally stopped abruptly
where it met the line of the neck (see fig. 13). From about 500
on, the line of the chin is generally continued, at least for a

short distance, to mark the contour of the jaw (see fig. 25).[1]

The hair is still generally a black mass with dots or short strands at the forehead and curling locks behind, which now fly backward with the motion of the figure. Occasionally a differentiation of the black mass is attempted by the drawing of wavy

FIGURE 20

lines on a background of diluted glaze. The contour is now reserved, but the practice of incision occurs sporadically for some time.

Several stages of development can be noted in the rendering of the drapery. We have seen that toward the end of the sixth century the lower edges of the draperies were drawn in zigzag lines in two directions, up and down from a central pleat (see figs. 16, 26). The general effect is highly schematic. Gradually the scheme becomes looser. At first the central pleat is not placed so high as before nor is it so broad, and the groups of pleats move nearer together; then the zigzags become less regular, the pleats are no longer arranged in groups, and most important of all, the lines of the chiton folds often assume expressive curves following the action of the figures.

Thus the drapery has acquired a separate entity and successfully suggests movement. The chitons by the Brygos Painter and Makron of about 480 are good examples of such renderings (see figs. 27, 61, 63). A little later the zigzags disappear altogether. The lower edge is then drawn by a wavy line or a series of arcs (see fig. 28) or merely by a curving line.

The rendering of the himation shows a similar development from the schematic to the more naturalistic. At first the zigzags are more or less pointed and

FIGURE 21

the folds are drawn in straight, radiating lines (see fig. 29). Gradually the zigzags become more rounded and the folds more diversified (see fig. 30). The rendering of the off lower edge of a garment (chiton or himation) by a wavy line or a simple curve, which was usual in the preceding period (see fig. 16), was continued throughout this period (see figs. 26–28).

In the technique also there are a few changes from the preceding period. There is an increasing use, at least by some artists, of thinned glaze for muscles, hair, folds of chitons, and even as washes here and there. This brown color note gives a pleasing variety, taking the place in this respect of the former red and white accessories, which now fall more and more into disuse (though red is retained for such things as inscriptions, fillets, wreaths, strings). Moreover, this soft brown, being less conspicuous than the black, helped the artist to distinguish between the more and the less prominent parts of his picture (see p. 29). He could make the contours of a figure and of its salient parts stand out by drawing them in black relief lines and marking the

FIGURE 22

subsidiary parts in brown. And he could suggest space and form. For instance, by drawing the folds of some parts of the garment

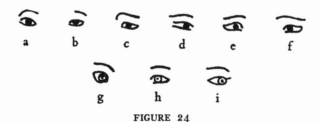

FIGURE 23

black and others brown, he could successfully indicate that one part was over another—the diploidion of a chiton over the kolpos (see figs. 59, 63); and he could differentiate the nearer from the farther distance—the drapery on the near side from that on the farther side (see fig. 60). By applying a wash of brown or by drawing brown brush strokes he could suggest the bulge of a shield or of a vessel (see fig. 53); in other words, he could model his forms. Though such instances are rare, they are important as progressions from the old two-

a   b   c   d   e   f

g   h   i

FIGURE 24

dimensional, linear drawing toward a three-dimensional conception. Further variety is obtained by the occasional use of applied clay, gilded—a technique which in the course of time became increasingly popular. White-ground vases continued along-side red-figured ones; some of the lines are now drawn in diluted glaze.

A comparison with contemporary sculptures is again instruc-
tive. Particularly striking is the parallelism in the drapery. The renderings which occur on vases at the turn of the century (see fig. 26 and p. 40) appear in the Mounting Charioteer from the Akropolis and in the Athena from the west pediment of the temple at Aigina. There, also, the lower edge is drawn in two zigzags up and

FIGURE 25   down from a central pleat which is broader than

the others and considerably higher than the lowest one. The drapery of the Athena from the east pediment of this temple corresponds to that noted on vases of the first decade or so of

the fifth century. The central pleat there is not so high in relation to the lowest pleat as it is in the Athena from the west pediment, and the zig-zag itself is not so regular. On the Boston and Ludovisi three-sided re-liefs (perhaps about 470) the zig-zags have practically disappeared, the lower edge being drawn by a wavy line. The folds of the himation in the

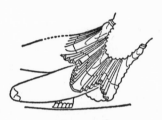

FIGURE 26

stele of Alxenor show a slight loosening of the strictly schematic rendering, comparable to that observed in the vases of the early fifth century. The rendering of the mantle of Aristogeiton (dated 477–476), with its loose folds displaying a certain variety, cor-

responds to that in the later vases by Makron and Douris.

For the facial type of the end of the period useful landmarks are supplied by the heads of Harmodios and Aristogeiton and by the head of Arethusa on the damareteion dated about

FIGURE 27   479.[2]

Besides sculptural parallels we have other important chronological data for this period. The mound at Marathon in which were buried those who fell in the battle of 490 B.C. contained, besides late black-figured vases, one fragmentary red-figured kylix.[3] In spite of the scanty remnants the cup can be assigned to the time of the Panaitios Painter,[4] who therefore must be anterior to the date of the battle. That this painter started his career before 490 is also indicated by the fact that on one of his earliest vases occurs the inscription "Leagros kalos," which is common at the end of the sixth century, whereas on his later vases the kalos name Panaitios appears.

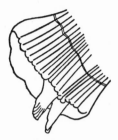

FIGURE 28

A potentially important landmark is given by the potsherds found in the Persian debris [5] on the Athenian Akropolis, which should antedate the year 480. But unfortunately this evidence is not so helpful as might have been expected; for, as other debris was added later, we find fragments of vases of the

early free style along with those of the styles of Epiktetos and Makron. If at the time of discovery more attention had been paid to stratification, we should doubtless be better informed. The fact, however, remains that by far the majority of the vase fragments are black-figured, early red-figured, and ripe archaic red-figured. Some refuse heaps apparently remained undisturbed, for in them all the vase fragments are early.

FIGURE 29

Among the shapes the kylix continues its popularity during this period. It was used by some of the foremost decorators, and there are superb examples extant, often of large dimensions. The offset mouth becomes less frequent, the preference being for one sweeping curve from foot to lip; the decorative apotropaic eyes are abandoned. Some of the larger pots—volute, calyx, and column kraters, amphorae of several forms (neck, pointed, Panathenaic, with twisted handles), hydriai, and stamnoi—are great achievements from the potter's point of view. The "Nolan" amphora, a smallish neck amphora with ridged handles, now makes its

FIGURE 30

first appearance and becomes increasingly popular. The smaller vases are often highly finished. It is clear that the potter's craft was in good standing and attracted gifted artists.

Ornaments are no longer used so freely as before. Many vase painters now prefer to use the major part of the surface instead of framing the pictures within borders.

In no other period of Athenian vase painting were there so many significant artists. Again we know the real names of comparatively few, but many have been recognized by their individual styles. They may be conveniently divided into three groups according to the shapes they preferred—large pots, small pots, and cups.

(1) THE KLEOPHRADES PAINTER, THE BERLIN PAINTER, AND OTHER PAINTERS OF LARGE POTS

The two most gifted painters of large pots are the so-called Kleophrades Painter and the Berlin Painter. THE KLEOPHRADES PAINTER [6] derived his name from the kylix in Paris [7] which is signed Κλεοφραδες : εποιεσεν : Αμασ . . . . s : The missing letters have been restored as ιος : hυυ. This restoration would make Kleophrades the son of Amasis. We now also know his real name,[8] for a pelike in Berlin [9] bearing the signature *Epiktetos egrapsen* has been identified as one of his late works. The name happens to be the same as that of an earlier vase painter, but the styles of the two artists are quite different. If the signature on the pelike had been an ancient forgery, as some have thought, one could have expected at least an attempt to imitate the style of the early Epiktetos. Instead, the drawing is frankly that of the Kleophrades Painter in his latest phase. Moreover by that time the fame of the early Epiktetos had doubtless been overshadowed by his many brilliant successors and there would have been no point in forging his signature. Titian would hardly have forged the name of Bellini to increase the value of one of his pictures. Why Epiktetos II signed only one late, insignificant work and none of his many masterpieces we do not know,[10] just as we cannot tell why Makron signed only one (possibly two) of his many extant products and the Berlin Painter, the Brygos Painter, and the Achilles Painter none (see p. 16).

Over a hundred vases have been attributed to the Kleophrades Painter [11] (we shall retain the familiar name as less confusing than Epiktetos II), including nine black-figured Panathenaic amphorae (two in New York).[12] His work reflects better perhaps than that of any of his contemporaries the strenuous and exalted spirit of the time. His best paintings have a grandeur and spaciousness, and are drawn with a flowing line which has seldom been excelled. He must have been active a considerable time, for we can trace several stages of development in his style. The earliest works—the amphorae in Würzburg,[13] the Vatican,[14] Munich,[15] and Vienna,[16] the psykters in Compiègne,[17] Paris,[18] and Athens,[19] and the volute krater with satyrs in a private collection[20]—resemble the work of Euthymides, from whom he clearly derived his firm drawing and monumental style. As he matured, however, he developed a personality with greater emotional power. The youths on the calyx kraters in Tarquinia[21] and New York (see fig. 47),[22] the warrior putting on his greave and Theseus performing his deeds on the two kylikes in Paris,[23] and the maenads on a pointed amphora in Munich[24] show him early in this mature stage. The next phase is seen in the majestic, somewhat more simplified Apollo and Herakles on an amphora in New York,[25] in the rhapsodist and flutist on an amphora in London,[26] and in the strangely moving Ilioupersis on a hydria in Naples.[27] Then his strength waned and he produced such second-rate pictures as those on the stamnos in the Villa Giulia[28] and the pelikai in Copenhagen[29] and Berlin.

Let us look at the two vases by this artist in New York. Both, as we have said, belong to his mature period. The calyx krater, which is unfortunately fragmentary, must have been very impressive, both as a pot and as a decoration. On the better preserved side we see two warriors arming. One holds out a helmet, the strap hanging, and puts the other hand on his head, perhaps to smooth his hair preparatory to putting on his helmet; a sword hangs from his shoulder, and on the ground is a shield (see fig. 47). The other youth is leaning on his spear and is holding out a sword in its scabbard, with the baldric hanging; his shield is lying on the ground beside him. The cuirasses are elaborately decorated with saltires, palmettes, a star, lizards, and dots; on the sword hilt is a strip of meander; on the helmet checkers. Every detail is drawn with the utmost care. The delicate folds of the tunics, the ornaments, the occasional indication of toe- and fingernails, all bespeak unusual finish. And yet this elaboration in no way detracts from the grandeur of the design.

The amphora with Apollo and Herakles is in good preservation, enabling us to appreciate more fully the original effect. Apollo is represented as advancing, one hand outstretched, the other grasping a handsomely carved bow; a quiver hangs at his back and he wears a mantle and a laurel wreath. He is in pursuit of Herakles (painted on the other side of the vase), who, in the act of carrying away the Delphic tripod, pauses to look back at his pursuer (note the large rolling eye). Herakles wears the lionskin over his head and back; his bow and quiver are hanging from a belt round his waist; and he grasps the club firmly in his hand. The firm, bold drawing, the velvety sheen of the glaze, and the beautiful form of the vase combine to make it an outstanding piece. It is one of several tall amphorae by this artist with a single figure on each side.

Among the many criteria by which the Kleophrades' style may be recognized [30] are the large nose with rounded line for the nostril, the brown (not black) circle and dot for the iris and pupil, the black edging of the lips with a fossette at the corner, the brown whiskers, the ear with a projecting lobe, the broad frontal knee, the hooked line for the ankle. In his representations of armor he draws the cuirass with high, straight neckpiece and squared shoulder flap, the scabbard with squared end and loops for the attachment of the baldric, the greave with modeled knees and indication of muscles. Some renderings, elaborate at first, are simplified as time goes on.[31] Occasionally he used washes of thinned glaze, giving roundness to his shapes thereby. He was evidently interested in the current problem of suggesting the third dimension.

THE BERLIN PAINTER derives his name from one of his most careful works, the amphora in Berlin with Hermes and two satyrs.[32] He must have started his career around 500 B.C. and worked for about forty years. More than two hundred vases (including fragments and a few black-figured Panathenaic amphorae) have been attributed to him,[33] and of these the best belong to the first two decades of the fifth century. They comprise such masterpieces as the Berlin amphora; the volute krater in the British Museum [34] with the contests of Achilles and Hektor and of Achilles and Memnon; the hydria in the Vatican [35] with Apollo sitting on his winged tripod and playing the lyre, while he travels over the sea; and many more modest works on Nolan amphorae and lekythoi. His figures have a litheness and elasticity, an angular grace which make them a good foil for the more massive types of the Kleophrades Painter. Single figures on tall vases particularly appealed to him. To give them the necessary width he generally placed large objects in outstretched hands. Satyrs with finely curving tails made specially good subjects and are accordingly popular. There are fine examples on the back of the Berlin amphora and on a Panathenaic amphora in Munich; [36] the portly ones on a Nolan amphora in New York [37] are not drawn with the same care, but are lively and well characterized.

One of the Berlin Painter's earliest works is the group of Achilles and Penthesileia on a hydria in New York (see figs. 17, 26).[38] Achilles is represented striding forward, plunging his spear into the Amazon, who falls back fatally wounded. She stretches out one hand in entreaty while the other still holds the bow. Blood flows from wounds in her thigh and beneath her breast. The scene is a less intimate, less emotional representation than the one of the same subject by the Penthesileia Painter on the famous cup in Munich (see p. 97); but though rendered in the impersonal, archaic fashion, it is grandly conceived. The sweep of the falling Amazon and the self-confident stride of the warrior make a finely contrasted composition. In the Achilles the three-quarter view is suggested by the placing of the rectus abdominis muscle on one side of the trunk, though its parts are not yet foreshortened. Penthesileia's right leg and foot are shown in full front; the left leg is bent, with the lower part not indicated, except for part of the foot and the frontal toes. The breasts are drawn far apart and in two profile views facing right and left. The black dot for the iris is nearer the upper lid than the lower, to suggest that she is dying.

A youth, a boy, and a dog, on an oinochoe in New York,[39] is a typical work of the Berlin Painter's early to middle period. The youth is playing the lyre, striking the strings, and moving to the rhythm of the music; the boy holds his master's stick and listens; the dog too is listening and lifts a paw.

An amphora, formerly in the Hearst Collection, now in New York,[40] shows the artist in the fullness of his power. On one side is depicted a youth playing the kithara, singing and swaying to the rhythm of the music (fig. 48), while on the other side is the trainer—or the judge, if the scene is an actual performance.

The late, less careful work by the Berlin Painter may be seen in several examples in New York—in a Nolan amphora with Poseidon and a youth,[41] and in two lekythoi, one with a woman running, holding a torch and a libation bowl,[42] the other with Poseidon pursuing a woman [43]—both perhaps school-pieces.

The Berlin Painter's scheme for expressing in linear patterns the complicated anatomy of the human body varies little during his long period of activity.[44] We find it already fully developed in his earliest works, for instance in the Achilles and Penthesileia in New York (see fig. 17). The eye is long, often open at the inner end and has a black dot for the iris; the nostril is marked by a deep, black arc; the lips are generally not edged, and often have a fossette at the corner; the ear has a hooked line for its inner marking. Two lines indicate the chief muscles of the neck; the clavicles recurve at the inner ends and do not touch the median line; the outline and divisions of the deltoid are marked by curving lines; at the junction of the breast lines a short, brown line is added forming a small triangle to indicate the depression at the bottom of the sternum; the nipples are generally rosettes of dots. On the arms two arcs convex to one another mark the biceps and triceps, three (or two) long lines the muscles on the forearm, a small arc the elbow, a small projection the wrist. The profile kneecap is drawn as an arc with a smaller arc below it; above, long curves mark the vasti, the thigh muscles, and the depression above the great trochanter; below, two long lines indicate the peroneal muscles, a curve outlines the calf. The outer protuberance at the ankle is regularly drawn as two black curves.

We can only mention a few of the many other pot painters active in the late archaic period. To THE NIKOXENOS PAINTER, called after the kalos name Nikoxenos on an amphora in Baltimore,[45] thirty-nine vases have so far been attributed, including thirteen in black-figure.[46] He had an angular, somewhat ungainly style,[47] but occasionally produced so moving a picture as the Death of Priam, on an amphora in New York.[48] In spite of the stiffness of the attitudes it makes us feel the pathos of Priam's death better than many more skilful renderings: Priam has taken refuge on the altar of Zeus, while Neoptolemos advances spear in hand; he neither shows fear nor begs for mercy, but merely puts his hand to his head as if dazed by his sufferings. We are

reminded of Priam's words to Neoptolemos in Quintus Smyrnaeus,[49]

> "Fierce-hearted son of Achilles strong in war,
> Slay me, and pity not my misery.
> I have no will to see the sun's light more,
> Who have suffered woes so many and so dread.
> With my sons would I die, and so forget
> Anguish and horror of war."

Something of this dignity of Priam in his extremity the artist has
been able to convey, in spite of his shortcomings, and also something of the ruthlessness of Neoptolemos as he advances "in mur-
derous mood" with his "resistless lance."

THE EUCHARIDES PAINTER,[50] named after the stamnos in Copenhagen [51] inscribed Eucharides kalos, must have been a pupil
of the Nikoxenos Painter, for a number of renderings are identical in both artists' works and unusual elsewhere; for instance,
the double-lobed ear.[52] The seventy works now attributed to him
include several black-figured Panathenaic amphorae.[53] His virile,
heavy, somewhat angular figures have a monumental character
which is enhanced by ample spacing. The pictures on an amphora in New York [54] are typical examples. Apollo in a long tunic
and mantle is playing the lyre, his left hand in the retaining band,
his right holding the plektron; Artemis picks up a fold of her
dress and holds up a lighted torch. On the other side of the vase
are a young athlete and his trainer; the latter grasps a long rod
and pegs for marking the ground.

MYSON was a potter as well as a painter, for he signed a column
krater in Athens egrapsen kapoiesen.[55] Most of the forty-seven
other works attributed to him are on column kraters and of
average workmanship.[56] His finest pictures—apparently early
works—are the Burning of Croesus on an amphora in the
Louvre,[57] the Release of Aithra on a calyx krater in London,[58]
and the Struggle for the Tripod on a Panathenaic amphora in
Florence.[59] His style marks the beginning of the mannerist movement (see p. 94). The figures are long limbed and rather affected, not so strong and vigorous as those, for instance, by the
Eucharides Painter, but more graceful. Instead of standing sol-
idly on the ground they move about as if in a rhythmic dance,
often looking back and down over their shoulders. The figures

on a column krater in New York [60] are typical—Dionysos, with
a cup and a large vine branch, walking and turning round as he
goes (see fig. 49), and a wreathed youth, evidently on his way
home from a party, balancing a cup on the palm of his hand and
grasping a knotted stick.

THE GERAS PAINTER [61] produced the remarkable painting on
a pelike in Paris [62] of Herakles clubbing Geras, Old Age. The
Greek love of youth and hatred of ugliness are here shown in
concrete fashion. Most of the Geras Painter's twenty-seven extant
pictures are on pelikai and consist of one or two figures, often
in unusual subjects. His tall, lean figures are generally in rather
stiff attitudes but have a pleasing vivacity. An attractive scene
is on a pelike in New York.[63] Dionysos is leaning on a knotted
stick holding out his kantharos to have it filled by a satyr (painted
on the other side of the vase), who is hurrying to him with a jug
and a full wineskin (see fig. 50).

THE HARROW PAINTER is named after one of his best works—
the boy with a hoop on an oinochoe at Harrow.[64] He decorated
chiefly neck amphorae and column kraters, often carelessly.[65] A
fragmentary jug in New York [66] has an unusual scene—a satyr
in a palaestra playing the athlete. One hand is on his hip, with
the other he grasps a pair of jumping weights (the tips of his fingers can be seen through the hole). On the ground lie a discus
with an owl [67] as emblem and a pickax used for loosening the soil
in the palaestra. The picture has an individual, almost comical
touch, and the accessories play a happy part in the composition.

Fifty-one works have been attributed to THE SYLEUS PAINTER,
so called after his picture of Herakles and Syleus on a stamnos
in Copenhagen.[68] He is represented in the New York collection
by three typical examples. A hydria with Herakles and the Nemean lion [69] is an early work: Herakles has thrown himself on
the lion and holds it tight with both arms, one hand on its belly,
the other on its forelegs. The lion roars with pain; stems its right
foreleg against Herakles' shoulder, its left hind leg against his
head; and lashes its tail. The tree in the background indicates
the valley of Nemea. An amphora and a hydria with youths in
statuesque poses [70] are products of the Syleus Painter's maturity.

THE COPENHAGEN PAINTER [71] and his "brother" THE SYRISKOS
PAINTER [72] are able, academic artists of this time. The former is
named after his attractive pictures, on an amphora in Copen-

hagen,[73] of an old man with a negro slave boy and of a youth buying an amphora; the latter after the vase in the form of a knuckle bone in the Villa Giulia Museum,[74] which he decorated with a Nike, an Eros, and a lion, and which is signed by the potter Syriskos: *Syriskos epoiesen.*

THE GALLATIN, DIOGENES, TYSZKIEWICZ, and TROILOS PAINTERS decorated mostly large vases in an ample style.[75] They lead gradually to the early classical period. An excellent example by the Gallatin Painter (who was perhaps the Diogenes Painter in an early phase) [76] is in New York.[77] It is an amphora, formerly in the Gallatin Collection, with scenes of Theseus and the Minotaur and of Theseus and Skiron (see fig. 51). Theseus has seized Skiron by one leg and is about to hurl him over the cliff. A scene on a hydria in New York by the Troilos Painter [78] shows Triptolemos in his winged chariot holding ears of grain, the whole skillfully composed on the strongly curving surface.

(2) PAINTERS OF SMALL POTS

(a) *IN RED-FIGURE*

The second group of late archaic pot painters—those who specialized in small vases such as Nolan amphorae, lekythoi, and oinochoai—includes several good artists. THE DUTUIT PAINTER,[79] to whom eighteen works have been attributed, is among the most attractive. He is named from his picture of Artemis caressing a fawn, on an oinochoe in Paris,[80] once in the Dutuit Collection. A Nike by him—holding an incense burner and gliding through the air with feet picked up in dainty fashion—is on a lekythos in New York (see fig. 52).[81] On another lekythos in New York [82] a woman is standing in front of an incense burner, holding a flower and a large scroll; behind her is a cushioned chair; a fillet and mirror are hanging on the wall. Hephaistos, polishing the shield of Achilles to give it to Thetis for her son Achilles, is represented on a Nolan amphora by him in Boston (see fig. 53).[83] Among the minor artists of this period he stands out as a singularly gracious personality. The kalos name Archinos occurs on two of his vases.

THE TITHONOS PAINTER,[84] who decorated a Nolan amphora in Boston with Eos and Tithonos,[85] recalls the Berlin Painter, but is more heavy handed. Nineteen works have been attributed to him. The stately Athena, on a lekythos in New York,[86] is a characteristic product. The goddess is represented standing in full array, holding her spear (the butt end down) and an Attic helmet with large crest, cheekpieces, and peak decorated with a fringe of hair. She wears a peplos with handsomely decorated borders and over it the aegis; also a diadem with leaves along the top. On another lekythos in New York [87] Hermes, with winged boots and a hat hanging down his back, is running rapidly to the left grasping the herald's staff (see fig. 55). One of this artist's most engaging pictures is on a lekythos in Boston.[88] A woman, wearing a chiton, himation, cap, bracelet, earrings, is looking at herself in a mirror before going out. The kalos name Diokles is inscribed on a neck amphora in London.

THE PROVIDENCE PAINTER [89] is another artist whose style resembles that of the Berlin Painter. His name is derived from his picture of Apollo on an amphora in Providence.[90] He decorated a few large pots, but most of his eighty-nine extant works are on Nolan amphorae and lekythoi. He began his work in the ripe archaic period, but continued into the early free; many of his paintings, therefore, really belong in the next period.[91] His figures have a quiet solemnity and a statuesque quality. Four pictures by him are in New York. On a lekythos [92] a flying figure, inscribed Nike, is represented holding a hydria—presumably a prize for a victorious athlete. On another lekythos [93] a stately Artemis is seen rushing through the woods, a deer by her side; she has espied a victim and is taking an arrow from her quiver to shoot it from her bow (see fig. 54). These two paintings rank among the artist's best works. The satyr pursuing a maenad, on a Nolan amphora,[94] and the woman running with a torch in each hand, on a lekythos,[95] are of only average workmanship. The kalos names Kallikles, Glaukon, Hippon occur on the Providence Painter's vases.

THE BOWDOIN PAINTER [96] also bridges the ripe archaic with the early free period; his work in fact continues into the third quarter of the fifth century. Over two hundred works have been attributed to him, mostly single figures—a Nike, a woman, a maenad, a youth—painted on lekythoi, some on a white ground. Two are at Bowdoin College,[97] hence his name. His pictures are in no way remarkable for technique or subject, but attractive in their simplicity. A typical one is on a lekythos in New York.[98] A woman is sitting on a chair, making skeins of wool which she pulls from a basket by her side; an Eros—perhaps suggestive of the trend of her thoughts—is flying toward her with a fillet; a tame quail is walking on the floor; on the wall hangs an alabastron (fig. 56). It is a simple Greek version of the later Dutch interiors representing women at work.

(b) *IN BLACK-FIGURE*

As we have said, the black-figured technique went on concurrently with red-figure for a considerable time (see p. 36). In the ripe archaic period THE DIOSPHOS PAINTER,[99] THE SAPPHO PAINTER,[100] THE ATHENA PAINTER,[101] THE HAIMON PAINTER,[102] THE THESEUS PAINTER,[103] and others decorated a host of lekythoi and other small vases in the old technique—often on a white ground (see p. 31)—but in the new, developed style of drawing. In the white-ground pictures the figures are occasionally depicted not only in silhouette but partly or wholly in glaze outlines—either full strength or diluted. These outline drawings on white slip mark the beginning of a class of vases which were presently to enjoy a great vogue in Attica (see p. 119). The subjects in the New York examples are varied and interesting. A lekythos has a scene of Perseus and Medusa by the Diosphos Painter.[104] Perseus has cut off Medusa's head and is flying off with his winged boots, his prize safely in his bag; from the neck of the collapsing Medusa springs the winged horse Pegasos (fig. 71). On a red-ground amphora by the same painter [105] Herakles is taking the dog Kerberos from the house of Hades; and on a white-ground lekythos by him [106] Achilles is dragging Hektor's body past the tomb of Patroklos. The comparatively rare subject of Herakles killing the sleeping giant Alkyoneus is depicted on a white-ground lekythos by the Haimon Painter.[107] Two red-ground skyphoi with wrestlers, boxers, Poseidon riding a hippocamp, and white herons, are by the Theseus Painter.[108]

A remarkable group of four white-ground lekythoi,[109] decorated by the Sappho Painter, are said to have been found in one tomb in Attica. The subject on one is unique. Helios, the sungod, is seen rising from the sea in his four-horse chariot, while the goddesses Night and Dawn are disappearing in their chariots, enveloped in streaky clouds. On the other side of the vase Herakles is squatting on a rock and roasting pieces of meat on long spits over a burning altar; his dog is lying at the foot of the rock, its head raised, as if smelling the food. Perhaps Herakles is sacrificing to Helios preparatory to asking him for the golden bowl in which he crossed the ocean in his successful expedition against Geryon. On one of the other lekythoi a Nereid is driving over the sea in a chariot with sickle-winged horses; on another Athena is fighting a giant; on the third Herakles is in Olympos, being escorted by Athena and Iris into the presence of Zeus, who sits on his throne, his cupbearer Ganymede behind him, Ares in the offing. Still another work by the Sappho Painter is on a lekythos in New York.[110] A satyr is sitting on a rock, an amphora and a drinking horn at his side, while a serpent is wending its way across the scene. The technique is unusual: The body of the vase is painted black; the satyr is incised; the inscriptions (three times kalos), the rocks, amphora, drinking-horn, serpent, and the satyr's hair, beard, and tail are painted white; above and below the scene are red bands.

(3) THE PANAITIOS PAINTER, THE BRYGOS PAINTER, MAKRON, DOURIS, AND OTHER CUP PAINTERS

The third group of late archaic vase painters—those who specialized in the decoration of cups, particularly kylikes—includes four great artists: the Panaitios Painter, the Brygos Painter, Makron, and Douris. Their names are among the best known in Greek vase painting. To judge by the many extant works attributed to them, their output must have been considerable. At the Greek symposia, cups painted by them were, we may be sure, in great demand. On such occasions, while the guests drank their wine, the pictures both in the circular field of the interiors and on the curving surfaces of the exteriors could be seen and enjoyed. An able painter had an opportunity to display his skill.

THE PANAITIOS PAINTER [111] is named after the kalos name Panaitios which frequently appears on his works. He decorated six cups signed *Euphronios epoiesen*. At one time it was thought that he was identical with the vase painter Euphronios, who signed several vases *Euphronios egrapsen,* but it is now realized that the two are different personalities (see p. 54). A cup in the Louvre signed *Euphronios epoiesen Onesimos egrapsen* has pictures of riders which resemble those by the Panaitios Painter in a late stage. It has therefore been suggested that Onesimos was the name of the Panaitios Painter; but the manner of drawing does not seem close enough for identity (see p. 85). Recently Beazley has tentatively placed fourteen cups which used to be regarded as very early works by the Panaitios Painter in a Proto-Panaitian group, and has assigned several kylikes which were also once considered early works by the Panaitios Painter to an artist whom he has called the ELEUSIS PAINTER.[112] This leaves six early works by the Panaitios Painter and thirty-five in his developed style. Leagros and Athenodotos occur as kalos names, in addition to Panaitios.

The Panaitios Painter was a master draughtsman. He not only could draw his figures in violent action, but he could imbue them with an abounding vitality. The breath of life seems to animate their movements and expressions. At the same time his compositions have a harmony and flow which distinguish them from even the best work of his contemporaries. The delicate curvature of practically all his lines is particularly noteworthy. Even forms which other artists are apt to indicate by straight lines he makes slightly curving. These undulating shapes give to his work its vibrant quality.

The Satyr sitting on a pointed amphora, on the inside of a kylix in Boston,[113] is one of his most powerful early works. His paintings on the kylikes signed by the potter Euphronios belong to his developed period. They are the famous Theseus and Amphitrite in the Louvre,[114] the Herakles and Eurystheus in London,[115] the komasts in Boston,[116] the Dolon in the Cabinet des Médailles,[117] the athletes in Amsterdam,[118] and the Herakles in New York.[119] The last is in bad condition, but what remains gives a good idea of this painter's style. On the interior Herakles is represented walking with a little companion (see fig. 59). He is evidently setting out for an expedition, fully equipped, using his club as a walking stick, his bow and arrow ready for action. The boy—perhaps his son Hyllos [120]—is wearing a wide-brimmed hat, a mantle, and high-laced sandals; a wineskin hangs from a

stick carried on his shoulder. The contest of Herakles with the
sons of Eurytos is depicted on the exterior. The fight is taking
place at a banquet, as indicated by the couches. Herakles, in the
center of the picture, has given young Klytios a crushing blow
with his fist; he has to fight with his bare hands, because his club
and bow have been taken from him and are being used against
him by his enemies. The brothers of Klytios are approaching
rapidly from either side. The confusion of the combat is admirably suggested by the draperies thrown hither and yon.

There are many other masterpieces by this gifted artist on unsigned vases; for instance, the animated youth reading aloud
from a book to two listeners, on a kyathos in Berlin (see fig. 57),[121]
and the exuberant satyrs on a kylix in Baltimore.[122]

Considerable variety is displayed in the Panaitios Painter's
renderings of individual forms. He had not the methodical tem-
perament of the Berlin Painter who developed a fixed scheme
and adhered to it with but few variations. The heads of his figures are relatively large with strong noses and finely curving
nostrils. On the neck is generally a single brown line; the clavicles
are black with long, brown recurves; the bold s-shaped breast
lines reach to the upper arm; long curving lines indicate the
muscles of arms and legs; hands and feet are finely articulated;
the mantles have heavy, bunched folds convincingly suggestive
of depth.

THE BRYGOS PAINTER [123] decorated five kylikes signed by Brygos as potter.[124] After the Panaitios Painter he was perhaps the
most gifted cup decorator of his time. Being fond of violent
movement, he painted scenes of pursuit, Dionysiac ecstasies,
revels, and battles; but occasionally he produced quiet, stately
figures. One hundred and seventy-one works have been attributed
to him. We can distinguish two distinct stages in his career. The
earlier works are characterized by a strong, incisive line and an
infectious joie de vivre. The famous Ilioupersis in the Louvre,[125]
the ecstatic maenads in Munich [126] (with the interior picture on
a white ground), the komos in Würzburg,[127] the wild satyrs attacking Iris and Hera, in London,[128] and Zeus pursuing Ganymede on a kantharos in Boston [129] are such animated pictures,
full of lifelike touches.

Several works by the Brygos Painter of this period are in New
York, and though they are not elaborate compositions they il-

lustrate his style well. Two satyrs are painted on the broad rim
of a molded kantharos.[130] One is stretched out full length,
propped against a support, playing the double flute—a picture of
comfort and contentment. His long hair is tied at the back with
a fillet ending in dangles, his tail is drawn in a decorative curve
alongside the support. On the wall hangs a wineskin. The other
satyr is also lying down, but is turning round to call his companion; he is playing the castanets, one leg raised as if beating
time; he leans against a wineskin, which is doubled up for better
support (see fig. 18). His momentary pose effectively contrasts
with the luxurious abandon of his companion. Another attractive
picture is on a skyphos.[131] On one side a maenad is playing the
double flute, a tall rock in front of her, behind her a thyrsos stuck
in the ground. She wears a chiton, a leopard's skin, and shoes.
On the other side a maenad is dancing to the flutist's music, a tall
rock on either side. She too wears a leopard's skin over her chiton,
of which she holds the sleeves extended, wing-fashion. The pictures are typically Greek in the simplicity of the rendering. The
stylized rocks sufficiently convey the impression of a mountainous
glen, we feel the wind blowing against the flute player's drapery,
we can catch something of the ecstasy of the dancer as she bends
forward, her arms outstretched, her hair flying. The majestic
goddess—perhaps Hera or Demeter—on a lekythos [132] is a good
example of this artist's work in a quieter mood. She stands in a
frontal pose, head in profile in one direction, left leg in profile
in the other direction. A figure in a similar pose on another
lekythos [133] is identified as Athena by her aegis, helmet, and spear
(see fig. 61). A reveler on the inside of a kylix,[134] though represented resting, conveys the impression of high-strung life better
than many scenes of intense action, for the rhythmical composition, expressive face, and nervous hand give it vivacity.

The later works by the Brygos Painter are weaker in style than
his early products, more attenuated, and also more refined. The
exuberance has gone; the lines have become thinner and the
pictures make an almost ethereal impression. These vases used
to be assigned to "the manner of the Brygos Painter," [135] but as
the renderings of the individual forms are the same as in the
Brygos Painter's earlier works, it seems best to attribute them
also to him as products of his old age.[136] Good examples of these
late Brygan pictures are the woman working wool on a lekythos

in Boston [137] and the Nike on a lekythos in Oxford.[138] A comparison of an Athena of this period on a lekythos in New York (see fig. 60) [139] with an earlier one (fig. 61), shows the change convincingly. The renderings of nose, lips, eye, earring, locks, draperies are strikingly similar in the two figures; but in the later one the lines are thin and delicate and the draperies with their long, parallel lines appear stiff and lifeless compared to the earlier more varied rendering; whereas the earlier Athena firmly grasps her spear, the later one hardly holds it. That there is an advance in time is also indicated by the drawing of the breasts. In the earlier Athena they are shown (on the aegis) in profile to right and left; in the later the three-quarter view is suggested by the placing of both breasts side by side in profile to the right. The attribute held by the later Athena—an ornament from the stern of a ship (*akroterion*)—appears on several vases of this period. Evidently the victory of Salamis and the growing importance of the Athenian navy made the vase painters see the presiding deity of their city in terms of this new outlook.[140]

The change in the Brygos Painter's style in later life is also apparent in his picture of a Thracian woman on the interior of a kylix in New York [141]—probably part of a representation of the Death of Orpheus. She is rushing forward, a spear in one hand, a large rectangular cloth, serving as a shield, along the other arm. Though she is depicted in rapid motion she seems tame and delicate compared to the exuberant creations of the master's earlier period.

The following are some of the many renderings characteristic of the Brygos Painter, found both in his earlier and later works: a long skull, low forehead, finely shaped lips, and strong round chin; a long, narrow eye, with upper lid curving strongly downward at the inner corner to meet the lower lid, the eyebrow high and strongly arched; a forehead-nose line slightly convex to the face, with a full curve for the nostril; a single, brown line for the chief muscle of the neck, arcs for the deltoid muscle, long curves for the biceps and triceps, a series of short arcs for the serratus magnus, dots or circles for the nipples, lines of varying lengths for the muscles of the lower leg, and a curved line for the protuberance at the ankle. In the chitons little arcs generally bound the sleeves, kolpos, and lower edge; the himation is often decorated with dots or little circles and with dotted borders.

There is a good deal of repetition in the paraphernalia which enliven the scenes—in the flute cases, the stools with fringed cushions, the earrings, bracelets, shoes, and headdresses, the baskets, wreaths, and lyres. Altogether his works are easily recognized.

Only three kalos names appear on the vases painted by the Brygos Painter—Diphilos, Philon, and Alkmeon, and one kale name—Nikophile.

MAKRON painted all except three of about thirty extant vases signed by Hieron as potter [142] (for the three see pp. 107, 108). Though over two hundred and forty works have been attributed to him,[143] his name is preserved only on one, possibly on two vases—a skyphos with Menelaos and Helen, in Boston,[144] which he signed jointly with Hieron (*Hieron epoiesen, Makron egrapsen*), and a pyxis in Athens,[145] on which the letters Makr . . . are preserved, but the verb is missing. He had not the vitality of the Panaitios Painter or the fire of the early Brygos Painter, but his paintings are made notable by his masterly line, especially in the rendering of the folds of women's clothes. Among his favorite subjects are men, youths, and women making love—sometimes in singularly harmonious compositions. He also painted mythological scenes, especially of the Trojan War. Briseis on a skyphos in the Louvre,[146] Triptolemos and an assembly of deities on a skyphos in London,[147] and the dancing maenads on a kylix in Berlin [148] are some of his masterpieces.

Several excellent works on kylikes, some of which are signed by the potter Hieron, are in New York. The earliest has an interior picture only.[149] A youth leaning on a stick, his right hand on his hip, is watching a slim young girl dancing. It is a charmingly lifelike picture. The outlines of the girl's legs are seen through the drapery, one in profile, the other in full front; the trunk is frontal, both breasts are in profile to the left. The youth's right hand, with its clumsy long first finger, is an instance of Makron's often careless drawing of details.

The pictures on another kylix [150] show Makron in his fully developed period. In the interior a satyr with a finely curved tail is playing the double flute; and to his music a maenad, thyrsos in hand, is dancing with rhythmical steps. The motion of the dance is suggested by her oblique posture, which also helps admirably to fill the circle. On the exterior is a banquet scene with six couches on which recline bearded men and hetairai. The meal is at an end; the three-legged tables are standing by the couches, but they are empty except for the gay branches (the equivalent of our flower pieces) hanging down their sides. A small slave boy—painted under one handle—is serving wine from a large, wreathed krater—painted under the other handle. His task is to fill the cups of the guests with his jug, pouring the wine through his strainer. Another strainer and a ladle are hanging from a candelabrum beside one of the couches, ready for use. On the candelabrum is a lighted lamp, lending a dim light to the evening scene. The groups of men and women are beautifully varied. We have here in fact a richer assortment of lovely poses than this artist is wont to give us. And the figures are drawn with an unhesitating brush that can draw contours of bodies, the multitudinous folds of rich garments, and locks of hair with equal ease and knowledge; it is only the hands which sometimes seem helpless and clumsy, as often in Makron's work. Unfortunately the surface is not well preserved and we miss many a lovely detail. The design as a whole has great beauty. The straight legged couches and tables with the black spaces between them form a decorative band and seem to supply an architectural base for the undulating lines of the figures above them. The signature *Hieron epoesen* is incised under one handle.

Men, youths, and women in beautifully balanced compositions appear on two other large kylikes in New York; [151] and the scene on still another kylix [152] is full of movement. On the interior, a maenad with streaming hair, thyrsos in hand, is trying to escape from a satyr; and the same theme of pursuing satyrs is repeated on the outside in several lively groups (see fig. 63).

There is much repetition in Makron's work, especially in his many conversation scenes. Figures in similar attitudes and groupings occur again and again with the same paraphernalia—stools, cushions, flowers, wreaths, sticks, sponges, strigils, baskets.

The renderings adopted by Makron serve as useful criteria for recognizing his work: The skull is long and flat; the eye long, narrow, and slightly oblique; the underlip droops; the chin is prominent; a hooked line serves for the inner marking of the ear. The hair is often drawn in black lines on a brown ground; the muscles on the neck are marked by two lines; the clavicles are continuous with the median line and do not recurve; the serratus magnus is occasionally placed very low. On the chest the divisions of the great pectoral muscle are marked by two converging lines running upward toward the clavicle instead of outward toward the arm. The hands are apt to be clumsily and carelessly drawn. The folds of the chiton sleeves are often indicated in thinned glaze, and two rows of arcs edge the chiton at neck and sleeves. The outlines of the figures are generally drawn in black glaze under the chitons, to show the transparency of the material. The heavy mantles have simple, expressive folds, drawn with an amazingly sure hand. The kalos names Antiphanes, Praxiteles, Hippodamas occur on his vases; also several kale names—Nauklea, Melitta, and Rhodopis. The last is the same name as that of the celebrated hetaira who made a costly dedication at Delphi [153] and was loved by Sappho's brother—about a century earlier.

Over two hundred vases have been attributed to DOURIS [154] and over thirty are signed by him as painter—*Doris egrapsen*. We know that he was a potter as well as a painter from the signature on a kantharos in Brussels,[155] *Doris egrapsen, Doris ep[oiesen]*, and from that on an aryballos by him in Athens,[156] *Doris epoiesen*. It does not of course follow that he potted all the vases he decorated. In fact some of them are signed by other potters—Kleophrades, Kalliades, and Python.

There were evidently two painters by the name of Douris, for the signature Doris egrapsen appears on a kylix in Berlin [157] decorated with a symposion in a style different from that of the well-known Douris, but identical with that of a group of other vases. The artist of this group has been called THE TRIPTOLEMOS PAINTER [158] after his picture of Triptolemos on a stamnos in the Louvre; [159] but his real name was presumably Douris, for there is no reason why he should have signed one of his works—executed in his characteristic style—with some other artist's name.

On five lekythoi—in Athens, Syracuse, and Berlin—the name Douris, without a verb, is inscribed in a "cartellino." Beazley has assigned these vases, and one uninscribed example, to the "CARTELLINO PAINTER." [160]

Douris was evidently active a long time. We can distinguish an early, a middle, and a late period.[161] The signed kylix in Vienna [162] with arming scenes and that in Boston with a discus thrower [163] are examples of his early style. At this time—soon after 500 B.C.—his figures are animated, his style has not yet become crystallized, the influence of the Panaitios Painter is evident. Specific distinguishing marks are the simple form of clavicle which does not recurve at the inner end (or has the recurve marked only in thinned glaze), the single shallow curve for the hip furrow, and the deep zigzags along the edges of the chitons. The favorite kalos name is Chairestratos. The names Panaitios and Athenodotos also occur.

The great majority of Douris' extant paintings belong to his middle period, the late nineties and eighties of the fifth century. They include such masterpieces as the Eos and Memnon on a kylix in the Louvre [164] and the satyrs on the psykter in the British Museum (cf. fig. 64).[165] A more typical work is the kylix with youths and men, in New York.[166] His style is now fully developed—distinguished, accomplished, academic—and henceforth remains remarkably uniform. The clavicle now has a hook at the inner end, the hip furrow is marked by two distinct curves instead of one, and the zigzags along the lower edges of the chiton are less deep than before. At first Chairestratos continues as a kalos name, then Hippodamas. Hermogenes, Aristagoras, Diogenes, Menon, Pythaios also occur.

The works of Douris' third and last phase (around 470 B.C.) belong to the early free period. They are not merely weak reproductions of earlier achievements, like those of some other long-lived artists, the Kleophrades Painter for instance, but they have a beauty of their own. Though some of the earlier vitality has gone, a new monumental quality has taken its place. Since Douris had always inclined to statuesque types, he felt at home with the ampler forms introduced at this time. The interior design on a kylix in New York [167]—two women putting away their clothes— is one of his ablest products in this last phase (see fig. 65). The women with their undulating contours and quiet poses show the new elevation of spirit. A maenad and two satyrs on the interior of a kylix in Boston [168] is a comparable work. The outsides of both these kylikes are decorated with more or less conventional conversation scenes, palmette designs round the handles, and an ivy twig, like a trademark, in the field. We may note the careful rendering of the expressive hands, a characteristic of Douris. A kylix in Munich [169] of this period has the kalos name Polyphrasmon.

The influence of Douris was widespread and lasted a considerable time. The quiet, classical style appealed and we shall find it especially potent in the succeeding period (see p. 106).

ONESIMOS [170]—who signed, with egrapsen, a kylix in the Louvre [171] which was also signed by Euphronios as potter (see p. 54)—may be said to have continued the work of the Panaitios Painter. Fifty-nine vases, all kylikes, have been attributed to him, including one in Perugia [172] with Achilles and Troilos, signed by Euphronios as potter. Panaitios, Erothemis, Lykos. and Aristarchos occur as kalos names on his vases.

His drawing is lively, accomplished, refined. It so closely resembles that of the Panaitios Painter in that master's latest phase that some archaeologists have even thought that the two were identical.[173] But it seems best to keep the two artists apart; for their styles, though close, seem to proceed from two different personalities. Onesimos is not an old, tired Panaitios Painter, but an artist who could produce paintings of great grace and delicacy, different in spirit from those by the Panaitios Painter at any time of his career.

THE COLMAR PAINTER,[174] called after his kylix in Colmar [175] with athletes, may also be placed in the cycle of the Panaitios Painter. He is fond of lively scenes and draws them with charm and animation, though often carelessly. He likes to attempt back and three-quarter views; and athletes and banqueters serve his purpose well. One of his most charming figures is the running archer turning round to shoot an arrow, on a kylix in Orvieto.[176] A kylix in New York [177] has on the interior a youth preparing to throw a javelin—holding it in his right hand and steadying it with his left before the actual throw. On the exterior is a banquet with youths reclining on couches and conversing in animated fashion; a provision basket with a cloth over it is suspended from the wall. On another kylix in New York [178] a youth, drawn in back view, holds a pair of jumping weights and two javelins. It is inscribed *Panaitios kalos*.

THE ANTIPHON PAINTER,[179] named after the kalos name on a stand in Berlin,[180] is likewise a member of the Panaitian circle. His works and those in his manner used to be assigned to the Lysis, Laches, and Lykos group, so called after three kalos names which often occur on these vases. Seventy-five vases have now been attributed to the Antiphon Painter, all kylikes except the stand in Berlin. His style has much in common with that of the Panaitios Painter, but lacks the latter's verve and vivacity, continuing rather the more modest tradition of the Colmar Painter (see p. 85). The chief theme is youth, preferably in action. Often the young men engage in violent exercise. All sorts of turnings and twistings are favored, drawn mostly in the archaic piecemeal manner, but occasionally with fairly successful three-quarter views. Youths with mantles, leaning forward on their sticks, are popular; often the hands are brought to the hips, or the head, or held up in graceful attitudes. The compositions are generally loosely spaced. Incision is mostly used for the contours of the hair (see p. 62).

Three typical works by the Antiphon Painter are in New York. On the interior of a cup [181] is a flutist, his double flute in one hand, the other brought up to his head to adjust the vertical strings of his mouth band. On the exterior are youths in various attitudes; one is holding a hare by the ears, showing it off to his companions. On another cup [182] is a youth, evidently going home after a party, carrying a cup and supporting his uncertain steps with a stick. The after-dinner scene is continued on the exterior with dancers and musicians. On a third cup [183] are athletes with javelins and strigils.

A superb kylix in New York,[184] formerly in the Gallatin Collection, was painted by a contemporary of the Panaitios Painter. On the inside, an armed warrior is seen leaning on his spear; before him are his round shield and crested helmet, behind him a little attendant (see fig. 58). On the outside are groups of boxers and their trainers. The scenes are painted with a wealth of detail in sure, flowing lines. Only two other works have so far been connected with this artist, one in Berlin, the other in the Thorvaldsen Museum in Copenhagen. Beazley has placed the three cups in "THE THORVALDSEN GROUP." [185]

THE MAGNONCOURT PAINTER is another gifted artist in the circle of the Panaitios Painter. He is named after a kylix in New York,[186] formerly in the Magnoncourt Collection. The pictures are not well preserved, but we can make out a finely composed group of a satyr and maenad on the inside and Dionysiac scenes with chariots on the outside. The words *Panaitios kalos* are inscribed. Three other works have been attributed to this artist,[187] two also with the kalos name Panaitios.

The Brygan cycle includes several gifted artists. THE FOUNDRY PAINTER [188] in particular is distinguished for his firm drawing and lively designs. The name is derived from his picture of a foundry with sculptors at work, on a kylix in Berlin.[189] The Lapith spearing a centaur, on a kylix in Munich,[190] is one of his most powerful works. The centaur, which is depicted as collapsing on the ground, is an interesting study in partial foreshortening. The head is drawn in three-quarter view, except the nose, which is in full front, seen from below; the body is in full front, seen from underneath; the legs, arms, and tail are in profile. In other words the figure is still pieced together from separately conceived parts, with here and there a successful attempt at foreshortening. The very fact, however, that so difficult a posture was attempted shows an ambitious interest in the problem.

A kylix in Philadelphia [191] has a cupbearer on the interior, preparing to ladle wine into a cup from a large krater, and on the exterior two lively combats, one of them a centauromachy. The cup was given to the University Museum in Philadelphia by the family of the late Henry C. Lea, in whose collection it had been. In the Metropolitan Museum [192] is a modern replica of the cup, purchased in 1896 with the Baxter Collection in Florence. Previous to that date, therefore, the Philadelphia cup must have been in Italy and have been copied by a forger. The only genuine example of the Foundry Painter's work in New York is a fragment of a cup with a man, perhaps a trainer (see fig. 97).[193] The rendering of the man's face, with the delicately curved lines for eyes and nostril, approximates that of the Brygos Painter.

THE BRISEIS PAINTER is another follower of the Brygos Painter. He derives his name from the picture of Briseis and Achilles, on a cup in London.[194] Fifty works have been attributed to him.[195] A good example is on a well-preserved kylix with offset rim in New York,[196] on which youths are represented singing to the music of the flute.[197] The locale is indicated as a colonnade with columns, architrave, and mutules. Another fine cup in New York [198] has scenes from the story of Theseus: his departure for Crete, and Athena welcoming him on his safe return to Athens (fig. 62).

THE PAINTER OF THE PARIS GIGANTOMACHY,[199] named after one of his chief works, in the Cabinet des Médailles,[200] also belongs to the Brygan circle. He was fond of scenes of movement—fights, athletes practising, and lively revelers. He sometimes closely approaches the style of his master, but never matches his fire and careless abandon.

Finally we may mention THE DOKIMASIA PAINTER,[201] still another follower of the Brygos Painter. The name is derived from his picture of a *dokimasia,* the examination of horsemen, on a kylix in Berlin.[202] His style is somewhat like that of the Briseis Painter, with the same mixture of liveliness and refinement.

III. EARLY FREE STYLE, ABOUT
475–450 B.C.

THE second quarter of the fifth century was a period of re-adjustment after the victories over Persia, of recovery from the devastations of the enemy. It was the time of the administration of Kimon (476–461), when Athens, placed at the head of the Delian Confederacy, rose steadily in power and influence. In the west, at the Battle of Cumae (474), the Etruscans were defeated by Syracuse and Cumae. Henceforth, though the importation of Attic vases to western Etruria did not stop, it was confined mostly to the cheaper wares. The grandiose vases of the period have been mostly found not in Etruria proper but in the Adriatic section and in the south.

The famous mural painters Polygnotos of Thasos and Mikon of Athens were active at this time. Their works have all perished, but we can obtain a slight idea of their stupendous compositions from the many references to them in ancient literature,[1] especially from Pausanias' detailed descriptions of some of their paintings—of the Ilioupersis ("Troy Sacked") and the Nekyia ("The Lower World") in the Lesche at Delphi, the Ilioupersis and the Battle of Marathon in the Stoa Poikile at Athens, and the battles of Greeks and Amazons and of Lapiths and centaurs in the Theseion at Athens. The salient points we glean from these descriptions are the nobility of the types, the expression of emotion in the faces, the disposition of the figures on different levels and at various depths (some above, below, or in front of others), and the interest in foreshortening. We shall see that these very qualities are conspicuous in some of the vases of this period. Considering the great fame of Polygnotos, it is natural to suppose that he was the leading spirit of his time and influenced his contemporaries, including the vase painters. The revival of artistic undertakings in Athens affected vase painting also in another way. Vase decorators of the first caliber, though they still exist, are on the whole fewer than before. The great artistic talent was evidently finding scope elsewhere.

In vase painting the exaltation over the Persian victories is reflected in a new breadth in the rendering of forms. The conception becomes nobler, ampler—comparable to that of the Olympia sculptures; and the feeling for space becomes more pronounced than before, both in composition and in the treatment of individual figures. Gradually vase paintings are becoming three-dimensional pictures rather than decorations. The old tradition of putting all the figures along one line in the front plane is not always followed; some figures are occasionally placed higher than others to suggest a farther plane (though they are still all drawn the same size; see p. 140), and the two feet of the same figure no longer always stand along one and the same line. Three-quarter views of trunk, head, arms, and legs are increasingly popular, and the farther side is convincingly foreshortened. Even female breasts, once the source of much difficulty, are successfully rendered in three-quarter views. Especially frequent is a foreshortened hand or foot, often, however, with the ankle misplaced. The use of shading lines to indicate roundness of form becomes more common than before.

Occasionally—and this is particularly distinctive of the period, though there were some examples in the preceding one (see p. 87)—bold foreshortenings involving the whole figure are attempted. A mounted Amazon in full-front view (see fig. 31), a centaur in back view turning round to defend himself (fig. 74), a warrior reaching for an arrow that has pierced his back are some of the complicated attitudes which painters of the period try to represent. Even here, however, the procedure is still the old one of piecing together different parts of the figure, separately conceived, into one whole. No attempt is made to represent these figures and objects viewed as a whole from one point of sight. Depth is suggested merely by the occasional overlapping of forms and by the placing of one figure higher than another. If rectangular shapes in furniture or architecture are introduced, only the front planes are indicated, and such objects as vases are represented in profile—not from above or below. When the farther leg of a chair is indicated it is merely added alongside the front ones, seemingly on the same plane. Artists only gropingly attempted a reproduction of the appearance of things.

We know that in this very period (probably about 460 B.C.) the underlying principles of linear perspective were discovered. Vitruvius[2] records that Agatharchos of Samos painted a scene for a tragedy of Aeschylus and wrote a commentary on it, and that this led the philosophers Anaxagoras and Demokritos to write further on the subject. As the passage is important we shall quote it in full: "Agatharchus in Athens, when Aeschylus was bringing out a tragedy, made a scene and left a commentary of it. This led Democritus and Anaxagoras to write on the same subject, showing how, given a certain central point, the lines should correspond as they do in nature to the point of sight and to the projection of the visual rays, so that from an unclear thing a clear representation of the appearance of buildings might be given in painted scenery, and so that though all is drawn on vertical and plane surfaces some parts may seem to be withdrawing into the background, and others to be protruding in front." [3] We shall see later the important consequences of this initial step (see pp. 116, 139 f.).

FIGURE 31

The eye is rendered in this period in a variety of ways. The profile view is now generally, though not yet always, drawn with the inner corner open and the iris moved toward that corner (see fig. 32). Sometimes two lines are used for the upper lid and one or more lines are added for the lashes. The expression becomes more natural and a greater range of emotion can be portrayed—a terrified nurse of Danae (fig. 32 b), an eager Jason (fig. 32 g), a dreamy boy playing the lyre (fig. 86), an aging father sorrowing over the departure of his son. Occasionally there are attempts at realism, a wrinkled old man or woman with curving eyebrows occurring in the midst of the generalized types. In a full-front or three-quarter view both eyes are drawn more or less in profile with the inner corners open, the outer ones closed, giving the appearance of a squint (fig. 32 j); sometimes, however, both outer and inner corners are closed and the iris is placed convincingly in the center (fig. 32 k).

The solid black mass of the hair is now increasingly varied by the drawing of separate strands either directly on the red ground or on a wash of diluted glaze. A wavy contour often takes the place of the separate lines and dots over brow and temple.

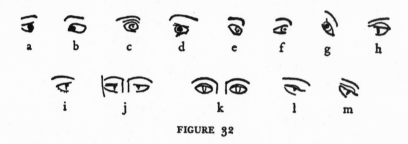

FIGURE 32

In the treatment of the drapery the advance of naturalism is apparent. The old schematic arrangement is evolving into a more realistic rendering. The folds assume natural shapes, they go in a number of directions, and they have depth. Sometimes even their shadows are indicated by washes in diluted glaze. The peplos, once the female garment par excellence but later ousted by the chiton, comes again into favor. Its heavy folds are rendered by a few lines, like those of the himation, often with bold, rounded zigzags along the edges. The bottom edge of the chiton is rendered no longer by zigzags but by a wavy line, by a series of arcs, or merely by a curve; and the indication of the farther edge, prevalent in archaic times, is given up.

The color scheme of the preceding period continues—red against black, enlivened by the brown of the diluted glaze and occasional touches of applied red; the last is now often put on white to make it more luminous (see p. 30). Rarely a bold spirit tries some new scheme; for instance, the Penthesileia Painter used on the Munich cups,[4] besides applied, gilded clay (found already in the preceding period), red-brown and purple-brown washes. But such deviations are the exception. As a rule the old scheme sufficed.

The influence of contemporary panel and mural paintings is also apparent in the increased popularity at this time of white-ground vases. As we saw, these had been in use during the earlier periods, with the figures drawn in black silhouette or in outline (see p. 75). By the second quarter of the fifth century the significant change of adding colored washes was made; the whole scene was drawn in outline in thinned glaze or dull paint, and the garments were painted in matt tones—red, brown, or yellow—with a few touches of black glaze. By these means colorful effects could be obtained which were impossible in the restricted scheme of red-figure. The favorite shape for the technique was the lekythos. It was used both in daily life and as a votive offering on graves, for we find it decorated with scenes from the life of women and with mourners at graves. Other shapes, such as the kylix and pyxis, also occur, often with mythological subjects [5] (see p. 98).

A comparison between the vases of this period and contemporary sculptures will show interesting parallels in the broader modeling of the human body and the more naturalistic draperies. In the Olympia sculptures, dated about 460, the former schematic box pleats have given place to a freer treatment. The himation and the now popular peplos fall in a few, significant folds, occasionally with bold, rounded zigzags along the edges, like those we observed on the vases. And the chiton has curving lines along the lower edge instead of the former zigzags.

An important chronological landmark for this period is furnished by the kalos name Glaukon—sometimes with the addition "son of Leagros" [6]—which occurs, for instance, on vases by the Providence Painter, the Nikon Painter, the Painter of the Yale Lekythos, and the Pistoxenos Painter. The Glaukon, son of Leagros, who was general at Samos in 441–440 and at Corcyra in 433–432 [7] may well have been a fair boy in 470; and this date fits the father Leagros whom we met as a fair boy in 510–500 and who was one of the generals killed in battle in 465 (see p. 45). This evidence suggests a date around 470 for the vases of the painters mentioned above.

In the choice of shapes we note a great change. The kylix, so popular with the great painters of the preceding periods, is eclipsed by other forms. Only the Penthesileia Painter and his school, and a few other, mostly minor, artists favor it. The stamnos, the pelike, and the various forms of amphorae are popular, and of course the different kraters for the more ambitious compositions; the column krater enjoys a special vogue. Among the smaller vases the Nolan amphora and the lekythos play prominent roles.

Over 130 different vase painters belonging to this period have been recognized. Some decorated chiefly pots, others preferred kylikes and skyphoi. Some favored large pots, others small ones, such as Nolan amphorae and lekythoi. Some carried on the styles of the great masters of the preceding period, others started new movements. Many continued their work beyond the middle of the century into the free period, others belong exclusively to the early free.

In this manifold activity we can distinguish several groups with different tendencies: (1) the mannerists, who cling to the formulas of the preceding age but develop them into a new, flowing style with graceful affectations; (2) an individualistic school, reaching out boldly in the direction of naturalism; (3) a group of artists who were strongly influenced by the contemporary large murals of Polygnotos and Mikon; and (4) painters who favored quiet compositions, foreshadowing the classicism of the Periklean period. Naturally these groups are not always clear-cut; and there are other artists who stood outside.

(1) THE PAN PAINTER AND OTHER MANNERISTS

THE PAN PAINTER [8] is the protagonist of the mannerists, carrying on the style of Myson (see p. 71), but in a new, individualistic way. He is one of the most engaging of Greek vase painters, delighting in scenes of movement and dramatic incident, consciously archaizing, and yet with a taste for the unusual and untried. And so his pictures, while retaining the late archaic quaintness and grace, are imbued with a new freedom. The forms are old but the spirit is new and highly individual. Over one hundred works have been attributed to him, on a great variety of shapes—cups, large pots, and small ones. His earliest extant ones are the psykter with Marpessa in Munich [9] and the lekythos with Artemis (on a white ground) in Leningrad (see fig. 66),[10] both somewhat stiff in design but, especially the Artemis, of an ethereal charm. The masterpieces of his mature period are the bell krater in Boston [11] after which he is named, with the death of Aktaion and Pan pursuing a goatherd (see fig. 67), and the pelike with Herakles and Busiris, in Athens.[12] They are magnificent in their exuberant vitality and dramatic force.

Several excellent examples of the Pan Painter's mature period are in New York. On a column krater [13] Dionysos is represented walking in stately fashion, dressed in a long tunic and a voluminous mantle—evidently on his way to an important function. He is followed by a satyr carrying his master's cup, an ivy branch, and a stool with a handsome cushion. Another satyr—painted on the other side of the vase—is coming toward them, carrying a cup; it is full, for he holds it at the bottom with evident care.

On a Panathenaic amphora [14] a kitharist is depicted in a long chiton, stepping forward, his head raised in rapture over the music he is making, while the judge (on the other side of the vase) quietly listens. The kithara is carefully drawn with the different parts clearly marked—the sound chest, the arms, the elaborately designed strengthening pieces, the crossbar with a disk at each end, the pegs, and the bridge. Hanging from the sound chest is a decorated cover, ending in a long fringe—a picturesque addition, especially if we imagine it gaily colored and swinging with the player's movements. The man's left wrist is put in the retaining band, whereby the instrument is kept in a vertical position and both hands are left free for playing. As a beautiful rendering of musical exaltation the kitharist may be compared with that by the Berlin Painter [15] and with the Orpheus in Berlin (see p. 129). The Pan Painter's figure is quieter than the two other musicians, but the stir of feeling is clearly conveyed.

The Ganymede on an oinochoe [16] is especially attractive (fig. 68). He is running at full speed, in one hand a cock, in the other a hoop and stick; his head is turned, presumably toward a pursuing Zeus (not here represented); his long hair is arranged in braids or rolls round the back of his head. The figure has the Pan Painter's grace and alertness, his highly finished drawing, his dramatic touch. Young Ganymede running away with his playthings from the chief of the gods is a subject which naturally appealed to this artist, and he painted it several times; for instance on a Nolan amphora in Boston,[17] where Zeus and Ganymede are combined in one group. The Theseus and Minotaur on a skyphos [18] in New York are not drawn with great care, but are well characterized. The rapid pursuit of Theseus, the flight of the monster, and the rocky landscape are all suggested with a few deft touches.

One of the Pan Painter's latest works is the bell krater in Palermo [19] with Dionysos and a maenad—a rhythmical but somewhat lifeless work. By that time his strength was evidently spent.

Among this artist's many characteristic renderings [20] we may note the black dot for the iris, the thin nose with delicate nostril line, the slightly pouting lips, the firm chin, the small round ear with arcs variously placed, the thick, short neck with one or two brown lines indicating the muscles, the clavicle drawn as a shallow curve not touching the median line and with a separate arc at the inner end, the short line often placed at the junction of the breast lines; the line at the armpit; the variously placed arc for the ankle.

THE PIG PAINTER [21] is an able mannerist of this time. His name is derived from the two pigs in his picture of Odysseus and Eumaios on a pelike in Cambridge.[22] Thirty-nine other works, chiefly on large vases, have been attributed to him. Two typical ones, on column kraters, are in New York [23]—a satyr pursuing a maenad, and a youth and a boy, both distinguished for their rhythmical compositions.

THE LENINGRAD PAINTER,[24] named after his two works in Leningrad,[25] is an artist of comparable caliber. His best-known painting is that of vase painters at work, on a hydria in private possession.[26] A lively scene of youths returning from a banquet is on a column krater in New York.[27]

THE AGRIGENTO PAINTER,[28] also a good mannerist, decorated the calyx krater at Agrigento [29] with Herakles and Nessos and the well-known hydria in London [30] with a music lesson. Most of his known works are kraters. Though not executed with special care they have a pleasing vivacity and swing. The scene of Herakles and Busiris on a column krater in New York [31] is a typical scene. Herakles, who was about to have been sacrificed at the altar by the order of the Egyptian king Busiris, is turning on his enemies. He has seized one of the Egyptians by the shoul-

der and is clubbing him so that the blood streams down the man's
face. The others are fleeing right and left, carrying the paraphernalia for the sacrifice—a torch, a table, a water jar, and a
basket. The barbarians wear long tunics and have long, flat
skulls, shaved crowns, pouting lips, heavy jaws, and drooping
mustaches. They are of the Ethiopian type, as in most similar
scenes.[32] The picture, though not comparable to the superb version of the theme by the Pan Painter (see p. 95), is depicted
with a good deal of dash.

The so-called NAUSIKAA PAINTER [33] is the mannerist who decorated the famous amphora in Munich [34] with Odysseus and Nausikaa. We now also know his real name, for he signed an amphora
in London [35] with women preparing oxen for sacrifice: *Polygnotos egrapsen*. As, however, at least two other vase painters called
Polygnotos are known (see pp. 97, 127), it seems best to retain
the assigned name. Though leaning to affectation and often careless in his drawing he was able to impart psychological interest
to his scenes and thereby to render them attractive. More than
forty vases have been attributed to him. A hydria in New York [36]
with Herakles strangling the serpents is one of the most dramatic: the infant Herakles is kneeling on a couch, calmly grasping a serpent in each hand, while his twin brother Iphikles, properly frightened, stretches out both arms to his mother Alkmene.
She is fleeing to the right, looking back in amazement. Her husband Amphitryon has taken his sword out of the scabbard, ready
to strike the snakes. Behind the couch stands Athena in godlike
calm, spear in hand. The lively scene brings to mind Pindar's
slightly earlier and equally vivid account of the story in his first
Nemean ode.[37]

Two minor works by the Nausikaa Painter in New York are
the Kronos and Rhea on a pelike,[38] and the Nike driving a chariot on a column krater.[39]

(2) THE PENTHESILEIA PAINTER AND HIS ASSOCIATES

THE PENTHESILEIA PAINTER,[40] named after one of his best
works—the Achilles and Penthesileia in Munich [41]—was one of
the chief exponents of the new naturalistic trend. He made the

old, familiar stories live in vivid fashion by giving them an individual interest. The paintings on more than one hundred
vases have been attributed to him. Besides the grandiose, highly
finished Achilles and Penthesileia, and Apollo and Tityos [42] on
the two large kylikes in Munich, he painted many slighter products in a spontaneous, sketchy style, mostly on cups. Pursuit
scenes, satyrs and maenads, youths with horses are favorite subjects. His interest in technical problems is shown in the accessory colors he used on the Penthesileia cup—red, brown, yellow,
and gold—and in the two polychrome, white-ground pieces in
New York. The latter rank among his best works. The Judgment
of Paris on the toilet box [43] is treated in a light, humorous vein.
Each figure is well characterized: Paris, a boy with pouting lips,
seated on a rock and looking up at Hermes (see fig. 73), who is
explaining his mission; Hera, with veil and scepter, turning to
the others as if hesitating to be the first to enter the contest;
Athena in full array; and Aphrodite, adjusting her mantle, while
her son Eros is looking up at her admiringly. The varied color
scheme, the finely designed shape, the careful execution, and
the exceptional preservation combine to make this an outstanding piece. The exalted Zephyros and Hyakinthos [44] and the Nike
crowning a victorious youth (fig. 69), on the New York double
disk,[45] are equal in caliber to the paintings of Penthesileia and
Tityos. The compositions have the same bold rhythm running
through them. The design of the Nike and youth in particular
—both figures placed diagonally across the circular field, one
moving gently forward, the other in strong backward motion—
is singularly vivacious, a happy solution of a difficult problem.

 Several less imposing works in New York show the Penthesileia Painter's average work. On a stemless kylix [46] are two lively
scenes; in one Eos, both arms outstretched, is pursuing Tithonos;
in the other Eos is running after a long-haired youth—Tithonos
or perhaps Kephalos; the eagerness of the goddess and the youth's
reluctance are well expressed both in the faces and in the attitudes. On a skyphos [47] are bearded men and youths with armor—
perhaps departure scenes, if we may judge by the dejected look
of one of the older men. A large kylix [48] has athletes on the exterior and on the interior a man fighting a boar with sword and
club in a rocky glen (fig. 70)—a well-spaced composition within
the circle. Two lively groups on a skyphos [49] are in the manner

of the Penthesileia Painter: a satyr capering before a maenad, his hands outstretched to ward off the blow she is threatening with her thyrsos, and a maenad fleeing before a satyr who is after her in hot pursuit. The satyrs are drawn in three-quarter front and back views.

The Penthesileia Painter's style is easily recognized by his characteristic renderings—the turned-up nose with delicate nostril line, the pouting lips, the obliquely placed eyes, the inclined heads, the wavy curls, the variously placed arc for the ankle. The open hand emerging from the mantle and the outstretched arm, holding staff, scepter, or spear, are favorite gestures. The inscription *ho pais kalos*, in two lines, occurs frequently.

THE PISTOXENOS PAINTER'S [50] style is closely related to that of the Penthesileia Painter. Some authorities have even thought that the two were the same person, that is, that the Pistoxenos Painter is the early Penthesileia Painter. But the spirit of their works is different and the two artists have now been convincingly separated again. Eighteen works have been attributed to the Pistoxenos Painter. His name is derived from a skyphos in Schwerin [51] signed *Pistoxenos epoiesen* which he decorated with young Herakles and the nurse Geropso, and with Linos instructing Iphikles in playing the lyre. A pyxis in Brussels [52] with women, and with five hares in charmingly lifelike attitudes on the lid, is signed by the potter Megakles. Several cups with white-ground designs on the interior are signed by the potter Euphronios [53] (see p. 54). They include one of the Pistoxenos Painter's masterpieces: The Death of Orpheus on a kylix in Athens,[54] now a mere fragment, but once a grandly conceived composition. His Aphrodite riding a goose, on a white-ground kylix in London,[55] is one of the most idyllic pictures in Greek vase painting. Her regal demeanor as she floats gently through the air marks her a goddess. We see here, better than words can convey, the enlarged concepts of a new age.

The only bit of painting by this artist in New York is on the fragment of a kylix [56]—the upper part of a woman wearing a chiton, a mantle, and a sakkos. The rendering of the eye with a black iris in the inner corner, the strongly curving lids, and the fluffy hair are in his characteristic manner.

The kalos name Glaukon occurs on several of the Pistoxenos Painter's vases; also once the name Lysis.

The Penthesileia Painter's broad, vivacious style appealed to his contemporaries and he had many imitators—THE SPLANCHNOPT PAINTER, THE PAINTER OF BOLOGNA 417, THE WEDDING PAINTER, THE PAINTER OF BRUSSELS R 330, and others.[57] Their decorations are chiefly on cups, and some can be dated as late as the end of the third quarter of the fifth century. Among the works of these Penthesileians in New York one of the most interesting is the Birth of Aphrodite by the Wedding Painter on a pyxis (see fig. 72).[58] She is represented as a young girl welcomed by Eros and surrounded by excited women bringing sashes, a perfume vase, a branch, and a chest. A similar representation occurs on a pyxis in Ancona. A kylix [59] decorated by the Painter of Bologna 417, has scenes of women in lively conversation and, in the interior, a picture of two women or girls walking together, one apparently being pulled forward against her will. The unwilling one is carrying a writing tablet, so a writing lesson may be the objective (though she seems rather big for this), or perhaps she has received a letter. The Splanchnopt Painter, named after his picture of a boy roasting splanchna (the viscera of animals), in Heidelberg,[60] is represented by scenes of Nikai and youths on a kylix.[61] In the interior a Nike confronts a boy holding a lyre—evidently the winner in a contest; bands of palmettes and laurel form an effective framing.

Beazley [62] has called attention to the fact that in the school of the Penthesileia Painter collaboration of two painters on one cup ("which occurs elsewhere, but seldom") is frequent. The inside of a cup is sometimes decorated by one painter, the two outside scenes by another. We have here a convincing instance of several artists working in one establishment. The Penthesileia Painter himself apparently did not so collaborate, to judge, at least, by his extant works.

(3) THE NIOBID PAINTER AND HIS ASSOCIATES

The Niobid Painter and his associates are the most ambitious vase painters of their time. Their imagination was evidently fired by the mural paintings of Polygnotos and Mikon, and their

Amazonomachies, centauromachies, and Iliouperseis, with their
elaborate compositions and bold attempts at foreshortening, can
give us some idea of the lost wall paintings described by Pausanias (see p. 89).

THE NIOBID PAINTER [63] is named after one of his chief works
—the death of the Niobids and the assembly of Argonauts on
a calyx krater in the Louvre.[64] The figures are no longer ranged
along one line in the front plane, but are composed on different
levels in hilly landscapes, and several are drawn in fairly correct
three-quarter views. In other words, spatial depth is attempted,
though not yet with a diminution of the figures in the farther distance. The quiet, statuesque postures of the figures reflect the
new elevation of spirit. The Athena in the Argonaut scene, for
instance, in her dignified, self-contained pose, brings to mind
the statue of Athena by Myron, the Athenas of the Olympia
metopes, and the statue from South Italy in New York.[65]

Many other grandiose compositions, chiefly on large kraters,
have been attributed to the Niobid Painter. In addition he
painted simpler designs on smaller vases in a somewhat formal
style. Triptolemos with Demeter and Persephone, on a hydria
in New York,[66] is a typical latish work of this kind (see fig. 75).
Triptolemos is seated in a winged chariot, holding a scepter and
the gift of grain which he is about to bring to mankind; before
his departure a libation is being poured. Two libation scenes on
a neck amphora in New York,[67] are rapidly drawn, without great
finish.

The picture of Kadmos and the dragon on a calyx krater in
New York [68] has been attributed to "the manner of the Niobid
Painter." It is beautifully composed, with Kadmos confronting
the serpent as the center of interest, Harmonia on a higher level
in the farther distance, and Ares and Athena, who are outside the
contest yet determine its issue, effectively framing the central
group. The four figures are drawn in three-quarter views. The
roundness of Kadmos' water jar is suggested by a wash of thinned
glaze; similar washes are used on Kadmos' hat and Ares' shield.

The Niobid Painter had a number of able associates—THE
ALTAMURA PAINTER, "an elder colleague," who is represented by
two good examples in New York: a pelike with a departing warrior, and a stamnos with the Story of Peleus and Thetis; [68a]

THE PAINTER OF THE WOOLLY SILENS, called after his picture on a bell krater in Syracuse; THE PAINTER OF THE BERLIN HYDRIA; THE PAINTER OF BOLOGNA 279; and THE GENEVA PAINTER.[69]

A large volute krater in New York [70] by the Painter of the Woolly Silens can give a good idea of the imposing products turned out by Attic potters at this time (fig. 74). On the body of the vase is a battle of Greeks and Amazons, composed in several groups: at the left a Greek, sword in hand, is seizing an Amazon by the arm to intercept her attack. Then comes an Amazon on horseback—presumably the queen, for she wears a rich costume; she is running her spear into a Greek who has fallen to the ground and is holding up his shield for protection; blood is flowing from the wound she has inflicted; he is drawn in three-quarter back view with the left leg foreshortened and the sole in full view; the sword blade is made quite short, again to indicate foreshortening. To the right a Greek, probably Theseus, is fighting two Amazons; he is attacking with his spear, they are swinging two battle-axes; one Amazon is in three-quarter view, with the breasts foreshortened and her shield drawn as an ellipse with the rim wider at the ends than at the sides. The scene continues under the handle with a Greek spearing an Amazon who collapses in front of him. From behind a hillock the upper part of a fallen Amazon is visible in front view, one arm over her head, the other hand on her breast. A wounded Amazon approaches with halting steps leaning heavily on her spear. Turning to the other side of the vase we see the continuation of the battle. An Amazon has shot an arrow which has struck a Greek in the back; he is reaching with his hand to his wound. Alongside, an Amazon, goad in hand, is driving a four-horse chariot at full speed; she is hurrying to the rescue of a hard-pressed companion (shown under the second handle). The latter has fallen on one knee (the leg is curiously foreshortened) and is wielding her sword to ward off a Greek advancing against her with his long spear. Above is visible the head of an Amazon surveying the scene from behind a hill. The hilly ground is marked by wavy lines drawn at different heights to indicate various levels; here and there flowering plants are growing on the hillsides.

The scene on the neck of the vase represents the combat of Lapiths and centaurs at the wedding feast of Perithous. It too is of great interest, so we may describe it in detail. There are

four banquet couches, placed end to end and spread with covers
and pillows; on a stand at one end is a large lebes, from which
the wine has been dispensed. The fight is in full swing. Lapiths
and centaurs have seized what weapons have come to their hand
for defense and attack—clubs, a pillow, an ax, and two long
swords. On the floor is an overturned tripod. In the center is
probably Theseus, swinging an ax, his attitude and drapery like
that of the well-known figure on the Olympia pediment. His opponent has taken a pillow from a near-by couch and is holding it
up to shield himself from the impending blow; the equine part
of his body is in three-quarter back view, his human trunk full
front, the legs, one arm, and the head in profile. Then comes,
perhaps, Perithous, drawn in back view, spearing a centaur.
Hurrying to the scene from the right is an old man with stick
and spear—presumably the bride's father. Equally animated are
the two groups at the left—a centaur seizing a Lapith by the
head (foreshadowing compositions of the Parthenon metopes),
and a centaur and a Lapith on opposite sides of a couch, both
wielding their weapons, the youth with his mantle pulled up
for a shield. On the other side of the neck is a more conventional
scene with youths and women.

The paintings on six other vases have been attributed to this
painter,[71] but none are comparable to the New York krater. It
is instructive to realize that a painter of seemingly average rank
if judged by his other work could rise to such achievements as
the combat scenes on the New York vase.

The battle of Greeks and Amazons on a calyx krater in New
York [72] by the Painter of the Berlin Hydria is another fine painting of this period. In the center is an Amazon on horseback, riding out of the picture toward us (fig. 31). Her head is in full front,
the head and body of the horse near a three-quarter view, while
her legs and the horse's go in different directions. Round this
central figure the battle is raging. On the left a bearded Greek
is aiming his long spear right across the center at two Amazons
who are attacking with spear and battle-ax. Below him an Amazon is collapsing before the onslaught of a young Greek, who in
turn is being attacked by an Amazon at his back (above the
handle of the vase). To the right of the central group is an Amazon, her feet hidden by a hillock, swinging her ax against a Greek.
The scene continues on the other side of the vase with two

groups. An Amazon on horseback is being attacked by a Greek while another Amazon comes to the rescue with drawn sword. To the right a Greek is threatening an Amazon with his sword. Behind them grows a tree. The hilly ground is indicated by wavy lines with flowering plants growing upward and downward. The composition admirably conveys the stress and confusion of battle. The figures—some of which extend over the ornamental borders—do not divide into the usual closely knit groups but are composed in unsymmetrical fashion, and the spears, swords, and arrows going in different directions and crossing one another at different points contribute to the general impression of turmoil.

As has often been pointed out, the crowded compositions in these and similar vase paintings, the bold foreshortenings, the suggestion of shadows in the draperies by washes of thinned glaze must have been inspired by the larger paintings of the time. But that the vase painter did not directly copy is clear from the fact that there are no repetitions of groups or even of single figures in the vase representations. An Amazon on horseback, an Amazon lifting an ax with both hands, an advancing Theseus, a collapsing Greek or Amazon appear again and again, but always in different attitudes and groupings. Moreover, as we have seen, the foreshortened figures on the vases are not sudden phenomena. Two generations of vase painters had already been at work on such problems (see pp. 37 f., 60 f.).

(4) THE VILLA GIULIA PAINTER AND HIS ASSOCIATES; "FOLLOWERS OF DOURIS"

THE VILLA GIULIA PAINTER,[73] named after his dancing women in the Villa Giulia Museum,[74] is the chief representative of the academic group which flourished side by side with the Niobid Painter and his associates, and which preferred calm, harmonious scenes to the latter's ambitious compositions. He produced such winsome pictures as Hermes and the infant Dionysos on a bell krater in London (see fig. 84),[75] and the family of satyrs, on a calyx krater in Karlsruhe;[76] but most of his paintings consist of quiet, serene figures with little animation or imaginative interest. Over ninety paintings have been attributed to him—

on large and small pots, a few on cups. Two are in New York.
The scene of Apollo, Artemis, and Leto on a bell krater [77] is
one of this painter's best products. Apollo, in the center, is holding his kithara and a phiale which Artemis has just filled from
her jug. Behind Apollo is Leto, also with a phiale. Libations are
about to be poured. The pictures on a stamnos [78]—a youth arming, surrounded by his family, and a libation scene—are less carefully executed. A white lekythos, also in New York,[79] has a scene
of a woman pouring a libation for a departing warrior, painted
in this artist's manner. It is drawn in glaze outlines with added
white for the flesh of the woman.

There is much repetition in this artist's work, the same figure
recurring often in different scenes—a woman moving away, a
woman holding a jug and a phiale, a bearded man grasping a
scepter. The himation is regularly drawn with one end thrown
over the left arm and with the zigzag folds often in thinned glaze.
The favorite headdresses are a broad band passing over the
chignon and fastened in front, and a narrow fillet wound round
the chignon and three times round the head, with ends hanging
down front and back. Long hair in men is mostly indicated by
a single tress falling down the back. The eye is generally drawn
with one or two lines for the upper lid (one strongly curving and
generally touching the other at both ends), one line for the
lashes, and a relatively small iris touching the upper lid only.[80]

THE CHICAGO PAINTER,[81] who decorated a stamnos in Chicago [82] with a scene of women at a Dionysiac festival, was a follower of the Villa Giulia Painter. The styles of the two artists
have much in common, but the Chicago Painter has a more
gracious personality. His figures are livelier, less statuesque.
They have not the Villa Giulia Painter's monumental quality,
but they have more lightness of spirit. To judge by the thirty-
five vases so far attributed to him, his favorite shapes were stamnoi, pelikai, hydriai, and oinochoai. Two hydriai in New York,[83]
both with Peleus pursuing Thetis, were evidently made as a pair.
Though not among the painter's best works, they are pleasing
and gay and the good preservation gives them added attraction.
A fragment of a bell krater in New York [84] has a charming head
of a woman in his characteristic style (fig. 99). The kalos name
Alkimachos occurs on two, perhaps three, of the Chicago Painter's vases and that of Chairis once.

The renderings of individual forms, though superficially like those of the Villa Giulia Painter, show important differences. Though both artists use narrow fillets wound three times round the head, the Chicago Painter generally lets both ends hang down the back, whereas the Villa Giulia Painter regularly has one end at the back and one in front. Both use the broad headband fastened in front, but the Chicago Painter regularly places it below the chignon, the Villa Giulia Painter above. In the Chicago Painter's works the dot for the iris is not nearer the upper lid but often reaches down to the lower, and the line for the lashes is apt to have a pronounced curve; the nose is larger and more pointed; the lines of the drapery are drawn with less confidence.

THE METHYSE PAINTER [85] belongs to the school of the Villa Giulia Painter and like him favored quiet, monumental scenes. Only a few works by him are extant, among them a magnificent bell krater in New York [86] with a Dionysiac scene. Though the subject is a revel, the figures march in a dignified procession: the maenad Methyse playing the lyre, her head raised in ecstasy (see fig. 78); Dionysos, holding a kantharos and thyrsos, his uncertain steps supported by a little satyr who clasps both arms firmly round the god's body; another maenad playing the flute; and a satyr with a kantharos and a wineskin. When we contrast these stately figures with the ecstatic maenads by the Brygos Painter and the boisterous satyrs by the Kleophrades Painter we can gauge the change of outlook. Greek art has lost the high spirits of youth and is assuming the serene outlook of the "classical" period.

Several artists who decorated chiefly cups show the same preference for quiet scenes. They, with the Villa Giulia Painter, the Chicago Painter, and the Methyse Painter, continued the tradition of Douris.[87] One of the most attractive is THE AKESTORIDES PAINTER, christened after the name he gave to the lovely boy on a kylix in New York.[88] The boy is sitting on a stool in front of an altar, playing the lyre and singing to its music (fig. 86). He is evidently much moved by the music, for he looks up as if inspired. We have few pictures of such grace and feeling expressed by means so simple. The figure is the embodiment of a modest, reverent Greek boy, comparable to the lyre player on the Boston three-sided relief; [89] but Akestorides has the added quality of exaltation, conveyed by the upward tilt of the head, the angle at which the eye is placed, and the rendering of the iris as a line instead of a dot. The composition is admirably adapted to the circular field. The hand marks the center of the circle; around it the lyre is drawn; the bag is balanced by the leg of the stool.

THE PAINTER OF MUNICH 2660 [90] (as well as of 2661 and 2662) decorated also a stemless cup in New York.[91] In the interior is a schoolboy, carrying a writing tablet; on the outside schoolboys, with writing tablets and rolls of manuscript are approaching the teacher—who looks just like the boys and may in fact be one of them playing at being teacher. The scenes have a charming simplicity, but the execution is not very careful and the proportions of the children are not convincing.

THE EUAION PAINTER,[92] so called after a kalos name on one of his cups in the Louvre,[93] worked in a similar vein. Over one hundred works have been attributed to him, mostly on kylikes. His favorite subjects are youths and satyrs in quiet compositions with little action, drawn with a delicate line. A satyr on a stemless cup in New York [94] is one of his liveliest products (fig. 87). He is represented stoking the fire in an oven on which his dinner is cooking. Though slight, the scene has a pleasing vivacity often absent in this artist's rather academic paintings; and the three-quarter back view of the satyr is ably drawn.

THE PAINTER OF LOUVRE C A 1694 [95] is close in style to the Euaion Painter. The two satyrs on an oinochoe in New York [96] are characteristic works by him.

THE EUAICHME PAINTER [97] also belongs in this general group. He is called after the name he gave to a figure on a skyphos in Boston. [98] Another skyphos, in New York,[99] with two male figures on either side (see fig. 85), has the inscription Isthmodoros kalos. The writing tablet hanging on the wall suggests a schoolroom; in that case the seated bearded man would be the teacher talking to one of the boys.

(5) OTHER PAINTERS

Among the many other painters of the early free period we can mention only a few of the most prominent. THE TELEPHOS PAINTER [100] is one of a number of artists whom Beazley has grouped as belonging to the school of Makron. He painted two remarkable kylikes in Boston, signed on the foot by the potter Hieron. On one [101] is a scene of Telephos in the house of Agamemnon, on the other [102] a picture tentatively interpreted as a festival in memory of the conquest of Salamis. Thirty-six other works have been attributed to this painter, chiefly on cups. His style is highly individual. Instead of the comely, heroic types prevalent at the time he used cadaverous figures in angular poses, with expressive gestures. The kalos name Lichas occurs on two of his vases.

THE CLINIC PAINTER [103] is another pupil of Makron with an interesting, vivid style. He is named after the remarkable scene of patients in a clinic, on an aryballos in the Louvre; [104] each in turn is being bled by a physician, bleeding being a favorite treatment in ancient times for many ills. A surgeon's basin and cupping glasses are ready to hand. Two other aryballoi and fourteen cups have been attributed to this artist, including a kylix in the British Museum [105] with Dionysos and Herakles dining together, waited on by two satyrs; one of the latter is surreptitiously stealing a cake while his mate self-consciously looks the other way.

A kantharos in Boston,[106] with Dionysos and Poseidon fighting giants, and with the inscription *"Hieron Medontos epoie"* painted on the foot, was not decorated by Makron, the decorator of most of the vases signed by the potter Hieron (see p. 81), but by THE AMYMONE PAINTER.[107] The name is derived from his picture of Poseidon and Amymone on a pyxis in Athens.[108] The antiquity of the inscription has been doubted. If it is ancient it supplies the name Medon as the father of Hieron, which is not elsewhere given.

HERMONAX's signature, with egrapsen, is preserved on six vases —four stamnoi in Paris, Orvieto, Boston, and Florence, and two pelikai, in Rome and Vienna. He continued the style of the Berlin Painter. Almost one hundred paintings have been attributed to him—mostly on pots, a few on cups.[109] One of the most pleasing is the Birth of Erichthonios on a stamnos in Munich.[110] A lekythos in New York,[111] with a running maenad as the principal picture (see fig. 77) and a crouching satyr on the shoulder, is an attractive work in a lively vein. Another maenad in a quieter pose is on a lekythos, also in New York.[112] More than most of his contemporaries Hermonax preserved the freshness and sense of movement characteristic of the preceding age. The manner in which he draws the eye—the upper lid convex instead of concave to the lower, and the iris a large black dot at the inner corner—gives the face an uncommonly alert expression. He marks the profile ankle in the same way as the Berlin Painter—with two lines, one more or less straight, the other strongly curving.

THE OIONOKLES PAINTER,[113] named after the kalos name which occurs on four of his vases, worked in the same tradition as Hermonax. He was a follower of the Providence Painter (see p. 74), who, like Hermonax, was a pupil of the Berlin Painter. His pictures are mostly lively pursuit scenes on Nolan amphorae and lekythoi. The satyrs and maenads on two Nolan amphorae in New York [114] are typical examples. How fresh and spontaneous, for instance, is the group of the fluting satyr marching along, followed by Dionysos with snake and thyrsos (see fig. 76)! They are off on a gay adventure to the strains of music. The youth advancing with drawn sword, on a large lekythos,[115] has a fine statuesque quality. In addition to Oionokles this artist uses the kalos names Akestorides, Kallias, and perhaps Hilaron.

Several artists of about the same measure as the Oionokles Painter are represented by good examples in New York: THE NIKON PAINTER [116] by a Nolan amphora [117] with Demeter and a woman and with the inscription *Kallikles kalos;* THE PAINTER OF THE YALE OINOCHOE [118] by an amphora [119] with a youth pursuing a woman, sword in hand; and THE PAINTER OF THE YALE LEKYTHOS [120] by a Nolan amphora [121] with a pursuit scene and by a small white-ground lekythos [122] with a warrior cutting a lock of his hair—presumably to put it on a tomb, like Orestes on the grave of Agamemnon. The scenes on three Nolans,[123] decorated with figures of a Nike, youths, and a man with a scabbard, are in the manner of THE PAINTER OF LONDON E 342. Two typical works are by THE SYRACUSE PAINTER [124]—a tall amphora [125] with lively scenes of Nike pouring wine for Poseidon and of Dionysos going off to a function and an unusually large oinochoe [126] with satyrs pursuing maenads in a highly decorative composition. An interesting scene of satyrs making wine [127] is by THE CLEVELAND PAINTER.[128] One is treading grapes in a wooden trough, holding up two corners of the cloth to make the juice pass through more easily. The juice flows into a large cauldron placed under the trough. A large amphora and a drinking horn are ready for use.

A cup,[129] delicately modeled in the form of a lamb's head with sprouting horns, has an attractive picture of a youth playing the lyre to listening friends. It is one of five works attributed to THE PAINTER OF LONDON E 100.[130]

We saw that the ability to give psychological interest to a scene by a few realistic touches was a characteristic of the Penthesileia Painter and his followers (see p. 97). Other artists occasionally made attempts in the same direction. THE AIGISTHOS PAINTER,[131] in his Death of Tityos on a calyx krater in the Louvre,[132] is able to bring out the contrast in expression between the triumphant Apollo and the frightened Tityos. THE ORCHARD PAINTER,[133] who produced many conventional figures, including the rather expressionless women in an orchard on a column krater in New York,[134] could individualize a Jason fetching the golden fleece, on a column krater in New York.[135] Instead of a conquering hero Jason here is a scared human being, wide-eyed and hesitant, though boldly accomplishing his task; he thus becomes an effective foil for the fierce dragon and the calm Athena. THE PAINTER OF BOLOGNA 228,[136] who painted a number of impersonal pictures including the war chariot on a column krater in New York,[137] also produced the prothesis in Athens,[138] one of the most moving representations of death and mourning in Greek art, and the dejected old warrior bidding good-bye to his son, on the neck of a loutrophoros in New York.[139] THE ALKIMACHOS PAINTER,[140] named after one of the kalos names which appear on his vases, could, in his Theseus in Hades on a lekythos in Berlin,[141] convey the surprised joy of the hero after his long suffering and the strength and determination of his deliverer Herakles. The contrast between the two figures is of course also indicated in the attitudes and gestures—Theseus sitting, supporting himself on two spears and stretching out a limp hand, Herakles vigorously clasping it, ready to depart; but the drama is heightened by the expressions, the rolling eye of Herakles, the upward, trusting look of Theseus. The Greek and Amazon by the same artist on a Nolan amphora in New York [142] are of the impersonal type prevalent at the time and show the influence of the Pan Painter. THE DEEPDENE PAINTER,[143] named after his amphora with Athena and Herakles which was formerly in the Deepdene Collection,[144] painted vivid scenes from the Danae legend on a stamnos in New York.[145] Each figure is convincingly characterized:

Danae, standing in the chest that is to be exposed on the sea, her eyes wide with terror; little Perseus with one hand projecting from the mantle as if in appeal; Eurydike, Danae's mother, her fingers raised to her lips in horror; the nurse holding her nose with two fingers to show her distress; and the carpenter, who had to prepare the chest, holding up one hand in consternation. Two other stamnoi in New York have representations of Eos pursuing Kephalos and of Menelaos threatening Helen; and on a hydria is shown a woman at her toilet.[146]

THE SOTADES PAINTER,[147] who decorated three vases signed by the potter Sotades, was another individualist, not so much in the characterization of his figures as in his liking of unusual subjects and shapes. The three pictures on white-ground cups with merry-thought handles in London [148] are among the most delicate in Athenian vase painting. They represent Polyidos [149] and Glaukos; a girl (in correct three-quarter view) standing on tiptoe and reaching up to pick apples from a tree; and an unexplained subject, sometimes interpreted as the Death of Opheltes. The Sotades Painter's most famous picture is on the vase in the form of a knuckle bone in London [150]—young girls dancing and floating through the air, perhaps symbolizing the Dance of the Clouds (fig. 79). Few artists have attained the lightness of touch he here displays. He also decorated several other molded vases of various forms—a sphinx, groups of a crocodile and a negro boy, heads of a hound and of a ram.[151] The lively satyrs and maenads on a kantharos in Goluchow and on a cup in the form of a ram's head in Leningrad [152] are particularly pleasing.

In addition to the three vases decorated by the Sotades Painter, five others bear the signature of the potter Sotades [153]: two phialai in London and Boston, with grooved exteriors (one with a plastic cicada on the central boss); two fragments with no paintings preserved; and a vase in the form of a mounted Amazon, from Egypt, in Boston, the pictures on which "are later than in the other signed vases and not connected with them in style."

A cup in New York [154] in the form of a cow's hoof has a scene which recalls the Sotades Painter in its individual treatment but is by a follower of the Brygos Painter, and the style is somewhat earlier (c. 480–470 B.C.).A herdsman, clothed in a tunic, shoes, furry pelt, and cap, is sitting on a rock (fig. 80). He is watching a herd of cows, of which two are wandering in different directions. At the other end a wolflike dog is emerging from a cave, down which hangs a tendril of ivy. He is rounding up the herd. In the center is a tree, under which a hare is crouching in a characteristic posture. A little to one side is a shrub. The whole is a sensitive picture of rural life, concisely told, in the manner of Greek epigrams. Thinned glaze is ingeniously used. A transparent wash suggests the smooth surfaces of cave and rock; mottling conveys the rough textures of the herdsman's pelt and of the coats of dog and hare; irregular shaded lines represent the foliage of the shrub; brown dots imitate the rough bark of the stylized tree; and on the vase itself the texture and color of the horn are rendered by brown striations. We could have no better example of the many different effects which the Greek vase painter achieved with his one black glaze.

THE LEWIS PAINTER [155] had a liking for skyphoi. The paintings on thirty-five examples have been attributed to him and so far on no other shapes. His name is derived from a skyphos in Corpus Christi College, Cambridge,[156] formerly in the Lewis Collection. We now also know his real name; for he signed two of his works *Polygnotos egrapsen*—a skyphos in Baltimore [157] and one in Tübingen.[158] He was, therefore, still another vase painter named Polygnotos (see pp. 97, 127). His pictures consist mostly of one or two figures, either quietly confronting each other or in some deliberate action, like a slow pursuit, with the pursued looking back at the pursuer. The rendering of the eye with two lines for the upper lid and with a line curving strongly upward for the eyelashes occurs often on the more careful works of his mature period.

THE ZEPHYROS PAINTER [159] is a close follower of the Lewis Painter. He is named after his picture of Hyakinthos and Zephyros on a skyphos in Vienna.[160]

THE SABOUROFF PAINTER,[161] the artist of a nuptial vase in Berlin [162] from the Sabouroff Collection, worked both in red-figure and on white ground. Most of his red-figured pictures are on kylikes, Nolan amphorae, and lekythoi; they are rarely great works of art, but form quiet, pleasant designs. The group of a woman and a youth on a lekythos in New York [163] is a typical example. She is sitting on a chair, holding up a mirror, while he looks down at her admiringly. The inscription "Archedike is fair" is perhaps a reference to the well-known hetaira from Naukratis, "the theme of song throughout Greece." [164] In the white-ground technique the Sabouroff Painter produced several masterpieces—the superb Hera on a kylix in Munich [165] and many lovely figures on lekythoi. The scenes on the latter, in addition to depicting life in the home, often relate to death, indicating that such vases were now often made to serve as tomb offerings (see p. 119). Men and women are seen mourning at tombs, or bringing sashes and ointments as offerings, or sitting by the grave making music. The woman kneeling by a tomb, with arms outstretched, beating her head in grief, on a white lekythos in the Schoen Collection,[166] is particularly moving. Three interesting pictures are in New York. One, drawn in glaze outlines, represents the lying-in-state of the dead, with mourners surrounding the bier (see fig. 82).[167] Another, drawn in matt lines, depicts Charon in his yellow boat, ready to ferry a youth across the river Styx (see fig. 81) [168]; the youth, wrapped in a mantle, has been escorted by Hermes to the river bank. The solemnity of the figures suggests that this is not an everyday incident but belongs to another sphere. A third, also in matt outlines, has a scene of two mourners standing by a tomb ornamented with sashes [169] —a subject which was soon to become popular (see p. 152). In all three pictures the colored washes—yellow, black, and red— are exceptionally well preserved. Most of the white-ground scenes by the Sabouroff Painter are drawn in matt outlines. He was one of the first to use this new technique, which presently became general.

A red-figured, squat lekythos in New York has a scene now attributed to THE PAINTER OF MUNICH 2363.[170] It has been suggested that instead of Achilles and Penthesileia, as has been thought, the subject represents two Amazons, one lying on the ground, wounded or asleep (her eyes are closed), the other coming to her.[170a] The Amazon on the ground wears the Oriental costume of tiara, tunic, jacket, trousers, and shoes; her quiver and bow are strapped to her side, her ax is on the ground. In contrast, the other Amazon (if it is one) wears a Greek short chiton and a Corinthian helmet, and carries a spear and a shield with a large eye as a device. The fact that the spear is in her left hand shows, it is argued, that the figure cannot have attacked, and is therefore not a Greek. Her gesture, however, suggests surprise or sympathy.

THE ETHIOP PAINTER is represented in New York by a dramatic painting: Kassandra, who has taken sanctuary at the statue of Athena, and the ruthless Ajax about to drag her away.[171]

A white lekythos in New York [172] by THE VOUNI PAINTER has the usual scene of mourners at a tomb, but instead of one grave stele two are represented—mounted on high platforms (fig. 83) —like those found in the Athenian Kerameikos. The shafts are bound with numerous fillets, and the mourners—a woman and a boy—have offerings in their hands. Jumping weights, a strigil, and an oil bottle (aryballos) are suspended from the right-hand platform, so one at least of the graves must have been that of an athlete. Behind the stelai is the funeral mound. The scene is drawn in glaze outlines on a yellowish-white ground with red, black, and white washes in exceptionally good preservation. The bright colors give the vase a striking appearance. The only other work by the painter of this picture is on a white lekythos found at Vouni in Cyprus,[173] hence his name. The style is related to that of the Pistoxenos Painter (see p. 99).

The so-called INSCRIPTION PAINTER,[174] was also a decorator of white lekythoi. A good example with a woman greeting a youth at a tomb is in New York.[175] The youth holds a spear and a helmet and his pensive, detached attitude contrasts with the animation of the woman; so he is probably intended for the dead soldier who was buried in the grave by which he stands.

Several minor painters of this period specialized in the decoration of small lekythoi and alabastra. THE AISCHINES PAINTER,[176] who used the kalos name Aischines on an alabastron in Boston,[177] is one of the most pleasing. Almost two hundred vases, chiefly lekythoi, with one or two figures, have been attributed to him. Two typical examples, each with a woman in an animated pose, are in New York.[178] THE TYMBOS PAINTER [179] decorated mostly small white lekythoi intended as offerings at tombs. THE CARLSRUHE PAINTER,[180] who decorated a small pelike in Carlsruhe,[181] worked in both red-figure and on white ground. THE IKAROS PAINTER,[182] named after a representation of a winged figure, perhaps Ikaros, in New York,[183] painted chiefly lekythoi, some on white ground. Though these modest painters produced no great works of art, they help us to realize the many-sided activity in the potters' studios at this time. Their works are like little trills supplementing the full chords of the more important artists.

IV. FREE STYLE, ABOUT 450–420 B.C.

THE period of the free style is concurrent with the administration of Perikles (461–429), which marks the height of
power of the Athenian state. The vast resources available
through the transference of the Delian Treasury to Athens (454)
and the Thirty Years' Peace signed between Athens and Pelopon-
nese (445) enabled Perikles to undertake important building op-
erations. The Parthenon, the Propylaia, and the Telesterion of
Eleusis all date from this time.

In the field of painting the great masters of the preceding
epoch—Polygnotos and Mikon—were still active and all influ-
ential.

In this period of great activity in the major arts of sculpture
and painting it was natural that the most prominent artists
should no longer work in potteries. And so vase painters now
tend to be mere decorators. Even so their work reflects the spirit
of the time. Something of the grandeur of the Parthenon sculptures appears in the simple compositions of standing and seated
figures which now come into favor. And the figures themselves
are drawn with a new ease and freedom. They are no longer
composites of separate formulas but are realized as a whole, with
contours suggesting the volume of the shapes enclosed. Shading
is suggested by occasional washes in thinned glaze alongside the
anatomical markings (see p. 128). This plasticity, though probably a gain for the large panel paintings of the time, detracts
from the decorative value of the vase paintings, for it seems out
of place in a design on a pot.

The experimental period being over, there was now less striv-
ing for difficult postures. Profile views or full-front views with
profile heads were still favored by most artists; but when three-
quarter views were chosen—for a chest, face, foot, hand, back,
or for the whole figure—they were drawn with comparative ease.

The rendering of the eye also becomes more natural. In profile
view it is now more or less triangular in shape with the iris hid-
ing the inner corner (see fig. 33). The iris itself is no longer
round but elongated, generally touching only the upper lid; the
latter is often rendered by two lines instead of one, and a curve

is added for the eyelashes. Thus a convincing rendering was attained by pure line drawing without any modeling or shading. In the full-front view the outer as well as the inner corner of the eye is now sometimes open, and the iris is usually placed in the center (see fig. 33 f.).

The hair has lost its former compactness and often appears as a loose mass with wavy contours at forehead and temples and fluffy curls at the sides.

The garments are drawn in flowing lines, which vary in direction, suggesting the round forms of the body underneath. As in

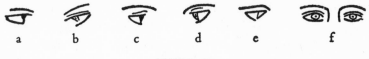

FIGURE 33

the preceding period, thinned washes are occasionally used for shadows to indicate the depth of folds.

Linear perspective, which, as we saw (pp. 90 f.), was applied to stage scenery in the preceding period and which occupied the minds of philosophers like Anaxagoras and Demokritos, only slowly penetrated into the consciousness of the vase painters. In the first two decades of the period under consideration rectangular objects like furniture, stelai, steps of stelai, altars are still regularly rendered only in the front plane (see p. 140). Only occasionally do we find an attempt at representing a receding side view, as, for instance, in the chest on a hydria in Boston by the Danae Painter [1] (about 450–440 B.C.); even there, however, the lines do not converge, but are drawn parallel to one another. From 430 B.C. such attempts are more frequent.[2] For instance, on an oinochoe of about 425 in New York a doorway and tiled roof are shown receding into the background (see p. 135).

The color scheme remains the same as before, but red as an accessory color (generally on an undercoating of white) and, toward the end of the period, gilding on applied clay become increasingly frequent. Relief contour is often dispensed with. Washes in thinned glaze to suggest shadows and volume become more frequent than before.

The white-ground technique popular in the preceding period

is continued alongside red-figure, but is now restricted more
and more to the lekythoi used as offerings to the dead. The subjects accordingly deal mostly with death (but see p. 121). The
figures are drawn in outline either in glaze or dull paint, presently in dull paint only. Applied white is discontinued, the white
ground serving for the flesh; sometimes a flesh color is added
over the white. The garments are covered as before with solid
washes; red and black are the favorite colors.

A comparison between the vase paintings of this period and
the Parthenon sculptures (447–432) reveals many similarities
of style, especially·in the draperies. The works of the Achilles
Painter and his group are related to the frieze (442–438 B.C.).
A little later, in the works of the Eretria Painter, the folds mul-
tiply and the garments gain in transparency, reflecting the renderings of the pediments (438–432 B.C.). In a few instances scenes
on vases seem to have been copied from specific figures. Thus
the youth mounting his horse, on a pelike in Berlin,[3] strikingly
resembles a group on the west side of the Parthenon frieze;[4] and
the two youths with a bull, on an oinochoe in Baltimore, may
be an adaptation from figures on the south side of the frieze.[5]
That sculptures were copied on vases during this period and
later is definitely shown by the representations, for instance, of
the Tyrannicides on a fragment in Boston[6] found in the burial
plot of Dexileos (see pp. 141 f.) and of Myron's Athena on an oinochoe in Berlin.[7]

Kalos names, which furnished such convenient evidence for
dating the earlier vases, become less common, except on white
lekythoi (see p. 152).

The types of vases used are much the same as in the preceding
period, but the forms gradually become more flowing in outline,
less crisp and sturdy.

Over eighty vase painters have been assigned to the free period.
Some decorated chiefly pots, others chiefly cups. The most prominent pot painters are the Achilles Painter and his followers, and
Polygnotos and his circle. The latter's broad style greatly influenced the art of the succeeding period. The Eretria Painter,
the Kodros Painter, and others decorated chiefly cups and the
smaller vases with delicately drawn scenes. They too have a great
future in the work of the Meidias Painter and his followers.

(1) THE ACHILLES PAINTER AND HIS
FOLLOWERS

THE ACHILLES PAINTER,[8] named after his stately amphora with Achilles and Briseis in the Vatican,[9] is one of the leading artists of his time. We find in his work, perhaps more than in that of any other vase painter, the serene spirit of the contemporary Periklean sculpture. Most of his pictures are on Nolan amphorae and lekythoi and consist of one or two figures doing the obvious things of everyday life, but with a quiet poise which gives them distinction. Occasionally he decorated large vases. Even in these more ambitious compositions, however, it is the beauty of the attitudes rather than the interest of the action that appeals.

So much of the work of the Achilles Painter has been preserved —on over 180 vases, including white-ground lekythoi and black-figured Panathenaic amphorae [10]—that we can form a good estimate of his style. In his early formative years he learned much from the Berlin Painter, and he drew his forms in a somewhat summary manner. The vases formerly assigned to the so-called Meletos Painter belong to this period; at least Beazley now thinks that this artist and the early Achilles Painter are identical. One of the most important examples of the "Meletos period" is a bell krater in New York [11] with an old warrior and a bearded man engaged in lively conversation. The old soldier's face is drawn in a remarkably realistic manner. The hooked nose, the strongly curving eyebrow, the wrinkles on forehead and cheek and around the eyes differentiate him from the current type. It is worthy of note that the Achilles Painter—if this vase is indeed by him—attempted such realistic renderings in his youth, whereas in his extant later work he adhered to the generalized types. Two Nolan amphorae in New York with Eos and Tithonos,[12] and a third with Athena and a woman [13] have likewise been identified as early products by the Achilles Painter.

As the Achilles Painter matured his style became surprisingly uniform. Especially in his slighter works the same poses and motives occur again and again with but few variations; in fact the mantled figures on the reverses of his vases serve almost as a trademark of his work. Most of his large important paintings belong to this period—the Achilles and Briseis on the amphora in the Vatican above mentioned, Euphorbos and Oedipus on an amphora in Paris,[14] the Dionysiac scene on a pointed amphora also in Paris, [15] and the Theseus and Amazons on a calyx krater in Ferrara.[16] A loutrophoros-amphora in Philadelphia [17] has several rare features. The principal decoration, instead of being the lying-in-state usual on such funeral vases, represents a combat; and though this picture is by the Achilles Painter, others on the same vase are by an associate—the Sabouroff Painter (see p. 112). We have here another certain instance of two artists collaborating in the same workshop (see p. 100).

The scene on a squat lekythos in New York [18] is a typical minor work, attractive in its simplicity. A woman has filled a phiale from her wine jug and is handing it to a warrior for a libation before his departure. He holds his shield and spear and wears a "Thracian" helmet and a short, heavy tunic. A stool with ornamented cushion is by their side. Both figures have close parallels on other vases by the Achilles Painter, for instance the woman on a pelike in the British Museum [19] and the warrior on a lekythos in the Louvre.[20]

Besides his red-figured work the Achilles Painter decorated many white lekythoi.[21] He was indeed the leading painter in this technique and was probably responsible for its great vogue during the second half of the fifth century. The development observable in his products is that current at the time. First the scenes are drawn in diluted glaze outlines, later in reddish or black matt outlines; in the earlier works a "second" white superimposed on the white ground for certain details was used, later it was abandoned. Among the Achilles Painter's many white-ground pictures several stand out by their excellence. In a famous one in Athens [22] a youth is departing for battle and bidding farewell to his wife; he is holding helmet, shield, and spear while she sits motionless looking into space. The poignancy of the parting is the greater for being merely suggested. Another masterpiece in this technique is in the Schoen Collection in the Ticino.[23] A woman sits on a rock and plays the kithara (see fig. 89), while a companion stands listening. The locality is identified as Mount Helikon and the women as Muses by the inscription *Helikon* on the rock. The stillness of the scene is conveyed by the quiet postures of the women absorbed in the music. The colors are exceptionally well preserved: yellow for the tunic of the seated figure, with a vermilion line near the hem, vermilion for her kerchief, wine-red for her mantle, reddish brown on the kithara; red lines on the tunic of the standing figure, vermilion for her mantle with black lines for the folds. The vivid colors, consciously interrelated, play their part in the harmony of the design. The vase is inscribed *Axiopeithes kalos Alkimacho,* "Axiopeithes the son of Alkimachos is fair."

Several attractive white-ground scenes by this artist are in New York. On one lekythos [24] a mistress and maid stand facing each other; the mistress is tying her girdle beneath the pouch of her tunic, the maid holds an alabastron ready for use; on the wall hang a mirror and two kerchiefs. On another [25] a woman and a youth are about to clasp hands; a kerchief hangs on the wall. The two vases are closely related and resemble two others in Toronto [26] and Broomhall.[27] All four were probably made at the same time. On a third lekythos in New York [28] two women are preparing to take offerings to a tomb; one carries a basket from which hang three fillets; the other holds up a vase with a cover, probably used for perfumes; a kerchief hangs on the wall. A fourth,[29] with a badly preserved picture of a youth and a woman at a tomb, has the mouth, neck, part of the shoulder, and the handle worked in a separate piece; it could, therefore, not have been actually used but must have been made as a tomb offering. All these scenes are drawn in diluted glaze outlines. A fifth example in New York [30] shows the new technique with matt outlines. A youth is sitting on a cushioned stool and is holding out a round fruit to a woman who reaches for it; an oinochoe, a mirror, and a kerchief hang on the wall. The youth's flesh is painted a light brown.

The Achilles Painter's renderings of individual forms [31] are as consistent as the Berlin Painter's. He draws the eye, for instance, with two almost straight lines for the lids and with the iris touching both lids (except in his elaborate vases when the eye is rendered in great detail); the forehead-nose line is slightly convex to the face, and the nostril has two short lines. The anatomical markings on the arm form an almost constant scheme— a brown curving line for the biceps, one black and two brown lines on the inside of the elbow, a brown curving line near the point of the elbow, two straight brown lines on the forearm, and a short black line separating the open hand from the arm. The profile knee is rendered by two straight lines for the patella and a curving line for the vastus internus; the frontal knee by several short straight and curving lines, one long and curving, one short and straight; the frontal ankle by two short vertical lines. And so on.

Kalos names occasionally appear on the Achilles Painter's red-figured vases, especially on his earlier ones—Meletos, Lichas, Alkaios, Epeleios, Axiopeithes, Kleinias, the son of Pedieus (perhaps the same Pedieus who was fair sixty years or so earlier). Some of these names reappear on the Achilles Painter's white lekythoi, as well as others, several with their fathers' names: Dromippos, the son of Dromokleides; Diphilos, son of Melanopos; Pistoxenos, son of Aresandros; Hygiainon; Alkimedes, son of Aischylides. If these white lekythoi were used as tomb offerings one would suppose that the names belonged to the youths to whose graves they were brought; but this can hardly be; for though several with the name Diphilos were found at Eretria, in other instances the provenances of vases with the same kalos names differ. The vases inscribed *Hygiainon kalos,* for instance, were found in Athens and in Kerateia; those with the name Axiopeithes in Greece, Gela, and Suessula; those with Dromippos in Eretria, Athens, and the Troad. It would seem odd to praise the beauty of other youths on a vase made for one who had just died. As a matter of fact, most of the scenes on the Achilles Painter's white lekythoi are not related to death but are from daily life—a mistress and her maid, a mother with her child, a woman making music—and the few paintings of mourners at tombs have no kalos names inscribed. Evidently most of his white lekythoi were not made to serve as grave offerings but, like his red-figured ones, simply as oil-containers. We may indeed surmise that the chief purpose of the white lekythos in the Achilles Painter's day was for daily use—as it had been earlier (see p. 75)—but that when the perishableness of the white slip and of the tempera colors showed that it was unsuited for everyday utensils its use was restricted to that of tomb offering. The Achilles Painter must have lived in the transition period when both uses were still current.

There were other painters of this period who specialized in the decoration of white lekythoi—for instance, THE BOSANQUET PAINTER, THE THANATOS PAINTER, THE PAINTER OF MUNICH

2335.[32] Though pictures from daily life occasionally occur on these vases, the majority relate to death. Several examples are in New York. One, by the Thanatos Painter,[33] has two figures at a tomb—a young girl with offerings and a woman who may represent the departed. An unusual feature is the stool on top of the stele shaft, perhaps symbolizing a seated statue. In another scene, by the same painter,[34] a maid is bringing a basket of offerings to her mistress. The serenity of the Pheidian period is conveyed in the quiet, aristocratic demeanor of these figures. A charming picture in matt outlines by the Painter of Munich 2335 represents Charon with his boat.[35] He is waiting to act as ferryman for a child who stands by the river bank with his toy cart bidding good-bye to his sorrowing mother. On another lekythos decorated by this painter [36] two women are bringing offerings to a tomb—a sash, a basket, and an aryballos. Two scenes by the Bosanquet Painter show mourners at tombs; [37] on the steps are vases and wreaths brought as offerings.

THE PHIALE PAINTER [38] is named after one of his most attractive works—the libation bowl in Boston [39] with a "visit to a school of music." He must have been a pupil of the Achilles Painter, with whom he has much in common; but into the Periklean serenity of his master he introduced a more lively spirit. His winsome figures, often in charmingly spontaneous poses, are chiefly on the smaller vases—Nolan amphorae and lekythoi—but occasionally he decorated successfully the larger fields of kraters and stamnoi. Among the latter the stamnos in Goluchow [40] with maenads and the infant satyr is one of the most successful. The group of Poseidon pursuing Amymone on a lekythos in New York [41] calls to mind Periklean sculptures. The Amymone resembles the "Iris" of the Parthenon pediment, combining in the same way a feeling of motion with a statuesque quality (see fig. 91). Another pursuit—of a youth and a woman—appears on a neck amphora in New York.[42] A scene of departure, on a lekythos in New York,[43] with a woman handing a youth his helmet, is painted in the artist's quiet, reposeful manner. A small pelike in Boston [44] has a rare subject, vividly rendered: two chorus men are dressing up as women; one is putting on his high boots, the other holds up a himation, neatly rolled up, and gesticulates energetically; a mask is on the floor. On a lekythos in Bowdoin [45] a girl is being taught to dance by her mistress. Another dancing lesson is on a hydria in London.[46] The kalos name Euaion is inscribed on a hydria with Thamyris in the Vatican.[47]

The Phiale Painter's work was not confined to red-figure. Several beautiful pictures by him are on a white ground. On a lekythos in Munich [48] a woman is seen sitting by a tomb on a rock, wrapped in her mantle and lost in thought; another woman is bringing a sash as an offering. The detachment of the seated woman shows that she is of a different world, that she is the dead woman sitting by her tomb. Her stillness and the reverent approach of her living friend are beautifully rendered. The lines are in matt reddish color, the washes red and yellow.

The picture on another lekythos in Munich [49] is equally remarkable. Hermes is sitting on a rock by a tomb, waiting. Opposite him a woman is approaching, fastening her wreath as she goes. She has died and is getting ready to go on her last journey, escorted by Hermes. Though she is engaged in an everyday action something unearthly in her appearance suggests that she no longer belongs to this world.

THE PERSEPHONE PAINTER [50] also belongs to the circle of the Achilles Painter. Only fourteen paintings have been definitely attributed to him—on both large and small pots—mostly slight works, like the two women on an alabastron in New York.[51] His masterpiece is the Return of Persephone, on a bell krater in New York (see fig. 92).[52] Persephone is rising out of an opening in the ground, her hand raised in a gesture of surprise; her guide, Hermes, stands by her side, holding his herald's staff; Hekate lights the path with two torches, while Demeter awaits her daughter, scepter in hand. Here too the figures have something of the grandeur of the Parthenon pediments. The artist has been able to convey the solemnity of the moment—the exaltation of Persephone as she returns to earth and again sees her mother, and the awe and expectancy of her companions. The attitude of Hermes, standing stiffly by Persephone's side, in full-front view, adds to the unearthly feeling. The picture indeed suggests the miracle which the story symbolizes—the return of life to earth with the coming of spring.

According to the Homeric "Hymn to Demeter," which is our chief source for the myth, Demeter [53] when she saw Persephone "rushed forth as does a maenad down some thick-wooded mountain"; on the New York vase she calmly awaits the return of her daughter. In two other particulars the artist has departed from the account of the hymn. Persephone and Hermes are on foot, not "in the golden chariot with the deathless horses" which "Aidoneus the Ruler of Many" had got ready for their journey; and Hekate is present at the actual return instead of later. Such variations in the translation of a story into a work of art are of course common. Instead of giving a snapshot of a particular moment the Greek artists represented the chief participants in characteristic attitudes, combined in a harmonious design. It is noteworthy, however, that in none of the other extant representations of Persephone's Return is a chariot shown.[54] Perhaps, therefore, the vase painters followed a version, now lost, different from that given in the Homeric hymn.

THE DWARF PAINTER [55] was another follower of the Achilles Painter. The numerous works attributed to him are on Nolan amphorae, small pelikai, and hydriai. He is named after his picture on a pelike in Boston [56]—a youth going out for a walk, followed by his dwarf servant, who holds a large dog by the collar. The erect, aristocratic gait of the youth is well contrasted with the humble attitude of the dwarf.

(2) THE MANNHEIM PAINTER AND OTHERS

THE MANNHEIM PAINTER [57] is a member of another group of artists, who, like the Achilles Painter, favored figures in quiet poses, but who worked in the tradition of the Villa Giulia Painter rather than that of the Berlin Painter. The name is derived from his oinochoe in Mannheim [58] with Amazons. His ten extant works are all on jugs. One of his best and liveliest is on an oinochoe in New York,[59] with a handsome scale pattern on the handle: Three Amazons are going into battle. The first rushes forward with shield and battle-ax, her quiver and bow hanging by a cord from her shoulder (see fig. 88). The second holds her horse by the reins and turns full face to the spectator, two spears in her hand; one leg is drawn in profile, the other in full front with the tip of the foot turned up. The last advances with crescent shield and two spears, her bow and quiver by her side. Their names are inscribed—Penthesileia, Antiopeia, Iole. The figures are beautifully drawn in a somewhat formal style, with a fine sense for composition and movement.

One of the artist's most interesting pictures is on a jug in the Vatican.[60] The king of Persia (inscribed *basileus*), the Persian queen (inscribed *basilis*), and another woman are represented in what seems to have been the Greek notion of Persian dress, with long-sleeved jackets and tiaras.[61] The queen is apparently preparing to pour a drink. A number of pictures of Persians occur on Attic vases. Those painted about 480 B.C. or so—in the period immediately following the Persian wars—generally represent Greeks fighting Persians. The later ones lay stress on the power of Persia, which was of course felt in Greece for a long time in spite of Persia's repulse from the shores of Greece.

THE DANAE PAINTER,[62] named after his Danae and Perseus on a hydria in Boston,[63] may likewise be placed in this group. Only eleven vases have so far been attributed to him with certainty, but he probably also painted the charming scene on a bell krater in New York [64]—a woman sitting on a cushioned chair and playing the lyre, while two young women stand before her, listening (see fig. 90). One of the listeners has put both hands on her companion's shoulders, and their hands meet in an affectionate gesture. Their faraway expressions suggest that they are listening to the music. They form an attractive group with a personal note unusual in Greek vase painting. The rendering of the musician is interesting. The head is drawn in three-quarter view, with eyes in two profile views; the fillet is in front view and so is the upper part of the body; the legs are in profile. Apparently the archaic tradition of piecing together various aspects of the body persisted with some artists for a considerable time. Another scene perhaps by the Danae Painter and comparable to the New York one is on a bell krater in Vienna,[65] with Apollo and two Muses, one playing the flute, the other the lyre.

Still another musical scene by an artist of this group—THE PAINTER OF LONDON E 497 [66]—is on a bell krater in New York (see fig. 93).[67] The subject is Orpheus among the Thracians. Orpheus is sitting on a rock and playing the lyre, engrossed in his music. A Thracian, wearing the typical Thracian cap, boots, and gaily decorated mantle—has been listening and now turns round toward a Thracian woman. She has just arrived—as indicated by her momentary pose—and has brought a curved knife to wreak vengeance on the great singer. The two Thracians symbolize respectively the crowd of Thracian men moved by Orpheus' music and the horde of women who tore him to pieces in their jealousy. The absorption of Orpheus in his music and his remoteness from the listeners are finely suggested. Spatial depth is indicated by the placing of Orpheus in the mid-distance, of the Thracians in the front plane. A bell krater in London [68] has a similarly composed scene of three figures, but they are ranged along one line in the front plane.

THE MENELAOS PAINTER,[69] called after his picture of Menelaos and Helen on a bell krater in the Louvre,[70] was perhaps an associate of the Danae Painter, for their styles are occasionally close. Only a few vases have so far been definitely attributed to him. Among them is a well-preserved bell krater in New York [71] with a procession of ecstatic maenads—playing the lyre and the double flute, singing, carrying thyrsoi, cups, and torches.

THE KLEIO PAINTER,[72] also a member of this general group, is called after the name of a Muse on a bell krater in Berlin.[73] His style closely resembles that of two other painters—THE EUPOLIS PAINTER,[74] called after the name he gave a satyr boy on a bell krater in Vienna,[75] and THE PAINTER OF ATHENS 1943,[76] who decorated four white lekythoi. It is even possible that all three artists were the same person. The famous pictures of three Muses and of Hermes bringing the infant Hermes to a silenos, on a calyx krater in the Vatican,[77] may be an early work by the Kleio Painter. They are in a polychrome technique on a yellowish-white ground. The "second" white used for the flesh of women and for the hair of silenos is a retention of an older practice (see p. 114). The statuesque figures and their quiet bearing impart a solemn note to the scenes. A white lekythos in New York,[78] attributed to the Painter of Athens 1943, has a sepulchral scene —a woman who has brought a wreath and an alabastron full of perfume as offerings to a grave; only minute traces are preserved of the second figure on the other side of the tomb.

THE CASSEL PAINTER [79] continues the style of the Kleio Painter. Twenty-three works have been attributed to him, among them a woman playing the lyre, on a bell krater in Cassel.[80] Kadmos and the dragon, on a bell krater in New York,[81] is a pleasing work by him. The regal attitude and quiet bearing of Harmonia are reminiscent of the seated goddesses of the Parthenon gables.

Two other painters belonging to this group are represented by characteristic examples in New York—THE POLYDEKTES PAINTER in a quietly composed scene of a young horseman leaving home (on a bell krater) [82] and THE RICHMOND PAINTER in a picture of a king with a woman pouring a libation (on a Nolan amphora).[83] They represent the output of the average artists of the time.

(3) POLYGNOTOS AND HIS CIRCLE

POLYGNOTOS [84] is the most important representative of a group of vase painters who flourished side by side with the Achilles Painter and his associates. His signature (*Polygnotos egrapsen*) is preserved on four vases—a stamnos in Brussels [85] with a centauromachy, a stamnos in London [86] with Herakles and a centaur, a pelike in Syracuse [87] with an Amazonomachy, and a neck amphora in Moscow [88] with Achilles in retirement. This Polygnotos must be distinguished from his more famous namesake, the mural painter Polygnotos of Thasos (see p. 89), and from two other vase painters—the Lewis Painter and the Nausikaa Painter, who we now know, were both named Polygnotos (see pp. 97, 112). An unpublished calyx krater in Munich [89] with a Dionysiac scene has a fragmentary inscription *Po[lygnotos]* *[e]g[rapsen]*. According to Beazley, it is "by a Polygnotan, but not by Polygnotos himself" (i.e., not the Polygnotos we are now discussing). If the inscription is rightly restored we should here have a fourth vase painter with this name. It was evidently a common one in fifth-century Attica.

Polygnotos, like the Achilles Painter, was imbued with the idealism of his time and was able to express it in the nobility of his types. His figures and those of his associates are less austere than the Achilles Painter's, rounder, fleshier, more suggestive of the third dimension. His tradition is that of the Niobid Painter. Most of the sixty-four paintings which have been attributed to him are on large vases—stamnoi, kraters, and amphorae. The signed ones, mentioned above, are among his best. A comparison of his Achilles and Penthesileia, on an amphora in London,[90] with the renderings of the same subject by the Berlin Painter

(see p. 69) and by the Penthesileia Painter (see p. 97) is instructive. Polygnotos' design is weaker and the effect of the whole
tamer than in the earlier paintings; but his drawing is more
naturalistic. Penthesileia's face, for instance, is ably rendered in
a three-quarter view, with the farther eye and even the mouth
correctly foreshortened.

One of the most important unsigned works by Polygnotos is
a pelike in New York [91] with Perseus in the act of cutting off the
head of the sleeping Medusa (see fig. 96) and with a king, named
Polypeithes, in the company of two women. It is characteristic
of this idealizing period that Medusa is no longer the terrifying
monster that she was in the archaic period (see p. 75, fig. 71),
but a beautiful woman. The musical scene on a bell krater in
New York [92] is of only average quality, but it shows well Polygnotos' serene spirit. A man is playing the kithara, striking the
strings with a plektron; he has carried his audience with him,
for they are all listening intently—a bearded man sitting in a
chair with a pensive expression; a youth leaning on a stick and
raising his hand in appreciation; and a man standing quietly behind the player. The vase is inscribed *Nikomas kalos.*

THE LYKAON PAINTER [93] is one of the most distinguished artists
of the Polygnotan group. He is called by the name he gave to a
departing warrior on a pelike in the British Museum.[94] His style
is related to that of Polygnotos, and his figures have the same heroic quality, the same roundness and fleshiness. To judge by his
comparatively few extant works, his preference was for the larger
vases. The Departure of Neoptolemos on a neck amphora in
New York [95] is comparable in quality to the London pelike. A
young warrior named Neoptolemos is bidding farewell to his
father, Antiochos, who is seated on a chair covered with a deer-
skin; his mother Kalliope, is ready to pour the libation; his friend,
Antimachos, holds helmet and shield. The washes of thinned
glaze in the folds and in the grooves of the anatomical markings
are characteristic of the Polygnotan group. The arc at the ankle
in the frontal foot successfully suggests a farther plane.

In contrast to this carefully executed picture, that on the other
side of the vase is hastily drawn, as so often in this period; for we
can now really speak of a "front" and a "back" of a vase.
Buschor [96] interprets the often recurring figures of such men and
women, holding sticks, torches, vases, etc., as "street scenes."

Two other masterpieces by the Lykaon Painter must be mentioned—the idyllic scene of Dionysos with satyrs and maenads on a bell krater at Goluchow,[97] and a picture on a pelike in Boston.[98] The subject of the latter is Odysseus on the reeded banks of Hades conversing with the shade of the unburied Elpenor (see figs. 94, 95). Odysseus, escorted by Hermes, has sacrificed the rams according to instructions and has sat down on a rock, when suddenly Elpenor rises from the ground. Odysseus' awe as he looks steadfastly at the unearthly figure is well suggested.

The death of Aktaion on a bell krater in Boston,[99] though a comparatively minor work, is interesting for comparison with the earlier rendering of this subject by the Pan Painter (see p. 95). The latter confined himself to the two chief participants of the story and represented them in a spirited action. The Lykaon Painter composed his figures more formally—Aktaion and Lysa, the personification of "Madness," in a central group, Zeus and Artemis as quiet, dignified onlookers on either side. The general effect of the picture is much tamer than in the earlier version, but naturalistically it is more advanced. Spatial depth is successfully suggested. Aktaion's head and left leg are drawn convincingly in three-quarter view. Zeus, with one leg placed on a rock, is correctly foreshortened. Instead of a two-dimensional decoration like that by the Pan Painter the scene has become a three-dimensional representation.

Several kalos names appear on vases decorated by the Lykaon Painter. The London pelike is inscribed *Euaion kalos,* the Goluchow krater *Alkimachos kalos* and *Axiopeithes kalos.* We have made the acquaintance of these names elsewhere (see pp. 107, 110, 121).

THE ORPHEUS PAINTER,[100] an artist on the outskirts of the Polygnotan group, is named after his well-known picture of Orpheus on a column krater in Berlin.[101] It is perhaps the finest musical scene of its period, more elaborate than the representations on the New York kraters (see pp. 125, 128): Orpheus is seated on a rock, playing the lyre and singing, while four Thracians listen. He is looking up inspired, while the Thracians are completely entranced by his sweet strains. They bend forward, sway to and fro, close their eyes, or stand apart. It is an extraordinary picture of emotion conveyed chiefly by posture

and gesture. A more conventional scene by the Orpheus Painter
is on a hydria in New York.[102] It consists of male and female figures composed in four groups; among them are a graceful woman
spinning with distaff and spindle, and an Eros giving a pair of
shoes with pointed toes to a woman.

Several other prominent painters belong in the Polygnotan
group—THE CHRISTIE PAINTER,[103] who decorated several largish
vases, including a bell krater with a komos, formerly in the
collection of the Lady Rosamund Christie; [104] THE HEKTOR
PAINTER,[105] who decorated a neck amphora in the Vatican [106] with
Hektor leaving home; THE PELEUS PAINTER,[107] who painted the
wedding of Peleus on a calyx krater at Ferrara [108] and the well-
known picture of Mousaios, Terpsichore, and Melousa on a neck
amphora in London; [109] and THE COGHILL PAINTER,[110] who decorated a calyx krater formerly in the Coghill Collection, now in
the Gulbenkian Collection.[111] A volute krater in New York [112]
with a spirited Dionysiac scene is perhaps also by the Coghill
Painter (see fig. 107). The artist has here caught the wild exuberance of Dionysiac life and has made of it a delicate, vivacious
design. The shape is unusual: the body is ribbed, and the foot
fits into a stand, which was made separately.

(4) OTHER PAINTERS OF POTS

Of the other painters of pots belonging to this period some
approximate the Polygnotan group, others are definitely outside it.

THE NAPLES PAINTER,[113] to whom forty-eight vases have been
attributed, decorated column kraters in Naples, Bologna, and
elsewhere with centauromachies. His output also includes nuptial lebetes and loutrophoroi with the scenes of women. We know
eighty works by THE PAINTER OF THE LOUVRE CENTAURO-
MACHY,[114] the majority on column kraters. A calyx krater by him
in New York [115] is decorated with spirited scenes of athletes practising—a discus thrower, two runners with jumping weights, a
pair of wrestlers, and a youth with a strigil looped round his
wrist.

A remarkable picture of the Lower World, on a calyx krater
in New York,[116] is by THE NEKYIA PAINTER, who is named after

this vase. The scene occupies the entire upper frieze: Herakles, with Hermes as escort, has gone to the Lower World to fetch Kerberos and finds Perithous and Theseus condemned to punishment for their daring attempt to carry off Persephone; the scene continues with Elpenor, Ajax, and Palamedes, three famous heroes who died tragic deaths, and Persephone in her chamber. Each figure is nicely characterized—Herakles, the evident newcomer, proceeding slowly; Theseus and Perithous, heroes of distinction, welcoming the visitor; Hermes detached; Persephone safe in her chamber; Palamedes brooding over his wrong; Elpenor and Ajax, quiet, lonely figures. At the two sides are other figures, evidently not heroes, but nameless souls wandering about. The feeling of mystery which pervades the scene, as if the participants were indeed ghosts in another world passing noiselessly to and fro, is extraordinary. All the persons depicted on the vase, except Herakles, formed part of the famous picture of the Nekyia by Polygnotos of Thasos in the Lesche at Delphi, which was described in detail by Pausanias; but the rendering on the New York vase differs so greatly from the Delphian that the two must be based on different traditions. Below the frieze on the New York vase are two panels, one with Zeus throwing his thunderbolt at a giant, the other with the punishment of Tityos by Apollo and Artemis. Only one other vase has been attributed to the Nekyia Painter—a calyx krater in Vienna,[117] also designed in two tiers.

THE TROPHY PAINTER [118] decorated several smaller pots, chiefly pelikai. Among them is one from the Deepdene Collection, now in Boston,[119] with a Nike erecting a trophy. An oinochoe in the Louvre [120] has a picture of Athena confronting a column surmounted by a child. The latter is evidently intended for a statue, for on the base of the column is a dedication (perhaps *Tisias anetheken*). Between the two figures is the inscription *Sophanes kalos*.

An able vase painter, to whom no other works have so far been attributed but who may be called THE ATHANASIA PAINTER, decorated a bell krater in New York [121] with the story of Tydeus (see fig. 100). Though only a few fragments are preserved we can distinguish several figures. Tydeus is seated on a rock, leaning his head on one hand; he is suffering from a wound in his leg, inflicted on him by Melanippos. At his feet is the head of the dead Melanippos, sent him by Amphiaraos. Approaching him is a young woman, inscribed Athanasia, "Immortality." She has been brought by Athena to heal Tydeus and make him immortal; but at the sight before her she raises a hand in surprise. Athena grasps Athanasia by the wrist to pull her away, for she too is struck with horror. This remarkable picture is the only extant Greek painting of the terrible end of Melanippos. It is characteristic of Greek art that the gruesome part of the legend —the sucking of Melanippos' brain by Tydeus, which disgusted Athena and lost Tydeus his immortality—is not actually depicted.

THE PENELOPE PAINTER [122] is the artist of two well-known vases which have often been reproduced for their subjects: Penelope, Telemachos, and Odysseus, on a skyphos in Chiusi,[123] and Odysseus slaying the suitors on a skyphos in Berlin.[124] He is a somewhat tame follower of the Lewis Painter (see p. 112) and like him painted practically only skyphoi. His most attractive pictures are on a skyphos in Berlin [125]—a satyr holding a parasol over an aristocratic young woman who is out walking, and a satyr pushing a swing on which a young girl is sitting with legs outstretched. Each figure is nicely characterized.

Fifty-nine vases have been assigned to THE MARLAY PAINTER,[126] a minor artist who decorated kylikes, stemless cups, and skyphoi, as well as other vases. He derives his name from a calyx krater he decorated which was formerly in the Marlay Collection and is now in Cambridge.[127] The rider on it resembles two other spirited horsemen on a column krater in New York,[128] and all three recall the Parthenon frieze. Two stemless cups in New York [129] have symposia on the interior, in the same sketchy, vivid style. A calyx krater in Berlin [130] has a scene of the rising Persephone amid wildly capering Pans—a very different conception of the story from the solemn representation on the krater by the Persephone Painter in New York (see p. 123).

(5) THE ERETRIA PAINTER AND OTHER PAINTERS OF CUPS AND SMALL VASES

Concurrent with the artists who decorated chiefly large pots were others who favored kylikes and the smaller pots. THE ERE-

TRIA PAINTER [131] is one of the ablest of these. He is so called because the onos in Athens [132] with his picture of the bride Alkestis was found at Eretria (see fig. 101). About half of the seventy-six works attributed to him are on kylikes, but the finest are on lekythoi, oinochoai, pyxides, etc. A kantharos in Paris,[133] decorated by him with pictures of the departures of Achilles and of Patroklos, is signed by the potter Epigenes. The inscription [Kal]lias kalos appears on a fragment of a kylix in Leipzig.[134]

The Eretria Painter is distinguished especially for his exquisite line. The delicacy of the curving strokes in his clinging drapery and curling hair has been equaled by few. His gentle faces and beautifully drawn hands impart an almost exaggerated air of refinement to his figures—whether of gods, or women, or satyrs. He was by nature a miniaturist and apparently at his best in small pictures. Many of these are masterpieces; for instance, the Alkestis and her friends on the onos from Eretria; the Nereids making preparations for a wedding, on a pyxis in London; [135] the Dionysos and his satyrs and maenads on a squat lekythos in Berlin; [136] and a mistress and maid on an amphoriskos in Oxford.[137]

Several fine pieces are in New York. An oinochoe [138] is decorated with the familiar subject of the return of Hephaistos to Olympos. The procession consists of a satyr playing the double flute, and a satyr boy leading a donkey on which Dionysos and Hephaistos are seated. Dionysos is leaning forward, holding his kantharos with both hands to prevent its contents from spilling; Hephaistos is gesticulating with one hand and in the other holds the implements of his craft, the tongs and hammer. All have ivy wreaths; for it is a festive occasion, since it was Dionysos' wine that succeeded in bringing Hephaistos back to Olympos. It is interesting to compare this scene with earlier versions of the story —on the François vase, on the krater by Lydos, and on a krater by the Kleophrades Painter (see p. 67, note 20). The strength and exuberance of the archaic period are gone and a quiet playful charm has taken their place.

On a squat lekythos [139] is a dainty scene of a woman dressing (see fig. 102). She is in the act of taking her tunic off a chair and slipping it over her head. In spite of the economy of line the action is convincingly rendered. A remarkable picture, which "somewhat recalls the Eretria Painter," is on a squat lekythos in

New York.[139a] It represents the wounded Philoktetes, abandoned on the island of Lemnos, sitting on a rock under a tree, his famous bow and arrows by his side (fig. 98).

Though no white lekythoi of the usual type by the Eretria Painter are extant, we know that he occasionally worked in polychrome on white ground; for a tall squat lekythos in Kansas City [140] has a scene of women and a baby in that technique. Another lekythos of the same shape in New York [141] has three zones of decoration—the middle one on white ground, the upper and lower ones red-figured—containing about thirty figures, all delicately and lovingly drawn. The white-ground picture represents Patroklos, Achilles, and Nereids. Patroklos is lying on a bier, covered with a cloth; Achilles sits beside him, both hands folded on his lap. He is mourning the death of his best friend, killed by Hektor and despoiled of his armor. Among the countless representations of death and mourning few are so poignant as this one —Patroklos a still figure with closed eyes, Achilles sitting motionless with head bowed. The scene continues with the approach of Thetis, Achilles' mother (see fig. 103), and her Nereid sisters, bringing the armor made by Hephaistos. They are riding across the sea on dolphins, bringing the gifts with which Achilles is to revenge the death of his friend. The motion of the sea is suggested by the wavy outlines of the dolphins. We must supply in our imagination the colors with which the mantles of the Nereids were painted and the gilding which made resplendent the armor, necklaces, bracelets, and parts of the headdresses (now in the dull buff of applied clay). The outlines of the figures are drawn throughout in diluted glaze lines. The upper red-figured zone, which is fragmentary, represented a chariot scene; the lower one has a battle of Greeks and Amazons, composed in seven groups at different levels on a hilly ground; the names of Theseus and of some of the Amazons are inscribed. Another battle scene by the Eretria Painter, with figures and appurtenances strikingly similar to those in the New York one, is on a squat lekythos in Boston.[142] Both belong to the painter's late years.

Several jugs decorated by the Eretria Painter have unusual subjects. The celebration of the Anthesteria, with a father putting his little boy in the swing while two bigger boys watch, on an oinochoe in Athens,[143] recalls a similar scene of this subject by the Meidias Painter in New York (see p. 148). The preparation for a feast of Dionysos is represented on another oinochoe in Athens; [144] on still another [145] is an uncertain subject.

Vases decorated by the Eretria Painter have been found not only in Greece and Italy but as far afield as Southern Russia and Spain; there was evidently a widespread demand for them.

THE KALLIOPE PAINTER [146] is called after the name he gave to a Muse on kylikes in New York [147] and in the Victoria and Albert Museum.[148] He must have worked in the same studio as the Eretria Painter, for a cup in Freiburg [149] was decorated on the inside by the Kalliope Painter, on the outside by the Eretria Painter. Sixty-one paintings have been attributed to him. They consist mostly of youths and girls in statuesque poses, confronting each other and holding objects. A cup from Spina at Ferrara [150] is inscribed *Alkimachos kalos*.

THE KODROS PAINTER,[151] named after a cup with Kodros in Bologna,[152] is another distinguished artist of this group. His thirty-two extant works consist entirely of kylikes, drawn in a finished style reflecting the Pheidian idealism. His favorite subjects are athletes and heroes performing deeds of prowess; but he also painted mythological subjects—the birth of Erichthonios, and King Aigeus standing before Themis at Delphi, on two cups in Berlin.[153] His refined drawing can be appreciated in the fragment of a kylix in New York [154] with the upper parts of two youths and two phialae in the hand of a third person. The youths are evidently departing, and a libation is to be poured on their behalf; one holds a spear and has his sword hanging from his shoulder; his mantle is hung over his arm; the other wears a mantle and three-cornered hat and is also girded with a sword. Every detail is drawn with exquisite care. An attractive cup by this painter in London,[155] decorated with athletes, is inscribed *Xenon kalos*.

An interesting picture—not yet attributed to a specific artist —appears on a jug in New York.[156] It is of the chous shape, used during the festival of the Anthesteria in honor of Dionysos. A man is represented coming home late after the festival and is pounding on the door with the butt end of his lighted torch. On the other side of the door is a woman with a lighted lamp. She has been roused by the noise and must let in her drunken husband. In the rendering of the house we see an early attempt at linear perspective. The door, floor, and tiled roof are shown as slanting or receding into the background; but the necessity of making the parallel receding lines converge toward a common vanishing point has not been understood (see p. 116).

THE PAINTER OF LONDON D14 [157]—an oinochoe with Herakles and Athena—also decorated a pyxis in New York.[158] Both pictures are in polychrome on white ground and are drawn with great delicacy. The scene on the pyxis is particularly attractive. It represents six women in the interior of a house (indicated by an Ionic column), doing the things of everyday life—dressing, putting away their clothes, playing with a pet bird, and so on. Their names are inscribed—Bentho, Galene, Kymodoke, Akteie (see fig. 104), Glauke, and Psamathe. So they are Nereids, not ordinary Athenian ladies; but instead of riding the sea on dolphins, they are at home. Each figure has the grace and simplicity of a Tanagra statuette, and together the poses, the accessories, and the paraphernalia on wall and ground make a subtly related composition in which each line and spot of color plays its part. The quiet theme thereby assumes an extraordinary animation.

THE KRAIPALE PAINTER [159] is named from his scene on a chous (see p. 135) in Boston [160] of two maenads and a satyr (fig. 105). One of the maenads, called *Kraipale,* "Hangover," has been drinking too much, and holds out her cup for more wine; but the satyr, Sikinnos, with a jug in his hand, hesitates; meanwhile the other maenad, Thymedia(?), is bringing a bowl of steaming liquid to help Hangover to recover. If we compare this scene with the riotous Dutch representations of drunken women we shall realize the restraint and serenity with which the artists of the Pheidian period depicted their scenes, regardless of subject. Kraipale is merely sitting quietly on a rock, a pensive, charming figure.

The only other work assigned to this painter is a small pelike in London [161] with torch racers and athletes.

THE WASHING PAINTER,[162] so called from his pictures of women washing, on small hydriai and pelikai, also decorated several large nuptial vases and loutrophoroi with wedding scenes. One of the best is in New York.[163] The bride is seated on a chair playing the harp. Her thoughts are of love and as she looks up she sees a little Eros flying toward her, a round fruit in each hand. Her expression is one of wonder and reverence. Her friends approach with round wicker baskets and a chest filled with finery for the wedding.

A similar scene is on another nuptial lebes in New York.[164] The bride is sitting on a stool, playing the harp. Her friends bring chests, a round wicker basket, and a loutrophoros (with water for the bridal bath) hung with fillets for the festive occasion. The three-cornered harp,[165] the Greek trigonon, occurs much less frequently on Attic vases than the lyre or the kithara, but it was apparently in favor in the late fifth and the fourth century B.C.

Another charming picture by this painter, on a hydria in New York,[166] represents a woman seated on a rock with Eros tying her elaborately strapped sandals and two youths holding spears on either side. The subject may be Helen with her brothers the Dioskouroi, or Helen with Paris and Aeneas about to take her fateful journey.

THE SHUVALOV PAINTER,[167] named after his Apollo on an amphora from the Shuvalov Collection in Leningrad,[168] decorated many small vases in a miniature style. The Eros offering a hare to a boy on a kantharos in the Louvre [169] is one of his best works. His scenes generally consist of two figures confronting each other. Two typical examples are in New York. On an oinochoe [170] two boys are standing before an incense burner (fig. 106); one is holding it by the ring handle and adjusting the lid; a jug is near by. On a small hydria [171] are two women; one has brought a small chest to the other, who is about to take something out of it; a wool basket is on the floor.

Of the many other minor painters of this period we can mention only a few. THE DISNEY PAINTER,[172] named after a small amphora in Copenhagen,[173] formerly in the Disney Collection, decorated small vases, mostly with athletes and youths. Among them is an archer on an oinochoe in New York; [174] his untidy hair and unmartial look suggest that he is Odysseus, returned from his wanderings, shooting Penelope's suitors. THE PAINTER OF THE EDINBURGH OINOCHOE,[175] to whom several small jugs with women have been attributed, resembles somewhat the Shuvalov Painter. A typical work in New York [176] shows two women, one handing a wreath to the other. THE KLÜGMANN PAINTER painted a number of red-figured and white-ground lekythoi,[177] including one which belonged to Mr. Klügmann in Rome. A good example in New York [178] has an Amazon throwing a stone with a sling, drawn in glaze outlines with added white for the flesh. THE XENOTIMOS PAINTER [179] decorated a stemless cup in Boston,[180] signed *Xenotimos epoiesen*, with two interesting scenes—Perithous in Hades, and Leda and the egg.

V. LATE FIFTH-CENTURY STYLE,
ABOUT 420–390 B.C

THE historical background of the late fifth-century style is the
Peloponnesian War (431–404 B.C.) and its immediate after-
math. The long-drawn-out hostilities, the plague, the disastrous
Sicilian expedition (415–413), gradually sapped the strength of
Athens and led to her downfall and final defeat at Aigospotamoi
in 405. The great edifice of power and empire laboriously built
up during more than a century crumbled, and Athens became
once more a small city-state with limited commercial opportuni-
ties—though she remained for some time the intellectual center
of Greece.

In the major art of panel painting the outstanding names are
Apollodoros of Athens,[1] Zeuxis of Herakleia,[2] and Parrhasios of
Ephesos,[3] all contemporary with the Peloponnesian War. Not
a scrap of tl.eir works has survived, and we must visualize their
style through the vase paintings and from the many references
to them in ancient literature.

To understand the innovations in composition and spatial
representation which appear in this and the succeeding periods
we must recall an interesting tradition about the contemporary
painter Apollodoros (about 430–400 B.C.), who was said to have
"opened the gates of art which Zeuxis entered,"[4] and to have been
the first to give to his figures "the appearance of reality."[5] Spe-
cifically his innovations seem to have been the use of shadows
and perspective,[6] and of mixed instead of pure colors.[7] Apparently he carried on the work of Agatharchos—who was credited
with having started linear perspective in scene painting a generation or two earlier (see p. 91)—and introduced this perspective into mural and panel paintings for such rectangular objects
as furniture and architecture.

From contemporary vase paintings we may obtain some idea
of these epoch-making changes. We can see there how form is
"mimicked" by color and by the "use of shadows" and foreshortening; how "mixed" colors such as mauve appear side by side
with the old primary colors (on the late white lekythoi); how
linear perspective makes its appearance in rectangular objects

such as shrines, altars, furniture, which from about 430 B.C. are drawn no longer always in front view but occasionally with receding sides, and with top or bottom showing [8] (see p. 135); how presently shrines are depicted with receding ceilings of which the beams slope downward, those on the right side toward the left, those on the left side toward the right; and how figures are occasionally not only placed at different heights—for that had been done before (see pp. 101, 102)—but some made smaller than others to indicate that they are in a farther plane.[9] In fact the graceful figured compositions current at this time might almost be conceived as three-dimensional pictures were it not for the uniform black surface which they are made to decorate. Yet, as the light strikes this lustrous, curving surface, illuminating portions of it and leaving others in shadow, it imparts a certain spatial quality—and this applies to all red-figured ware.

Naturally the new "realism" met with criticism from contemporary "conservatives." Plato,[10] for instance, who lived at the time of Apollodoros and Zeuxis, disliked the innovations because they created illusions that were deceptive and made things appear larger or smaller than they really were and than they could be shown to be by actual measurements. To him "perspective" was a kind of trick that took advantage of the weakness of our senses.

It is important, however, to realize that the linear perspective on these late Greek vases is only a partial one.[11] Instead of viewing the whole scene from one point of sight and adopting one vanishing point toward which all receding parallel lines converge, several vanishing points were used, with varying points of sight. The space of the picture was not yet realized as a unity. This partial perspective obtained throughout antiquity. Hellenistic, Roman, and mediaeval art utilized but did not carry further the inventions of fifth-century Greece. Though the compositions are often more complex than before, no new knowledge of perspective is introduced. Each object is still viewed separately, not as part of a unified whole. It was not until the Renaissance of the fifteenth century that perspective as we understand it— with one single vanishing point for the entire picture—was developed and used.[12] And not until still later were rules formulated for the two-point, angular perspective which is in common use to-day.

The vase paintings of the late fifth century continue the line of development begun in the preceding period; but the stately figures become more effeminate, the garments richer, the drawing more refined. The hair is now generally indicated by separate strands on a reserved background instead of as a solid mass. The rendering of the eye is as before, but the line for the lower lid is often very short. The subjects are mostly taken from domestic life—as if the artist had tried to find an escape from the turbulence around him in the peaceful occupations of the home. Women dressing, adorning themselves, being courted, playing with their children are the principal themes. Of the gods only Dionysos with his satyrs and maenads and Aphrodite and her retinue remain popular.

Notes of white and yellow are now increasingly added to the sober color scheme of red and black. Light incisions on the glaze, made before firing, are often used for the indication of the ground or other details. As before, some parts are occasionally rendered in applied clay, gilded, and made to stand out in relief.

White-ground vases continue alongside of red-figure. The scenes are drawn throughout in dull paint with a rich variety of washes, as many as four or five colors sometimes being employed on one vase (see p. 152). The subjects consist almost entirely of mourners at the tomb, among whom the dead usually appear, often seated on the steps (see pp. 152 f.).

The vases of this period present marked similarities to the sculpture of the late fifth century. The thin, clinging draperies with multitudinous folds following the contours of bodies and limbs, which are characteristic of Meidian vases, are found also on the reliefs of the Nike balustrade (dated about 410), the frieze of the Erechtheion (409–406), and the "document" reliefs [13] of the last two decades of the century.

Besides these connections with sculpture the following data have helped to determine the chronology of the vases of this period.[14]

(1) No vases of the style we are discussing have been found in the graves which were transferred to Rheneia from Delos during the purification of that island in 425.[15] It is reasonable to suppose, therefore, that the development of that style is posterior to that date.

(2) Several of the fragments of vases found in the burial plot

of Dexileos, who fell at Corinth in 394, are in the style of the
period we are discussing.[16] Though this burial plot was apparently used for a considerable time and Dexileos himself was not
actually buried there,[17] but in a public sepulcher, the date 394
nevertheless gives an approximate time—within two or three
decades—for the period of the style.

(3) On a volute krater in Naples a flute player (see fig. 120) is
named Pronomos; there is a reference to a Pronomos in the *Ekklesiazousai* of Aristophanes (early fourth century),[18] and the
name also occurs in an inscription of 384–383.[19] It is possible
that in all three cases the allusion is to the famous Theban musician Pronomos.[20] Though the fame of this flute player lasted
for a considerable time (he is said to have taught Alkibiades,[21]
and his music was played while the walls of Messene were building [369]),[22] it is not likely that a Theban enemy was honored on
an Attic vase during the Peloponnesian War. So—if the assumption regarding Pronomos is correct [23]—the date of the Naples vase
should be posterior to that war, that is, the end of the fifth or
the early part of the fourth century.

(4) A fragment of a vase in the general style of the Suessula
Painter has recently been found in the Athenian Kerameikos, in
the Tomb of the Lacedaemonians, who fell in 403 B.C. (see p.
151). This shows that the vase paintings in that style, which used
to be assigned to the early fourth century, can also have been
produced in the concluding years of the fifth.

We can distinguish three chief styles in this period. One, derived from the Polygnotan group, shows a broad treatment—
round, fleshy forms, loose draperies with well-defined folds, and
a developed spatial sense. It is sponsored by the Kleophon
Painter, the Dinos Painter, and their followers. They chose
chiefly Dionysiac subjects and favored the larger vases, particularly the different forms of kraters. Another style of delicately
curved lines, pretty postures, and clinging draperies, often richly
patterned, is sponsored by the Meidias Painter and his followers.
Their pictures, which deal chiefly with the life of women, are
derived from the renderings of the Eretria Painter, but the rich,
swirling draperies, the elaborate coiffures, and the more frequent use of accessory colors add a softer, more luxurious note.
They are mostly on the smaller vases—the squat lekythos, the
pyxis, the lekanis—as well as the hydria. Lastly, at the end of the

century, a highly ornate style is developed in which the uneven thickness of the lines, the dark stripes and checkers in the patterns of the garments, and the copious additions of white, often with yellow details, lend a picturesque but overladen appearance. The Talos Painter, the Pronomos Painter, and the Suessula Painter are the prominent exponents of this style. Side by side, however, with these florid paintings on large vases, a simpler style persists, in which the red and black color scheme, with only slight touches of accessory colors, is retained. It is found particularly on the smaller vases by minor artists, but is also sometimes adopted by the very artists who painted the florid vases (see p. 151).

(1) THE KLEOPHON PAINTER, THE DINOS PAINTER, AND OTHERS. LATE FOLLOWERS OF POLYGNOTOS

THE KLEOPHON PAINTER [24] is the outstanding artist of the late Polygnotan group. His name is derived from one of his best works —the scene of banqueters on a stamnos in Leningrad [25] with the kalos names Megakles and Kleophon. He belongs to the transition period between the Free and the Late Fifth-Century style. His figures and especially his heads retain much of the grandeur and serenity of the preceding age, but are fleshier, more plastic, and there is a new fluidity in the lines of bodies and draperies. Fifty-two works have been attributed to him, chiefly on the larger vases—the stamnoi, kraters, pelikai, and amphorae. His Return of Hephaistos on a pelike in Munich [26] shows well the quiet amplitude of his style. The Departure of a Warrior on a stamnos in Munich [27] is painted in a somberer mood, in the tradition of the Achilles Painter. The same subject recurs on several vases by him, for instance, on a pelike formerly in the collection of Lord Melchett, now in the British Museum,[28] where a youth clasps the hand of a woman (see fig. 108), and the father stands sorrowfully by. A lekythos in New York [29] with Eos pursuing Kephalos is a typical minor work. We may note the characteristic rendering of the eye with the strongly curving lids and the dreamy expression.

THE DINOS PAINTER,[30] named after one of his chief works, a dinos in Berlin [31] with Dionysos reclining, continued the style of the Kleophon Painter. The Pheidian tradition is waning and is replaced by a new restlessness. The forms have become still rounder and fleshier, the draperies looser (note the many short, hooked lines), and there is more feeling for depth. The Dinos Painter's style, in fact, represents a new movement which leads directly to the ornate vases of the end of the century. Among the thirty-odd works which have been attributed to him—all on large vases—are the imposing Atalante on a calyx krater in Bologna,[32] the Dionysiac festival on a stamnos in Naples,[33] and the remarkable scene with Prometheus as fire-lighter on a calyx krater in Oxford.[34] A fragment of a dinos in Palermo [35] with a symposion well illustrates his delicate drawing. The boy standing with jug and colander by a krater, ready to fill the guests' cups with wine, is drawn with great freedom. The momentary, swaying pose marks a new departure in Greek art. On a fragment of a bell krater in New York [36] is the upper part of a reclining youth, beautifully drawn in a three-quarter view, evidently part of a symposion (see fig. 111).

THE CHRYSIS PAINTER [37] is called after the name he gave to one of the women on a hydria in New York.[38] His style is similar to that of the Dinos Painter, but more schematic, less refined. Seven hydriai and two bell kraters have so far been assigned to him. The scene on the New York hydria—women in an out-of-doors setting—is skillfully composed in a number of planes; but the execution is not careful, and the lines are rather coarse. An attractive picture of Dionysos dining, on a pelike in New York,[38a] is now attributed to the manner of the Chrysis Painter.

The signature of POLION,[39] with egrapsen, is preserved on a large volute krater in New York.[40] His broad style, which is related to that of the Polygnotan group, can be well studied on his signed work. A continuous scene of gods and goddesses occupies the body of the vase. The chief motive is a four-horse chariot. Hermes (under the left handle), in winged sandals, is holding one of the horses by the head; alongside stands Athena; Artemis, identified by her quiver and bow, holds the reins and the goad and turns round toward her brother Apollo; for it is evidently he who will mount the chariot. He is in gala array and stretches out both hands to take a kithara which his mother Leto is handing to him. A little Nike hovers above the chariot hold-

ing a leafy spray. Behind Leto are Poseidon with his trident and
Herakles with lion's skin, club, bow, and quiver. Finally come
three magnificent figures—Dionysos with thyrsos and kantharos,
Hera holding the royal scepter, her hand raised in salutation,
and Zeus with a scepter to match that of his consort. The names
are inscribed. The Pheidian idealism in these regal figures is still
potent especially in the imposing figure of Hera, in the Apollo,
and in the quiet, stately Hermes, but the effect of the whole is
rather empty. From this august scene of Mount Olympos we turn
to the lively one of an Athenian gymnasium on the neck of the
vase. Comely figures of young boys are busily exercising under
the supervision of trainers (see fig. 112). Two are engaging in a
boxing bout, sparring with open hands; the others are running,
jumping, and preparing to throw a discus. Noteworthy are the
thin, flowing lines of the drapery, the often high crowns of the
heads, and the delicate drawing of the faces.

Sixteen other works have been attributed to Polion, among
them a bell krater, also in New York,[41] with an interesting scene
—a wreathed flute player and three bearded satyrs playing the
kithara and singing (their mouths are open). Each wears a shaggy
garment of white fleece (μαλλωτοὶ χιτῶνες [42]) while the flutist has a
long-sleeved, foldless chiton, the regular costume of musicians.
That these are not ordinary satyrs we learn from the inscription
above them, ōdoi Panathenaia, indicating that they are singers
at the festival of the Panathenaia. What kind of performance is
going on is not certain. Hardly a satyric drama, for we have no
reliable evidence that plays were acted at the Panathenaia. Perhaps a dithyramb, for Lysias mentions a performance of one at
the Lesser Panathenaia in 409–408 B.C.[43]

A volute krater from Spina at Ferrara [44] is comparable to the
New York one. Here too we have the contrast between the stately
scenes on the body of the vase—the return of Hephaistos, and
Thamyris with the Muses—and the less august but livelier torch
race on the neck of the vase. Two simple compositions appear on
a skyphos in New York [45]—a bearded man in three-quarter back
view between two boys, and a boy leaning on a goal pillar in a
palaestra, extending his hand to a bearded man. The men are
not trainers, for they have walking sticks; they are spending their
time at the palaestra watching the athletes—as described by
Plato in the Charmides.

The kalos name Nikon is inscribed on a fragment of a calyx krater in Chicago,[46] decorated with satyrs.

AISON [47] is another artist of whom a signed work, with egrapsen, has survived—a kylix in Madrid [48] with exploits of Theseus, delicately and ably drawn. We may note particularly the successful three-quarter views of Theseus and the Minotaur. Twenty-one other works have been attributed to him, mostly on the smaller vases. The spirited fight of Theseus and Amazons, on a squat lekythos in Naples,[49] is one of his best works. A kantharos in New York [50] with a molded body in the form of two heads has libation scenes for departing warriors (see fig. 110). The figures have a dainty grace which makes them appealing. We may note the delicate heads, pointed noses without nostril line, small mouths with short upper lip, the staccato lines for the bunched draperies, and the characteristic attitudes, with the weight resting on one leg and the figure appearing to lean slightly backward.

A small, pointed amphora in New York [51] has two delicately painted pictures—Apollo with two Muses, and Adrastos in his chariot. No other attributions have been made to this painter.

THE KADMOS PAINTER,[52] who decorated a hydria in Berlin [53] with the story of Kadmos, painted chiefly kraters in a style resembling that of the Chrysis Painter. Several scenes illustrate the story of Apollo and Marsyas. THE POTHOS PAINTER,[54] called after the name he gave to a winged boy on a bell krater in Providence,[55] is related to the Kadmos Painter, but of inferior caliber. He too decorated chiefly kraters, and his favorite subjects are Dionysiac scenes.

(2) THE MEIDIAS PAINTER AND HIS SCHOOL

THE MEIDIAS PAINTER,[56] who decorated the famous hydria in London [57] signed *Meidias epoiesen,* is one of the last great figures in Athenian vase painting. He carried on the tradition of the Eretria Painter, but in a softer, more luxurious form. His graceful figures with rich, clinging draperies are the counterparts in vase painting of the reliefs on the Nike Balustrade. They, like the late fifth-century sculptures, initiate the art of the fourth century in which a gentle loveliness replaces the early sturdiness.

The Meidias Painter had many followers and it is sometimes

difficult to distinguish their work from careless products of the master. Beazley attributes to him fourteen certain works—in addition to the London hydria. The latter is one of his master-pieces, both in execution and composition. The decoration is in two tiers—above, the Rape of the Leukippids, below, Herakles in the garden of the Hesperides. The curving surfaces of shoulder and handle zone are utilized for the upper picture which is composed in several planes, with the two chariots at the top, the seated and fleeing figures below, and the group of Kastor seizing Eriphyle as a connecting link. It is an amazingly bold and successful design. If we compare the two-wheeled chariot and the four galloping horses in three-quarter view with the earlier two-dimensional renderings, we shall realize how far Greek artists have traveled in a short century on the road toward naturalism.

The painting of Mousaios on a pelike in New York [58] is another excellent work by the Meidias Painter. Here too the decoration is composed in several planes, suggestive of depth. In the center is a youth in a richly decorated costume playing the kithara. All around him are female figures, some with musical instruments—harp, tambourine, and lyre; one holds a tame bird to which a child is stretching out its hand. Trees, hillocks, and flowers indicate an outdoor setting. One might think we had here a picture of Thamyris and the Muses, for the scene is similar to that on a squat lekythos in Ruvo [59] where the singer is identified as Thamyris by an inscription. However, the name of the singer in the New York scene is also given, and it is not Thamyris but Mousaios, who according to some sources came from Thrace— hence his barbarian costume. Moreover the child and the woman with the bird are also named—Eumolpos and Deiope, the son and wife of Mousaios. The inscribed names of the other figures identify them as Muses, except the radiant one sitting with Eros, who is Aphrodite (see fig. 114). We have here, then, a representation of Mousaios with wife and child making music in the presence of the Muses and of Aphrodite and her retinue.

The scene on the other side of the vase represents Herakles with his wife Deianeira and two women of unknown identity. The figures are among the tallest known by the Meidias Painter, the standing ones being over 21 cm. high. They are not so carefully drawn, however, as those on the "front" side. The black glaze of the background has mostly disappeared, leaving the contour stripes—where the glaze had a double thickness (see p. 29)—to stand out prominently.

Two hydriai from Populonia [60] in Florence with Phaon and with Adonis (see fig. 115), and the squat lekythos in Ruvo with Thamyris above mentioned are closely related in style to the London hydria and the New York pelike. There are many obvious similarities between the figures in all five works: heads in three-quarter view looking upward and downward; slender hands with tapering fingers, sometimes holding objects without properly grasping them; soft, transparent, swirling draperies rendered by multitudinous curving lines which model the forms of the body; lower legs drawn crossing each other; large feet in three-quarter view with cushioned toes, of which the big toe is sometimes disproportionately large; curving lines incised lightly in the glaze to indicate the hilly ground and the trailing plants; flowers in superimposed clay. And throughout we find the same masterly quality of line—so thin and equable and drawn with such swing and freedom that it is almost incredible that it was traced in glaze. These five paintings must be about contemporary and they represent the high-water mark of the Meidias Painter's work.

The picture by the Meidias Painter on an oinochoe (chous) in New York [61] has recently received a new interpretation. Instead of a laundry scene it represents women perfuming clothes in preparation for the feast of the Choes (the second day of the Anthesteria). As in the picture of the same subject on a jug by the Eretria Painter (see p. 134), a swing and a chair with folded garments are introduced; also a boy watching the proceedings. That a swing was used in connection with the Anthesteria seems certain from our literary sources, and the shape of the vase connects the scene definitely with the Choes. At the top is the inscription *Ganyme(des) kalos*.

Most of the other paintings by this artist are on the smaller vases—the squat lekythoi, lekanides, and pyxides. The favorite subjects are Aphrodite, Eros, and women. The sensitive rendering of the hands, frequently held half open, is noteworthy. The inscriptions *Epicharis kale* and *Myrrhiniske kale* occur on a lekanis in Naples.[62]

"Meidian" pictures, that is, vase paintings in the manner of

the Meidias Painter but not by him, occur mostly on squat leky-
thoi, oinochoai, pyxides, and lekanides. The graceful figures
and attractive compositions are directly derived from the Meidias
Painter's creations, but they have not the master's delicate touch.
The drawing is less able and the lines are coarser. Several examples are in New York—a squat lekythos [63] with Chrysippos,
Pompe, and a processional basket; a pyxis [64] with a scene of
Aphrodite and her attendants: Persuasion, Health, Luck, Good
Repute, Freedom from Toil, and Paidia, "Play" (the names are
inscribed); and a "toy" oinochoe [65] with children playing at being revelers. "Toy" jugs, frequent at this late period, were evidently connected with the celebration of the Choes festival by
children.[65a]

Several well-known paintings which were attributed to the
Meidias Painter by many authorities have now been detached
from him by Beazley; for instance, the Pelops and Hippodameia
on a neck amphora in Arezzo (see fig. 113),[66] and the Judgment
of Paris on a hydria in Carlsruhe.[67] He considers them close to
the master but not by him. Apparently the Meidias Painter influenced not only minor painters, but also some of his more
prominent contemporaries. Certainly the figure of Pelops on the
Arezzo amphora—guiding his galloping horses and turning
round in a three-quarter view—is the work of a great artist.

The painter ARISTOPHANES [68] signed several of his works. Two
kylikes—one in Berlin [69] with a gigantomachy, the other in Boston [70] with a centauromachy—are inscribed: Erginos epoiesen,
Aristophanes egraphe; and Aristophanes egrapsen occurs on a
fragment of a bell krater with a male figure in Agrigento.[71] Two
other paintings have been attributed to him—a kylix in Boston,[72] a replica of the signed one there, and an acorn lekythos in
Berlin,[73] with a picture of Adonis. His style is very close to that
of the Meidias Painter, and some authorities have even thought
that the two were identical, that is, that Aristophanes was the
Meidias Painter in an early phase. But in spite of an obvious
similarity there is also a marked difference. Aristophanes' line
is also excellent, but his compositions have not the swing and
ease of the Meidias Painter's, and his figures, though in lively
poses, make the impression of statues in arrested motion.

Fragments of two lekanides in Athens [74] have several letters
belonging to signatures by a potter named MIKION and by a

decorator perhaps named EUEMPOROS. If the restoration of the inscriptions is correct, we should know another name of a vase painter of this late period.

THE NIKIAS PAINTER'S [75] name is derived from the picture of torch racers on a bell krater in London [76] signed "Nikias, the son of Hermokles, of the deme of Anaphlystos, made it." He is an artist in the Meidian tradition, who decorated chiefly large vases. A sacrificial scene on a bell krater in New York [77] is a typical work.

(3) THE TALOS PAINTER, THE PRONOMOS PAINTER, AND THE SUESSULA PAINTER

A volute krater in Ruvo [78] with the death of the bronze giant Talos has supplied the name TALOS PAINTER [79] to an outstanding artist of the end of the century. The vase is one of the best known of antiquity, for it is an imposing piece and well exemplifies the ornateness which becomes a dominant characteristic of Attic pottery at this time. The scene is crowded with figures which are not only placed in different planes but are drawn one behind the other; figures in the distance are sometimes made smaller than those in the foreground; the three-quarter view has become the prevailing one; and, above all, white with yellow markings is profusely used; in fact the whole figure of the dying Talos is painted white, and so stands out unduly from his surroundings. The shape of the krater has also become more complex and the divisions of mouth and foot have multiplied.

Only three other works, all fragmentary, have been attributed to the Talos Painter. One is a stand, perhaps of a nuptial lebes, in New York (see fig. 109).[80] The figures are about ten inches (25 cm.) high. One can make out Athena, Herakles, and Iolaos, and two other figures. Their noble bearing and exceptional size show that the picture was an imposing work. The bearded head is a close counterpart of the Poseidon on the Ruvo krater.

A volute krater in Naples [81] with a representation of a satyr play is another famous vase, which has often been reproduced. The artist who decorated it has been called THE PRONOMOS PAINTER [82] from the name he gave to a flute player on this vase (see p. 142). The scene is of great interest and shows the influence of the theater on the painting of the period. Dionysos, the sponsor of Greek drama, is sitting on a couch with Ariadne, surrounded by three tragic actors, twelve dancers of a Satyric chorus, the poet, a lyrist, and the flutist Pronomos (see fig. 120). The many figures arranged on different levels, the profusely ornamented garments, the decorated neck, lip, and handles of the vase, combine to give an overladen effect. The style is in the tradition of the Dinos Painter. The Dionysiac scene on the back of the vase is somewhat less ornate, and so are the paintings on three other vases attributed to this artist.

THE SUESSULA PAINTER [83] decorated six neck amphorae with twisted handles, four of which have been found at Suessula in Campania and three of which are now in New York. The most ambitious and largest is that from Melos in the Louvre [84] with a gigantomachy. The copious additions of white and yellow, the richly ornamented garments, the uneven thickness of the lines, and the restless composition arranged in several levels—are all in line with the style of the period. Similar combats on a smaller scale are painted on two amphorae in New York (see fig. 122).[85] It is instructive to compare these scenes with those on the large kraters by the Niobid Painter and his school (see pp. 100 ff.). Violent foreshortenings and three-quarter front and back views, which fifty years ago were boldly but unsuccessfully attempted, are now convincingly rendered. The third amphora in New York [86] has a scene of a soldier leaving·home. He holds his horse by the rein and grasps two spears. On one side are his old father, leaning on a stick, and his young companion in arms; on the other his mother, with phiale and jug, ready to pour the libation.

We have an important piece of evidence for the dating of the Suessula Painter's work. A fragment of a bell krater with a youth in a style approximating his was found in the Athenian Kerameikos [87] in the tomb of the Lacedaemonians who fell in 403 B.C. (see p. 142). He must therefore have lived in the concluding years of the fifth century, though many of his works may of course belong to the early fourth.

(4) PAINTERS OF CUPS AND SMALL VASES

Many minor painters were naturally active in the late fifth century alongside the more important ones. A number of them have recently been segregated and their works classified. They decorated mostly the smaller vases—cups, pyxides, oinochoai, and especially the squat lekythoi popular at this time. The decoration generally consists of one or two figures—a woman seated or standing, dancing, playing with a ball; a youth leaving home; an animal or a monster; the head of Hermes or of a woman. Beazley has given them various names after their chief works, characteristics, provenances, locations: THE PAINTER OF LONDON 106, THE MOURET PAINTER (both cup painters), THE STRAGGLY PAINTER, THE MINA PAINTER, THE WORST PAINTER.[88] Two pyxides, in Copenhagen [89] and London,[90] are signed by their potter, GAURION (with *epoie*). On the lid of the former is painted a calyx krater, on the latter an arm with a sheathed sword.

(5) WHITE-GROUND VASES

In this period also, the white-ground technique was used concurrently with red-figure; but it is now confined to sepulchral lekythoi, and the artists who decorated them seem to have specialized in this one field. The lines are now always drawn in matt colors—red or black—and a large palette is often used for the colored washes—blue, purple, green, mauve, yellow, and different shades of red. The sometimes large size of the vases and of the figures give them a monumental quality. A change in the representations is noticeable. The artists of the preceding period suggested the pathos of death subtly, in attitude and gesture, and thus created gentle and deeply moving pictures. The painters of the late fifth-century lekythoi often showed the sorrow of parting more directly. As before, the scenes generally consist of figures at a tomb and the dead are often represented sitting or standing by their graves with one or two mourners bringing offerings. But the attitudes and expressions are no longer detached; instead of resignation actual grief is suggested in the restless poses and the sad, almost rebellious expressions. It was the time when the Peloponnesian War was drawing to a close and Athens' long struggle ended in defeat. As Sir John Beazley [91] put it, "something of that angry sunset has passed into the work" of these artists.

On several good examples in New York we see a youth or a

woman seated on the steps of the tomb, attended by mourners. The pictures are painted by the prominent artists of the time, or by their associates. One is in the manner of THE WOMAN PAINTER (see fig. 116),[92] another is by a member of GROUP R (see figs. 118, 119),[93] a third is by THE TRIGLYPH PAINTER,[94] a fourth is not yet attributed (see fig. 117).[95] A fifth,[96] by THE REED PAINTER, has a spirited battle scene with a foot soldier attacking a horseman—presumably the action in which the youth who is commemorated was killed. In some of these pictures the washes are fairly well preserved, giving a good idea of the original colorful effect.

VI. THE FOURTH CENTURY

THE Peloponnesian War and its disastrous ending had seriously impaired the commerce of Athens. Nevertheless, in a few years she was able to regain to some extent her Western markets—at least so we may surmise from the early fourth-century Attic vases which have been found in considerable numbers in Italy. Gradually, however, as South Italy rose in power, the local Apulian, Lucanian, Campanian, and Paestan vases took the place of these Athenian stragglers. By the second quarter of the fourth century the ceramic trade between Athens and Italy which had flourished for almost two hundred years came virtually to a stop. In its stead Athens acquired an extensive market in the cities of the Greek colonists of southern Russia. Quantities of Athenian pottery have been found at Kerch (Pantikapaion) and Olbia near the Black Sea; and though the same type of pottery has also come to light elsewhere [1] (for instance at Alexandria, in the Cyrenaica, and of course in Greece), the style is generally referred to as "Kerch," after the chief finding place. The period assigned to it—about 370 to 320 B.C.—is politically that of the Arcadian League and the beginning of the Macedonian domination.

The chief panel painters of the time—whose works have all perished, but whose names we know from the statements of ancient writers—were Eupompos and Pausias of Sikyon and Aristeides of Thebes, then Nikias of Athens and the great Apelles. [2] They utilized and expanded the innovations of the preceding age in the direction of naturalism (see pp. 139 f.). Pliny's [3] well-known anecdotes of the painted grapes by Zeuxis and of the horse by Apelles well illustrate this *trompe l'oeil* ideal. The vase paintings can reflect it only to a limited extent, for it must have largely depended on modeling by light and shade and on the use of many gradating, blending colors.

During the first quarter of the fourth century the vase paintings continue and develop the styles of the preceding period. In fact, many of the artists who were active at the end of the fifth century of course worked also in the early fourth. Interest in perspective was keen, and we find rectangular objects and buildings drawn with receding sides (see p. 158); chair legs are no longer always drawn all in the front plane. A florid and a plainer style flourished side by side. Gradually, however, the lines become thinner and weaker, and by about 370 the so-called Kerch style is evolved. It represents the last phase of Athenian vase painting. Instead of delicate curves and effective contours there are many short, very thin lines to indicate the actual structure of the folds and the plastic shapes of the body. The renderings of hair and eye are the same as in the foregoing period. The hair is drawn in separate wavy strands on a reserved background, the eye with the lower eyelid very short—the linear equivalent of shallow carving. The subjects continue to be taken largely from the life of women, but cult scenes are now also favored and mythological scenes are common. Dionysos and his retinue, as well as Herakles, are especially popular.

As in the preceding period other colors—chiefly white, pink, and gold leaf, occasionally blue and green—were added to enrich the red-and-black scheme. Thinned glaze was still used, especially for parts of the hair and for lines on the white; not so much for anatomical markings on a reserved ground. Occasionally some of the figures were rendered in applied clay and made to stand out in relief (see p. 157). Vases in this dual technique are the forerunners of the vases with the decoration entirely in relief, which finally ousted the painted ware (see p. 162). The white-ground lekythoi continued for a decade or so into the fourth century and then stopped. Inscriptions, so frequent in the early days and popular also in the late fifth century, now occur only rarely.[4]

In general the easy poses and soft draperies of the paintings of the first quarter of the fourth century can be compared with the akroteria and pediments from Epidauros and the "document" reliefs of that time.[5] The period of the Kerch vases is that of Praxiteles, Skopas, and Lysippos, whose influence was evidently potent even in vase painting. For instance, a figure on an oinochoe in New York recalls the Knidian Aphrodite and the figures on a hydria from Alexandria Lysippian statues (see p. 161). Comparisons with dated "document" reliefs of the fourth century are especially useful; for instance, with that of Korkyra (375 B.C.) and that dated in the archonship of Molon (362–361).

There are several important landmarks for the chronology of fourth-century vases. We have noted the evidence obtained from the vase fragments found in the burial plot of Dexileos, from the krater with a flutist named Pronomos, and from the fragment found in the Tomb of the Lacedaemonians who fell in 403 B.C. (see p. 142). And there are other clues: [6]

(1) The commercial relations between Athens and Cyprus, active during the reign of Evagoras I of Salamis (411–374/3), stopped with the end of his rule; in the tombs at Marion in Cyprus many Athenian vases have come to light, all in the late Meidian and ornate styles, none in the succeeding Kerch one.[7] From this we may infer that the sub-Meidian and ornate styles continued during the whole of the first quarter of the fourth century and that the Kerch vases are subsequent to that time.

(2) The Panathenaic amphorae datable (by the names of the archons which are inscribed on them) in the first third of the fourth century [8] show Athena clothed in a garment richly decorated in the manner of the ornate style.[9] In spite of archaizing tendencies the contemporary fashion was evidently followed. The figures on the Panathenaic vases of about 370–310, on the other hand, show many points of similarity with the Kerch vases. They are drawn in a similar way with the same kind of short lines, bringing out the structure of folds and bodies.[10]

(3) The fact that a plate of the Kerch style was found at Olynthos [11] suggests that it was painted previous to the destruction of that city in 348.

(4) Kerch vases have been found in graves with coins of Philip II of Macedon, of Alexander, and of Lysimachos (the last dated soon after 305), as well as with coins of Pantikapaion assigned to the second half of the fourth century.[12] Thereby we obtain approximate dates for the burials.

(5) Kerch vases have come to light at Alexandria,[13] which was founded in 331, and they represent the concluding phase of the style.

The shapes of the fourth-century vases are slenderer, more elongated than before, with a tendency to ogee curves. The favorites among the larger vases are the hydria, the pelike, and the bell krater; also common are the lekane, the skyphos, the oinochoe, and the squat lekythos. The calyx krater has a vogue in the late Kerch period. The kylix proper dies out at the beginning of that period, and the stemless cup at about the same time.[14]

(1) *FIRST THIRD OF THE CENTURY*

(a) THE ORNATE STYLE: THE PAINTER OF THE NEW YORK CENTAUROMACHY AND OTHER POT PAINTERS

The chief exponent of the ornate style among the pot painters of the fourth century is THE PAINTER OF THE NEW YORK CENTAUROMACHY,[15] named after a scene on a fragmentary volute krater in New York.[16] His style is a continuation and amplification of that of the Dinos Painter. The Theseus and Lapiths on the New York fragment and the Herakles on a fragment of a volute krater in Leningrad [17] still retain something of the fifth-century grandeur, but the restless composition and the many superimposed colors point to a different epoch. Two fragmentary cups, in Leningrad [18] and Bryn Mawr,[19] are the only other works so far attributed to this painter.

THE MELEAGER PAINTER [20] is related to the Painter of the New York Centauromachy, especially during his early years before his work deteriorated. Forty-seven works have been attributed to him, including several with Atalante and Meleager. The subject occurs, for instance, on one of his chief works, a volute krater in Vienna,[21] and again on a calyx krater in Würzburg.[22] The Vienna krater has, on its other side, an Oriental king being entertained by dancers. Most of the Meleager Painter's scenes are Dionysiac and are composed in several tiers on large vases.

THE XENOPHANTOS PAINTER [23] also belongs to this group. He decorated the two famous squat lekythoi in Leningrad,[24] each with the signature *Xenophantos epoiesen Athen[aios]*, "Xenophantos, the Athenian, made it." Both were found in South Russia and were evidently made by an Athenian in that region. The representations are the same in both—on the body Persians hunting, on the shoulder Nikai driving chariots, a centauromachy, and a gigantomachy. The scene on the shoulder is entirely in relief, that on the body partly so.

Among the other pot painters of the early fourth century be-

longing to this group we may mention THE PAINTER OF THE OX-
FORD GRYPOMACHY; THE RETORTED PAINTER (so called "because
the eyes of his reverse figures are often turned in instead of out
—*oculi retorti*"); THE BLACK-THYRSOS PAINTER, who introduced
black thyrsoi into his Dionysiac scenes; and THE OINOMAOS
PAINTER, who decorated a bell krater in Naples with Pelops and
Oinomaos.[25]

The partial perspective in use at this time can be well seen in
the picture of Dionysos sitting in front of his temple on a fragment in Jena.[26] The artist has represented not only the front
view of the building but a receding side view, and part of the
ceiling beneath the gabled roof; but the parallel receding lines
do not meet at one vanishing point and the various parts are
viewed not from one point of sight, but from several; nor do the
farther columns diminish in size. The result is somewhat confusing.

(b) THE PLAINER STYLE: THE ERBACH PAINTER, THE JENA PAINTER, AND OTHERS

Side by side with the ornate pot painters there were others
who adopted a plainer style. One of the most pleasing is THE
ERBACH PAINTER,[27] to whom eight vases have been attributed,
one of them at Erbach. All his paintings are on kraters and deal
with Dionysiac subjects. Among the other artists in this class are
THE PAINTER OF LONDON F 64,[28] who painted several scenes of
the Apotheosis of Herakles, and his close associate, THE PAINTER
OF LONDON F 1.[29]

THE JENA PAINTER[30] is one of the chief cup painters of the
early fourth century. Seventy-two works have been attributed
to him, all except two on cups. The majority are fragments found
in a potter's workshop in Athens and now in Jena[31]—hence his
name. His scenes are drawn in a delicate, broad manner with
thin, flowing lines, without the overladen, ornate effects of some
of his contemporaries. One of his loveliest products is the fragment with Eros sitting on the lap of Aphrodite and playing the
harp.[32] The delicate rendering of the face of Aphrodite fore-
shadows the Kerch style. On a hydria in Berlin[33] is a picture of

Paris and of Helen holding a mirror and sitting on the edge of an open chest filled with her belongings.

THE Q PAINTER [34] and THE PAINTERS OF VIENNA 155, 202, AND 116 [35] belong in this group.

While some painters specialized in the decoration of cups, others painted chiefly jugs. A large number of oinochoai with fat athletes, cursorily painted, have been put together as the works of THE FAT BOY GROUP.[36] A few other jugs, all from Spina, are attributed to "THE BROWN-EGG PAINTER," [37] for they have a brown, not a black, egg pattern below.

An unattributed pelike of this period in New York [38] has an interesting subject—Herakles in the garden of the Hesperides. In addition to the usual tree, serpent, Herakles, and Hesperid, the figure of Okeanos, horned and leaning on a stick, is introduced. Ocean is rarely represented in Greek art. His presence here marks the locality as the shores of the river Okeanos. The delicate, broad style of the drawing places the picture in the group of the Jena Painter.

Another noteworthy scene by an artist belonging to this group is on a hydria in New York.[39] Poseidon, mounted on a sea horse and grasping his trident, extends his hand in welcome to a youth (see fig. 121). The seaweed (or spray?) beneath the horse's body indicates that the encounter takes place by or in the sea. One might think that the youth was Theseus, who, when his divine origin was challenged, descended to the bottom of the sea to prove it. His meeting with Amphitrite is represented on the famous cup in the Louvre (see p. 77) and that with Poseidon on several other vases. But on the New York vase Poseidon is on a sea horse. As he would hardly be riding at the bottom of the sea, either we have here a different version of the legend, or the youth is not Theseus but Pelops, standing on the beach and asking Poseidon for help in his race with Oinomaos.[40]

(2) THE KERCH STYLE, ABOUT 370-320 B.C.

The early Kerch vases are of course the direct outgrowth of those of the preceding period. They resemble in a general way the work of the Jena Painter. A hydria in London [41] with Europa and the bull, a pelike in London [42] with Artemis and a deer, and a hydria in New York [43] with Poseidon and Amymone are typical examples, datable about 370 B.C. and later. The compositions are relatively simple and the lines still retain something of the early flow.

By the middle of the fourth century the Kerch style had reached its acme and many of its masterpieces may be assigned to this period. The crowded compositions, the sketchy lines, the addition of washes in diluted glaze to suggest shadows, and the often profuse accessory colors—white, pink, blue, red, green, and gold—lend to these vases a rich and sometimes restless aspect. We may look at a few examples.

A hydria in New York [44] with Herakles and the Hesperides is exceptionally well preserved (see fig. 124). The tree with the golden apples and the serpent occupy the center of the scene. Herakles stands at one side, resting on his club; at the other is a Hesperid, leaning against a tympanon and listening to Herakles. The other figures, placed on different levels, all in three-quarter views, are two Hesperids, a youth presumably Iolaos, a Pan with club and leopard's skin, and a satyr. On the ground is an omphalos covered with fillets and mounted on a low platform. White with yellow markings is used for the serpent and for the flesh parts of two Hesperids and Nike. The combination of Pan, a satyr, the Bacchic tympanon, and the omphalos in the garden of the Hesperides would be surprising on a fifth-century vase. But in the fourth century the ascendancy of Dionysos is so general that his companions and attributes are introduced into many scenes not strictly Dionysiac. The omphalos is of course explained by Dionysos' connection with Delphi, where he was worshiped during the three winter months. He is represented seated on the omphalos on a Kerch hydria in Lyons,[45] and he welcomes Apollo upon the latter's return in the spring on a late fifth-century krater in Leningrad [46] by the Kadmos Painter.

A lekane in Leningrad [47] is a famous piece and has often been described. Women are represented engaged in various activities, in a crowded composition, effectively composed on the lid of the bowl. The subject seems to be the preparation for a wedding, but we obtain at the same time a pleasant glimpse into a fourth-century Attic home. We see women busily washing, adorning themselves, and making cakes, surrounded by their household objects: chests, vases, a wash basin, a basket, an incense burner, and a herm, as well as pet animals—a dog and two birds, one in a cage.

An oinochoe in New York [48] has a scene of particular interest, beautifully executed (see fig. 123). In the center is a woman, identified as Pompe, "Procession," by an inscription; she has a wreath in her hands and is turning toward Dionysos, who is sitting on a chair holding his thyrsos. On the ground is a processional basket in applied clay, gilded. Beside it Eros is tying his sandal. The presence of Pompe, Dionysos, and a processional basket shows that the occasion is a Dionysiac festival. The scene is drawn with very fine lines and with copious additions of white, pink, and gold, and seems more like a miniature painting than a vase decoration. The graceful pose of Pompe recalls the Knidian Aphrodite of Praxiteles. The tying of a sandal with one foot raised is a familiar motive in statuettes of the fourth century. The seated Dionysos is ably drawn in three-quarter view; all four legs of the chair are indicated, as well as parts of the farther sides of the back and of the seat.

On a skyphos in New York [49] of about the same period we again see a processional basket, held here on the lap of a seated woman. It too is rendered in applied clay and gilded. As a satyr is present, the subject is evidently also the preparation for a Dionysiac festival. On the other side of the vase are two women with a satyr and Eros, carefully drawn with very fine lines (see fig. 125).

Mythological scenes occur occasionally. There are representations, for instance, of Apollo and Marsyas, of Oidipous and the sphinx, of Themis advising Zeus to start the Trojan war, etc. It is clear, however, that the belief in these ancient myths was waning. Interest centered in the activities of daily life.

Cult scenes are in special favor on Kerch vases. Several have been identified as representations of the Adonia, which was celebrated by Athenian women with lamentations for the dead Adonis and with the planting of "gardens" in pots or potsherds. One of the ceremonies was the bringing of such "gardens" to the roofs of houses, and this seems to be represented in the scenes with women standing on ladders and with plants sprouting in pots.[51] One such scene, somewhat fragmentary, may be seen on a squat lekythos in New York.[52] Traces of gilding, pink, red, and green remain. A woman burning incense on an altar is depicted on a hydria in New York.[52a]

The fragment of a hydria in Leningrad [53] with a seated Zeus recalls contemporary sculpture, for instance the "Maussolos" of Halikarnassos. It is drawn in a broad, sketchy manner, with many short lines, suggesting the volume of the figure, and resembles a modern drawing more than a Greek vase painting. We have here the complete abandonment of the early Greek silhouette style.

The same marked feeling for volume appears in a scene on a lebes in Leningrad [54] with the bringing of wedding gifts to the bride. The figures are, as is usual at this time, practically all in three-quarter views; a sense of movement is imparted by the swirling draperies and the momentary poses. The curving surface of the vase accentuates this quality.

The picture on a pelike in Leningrad [55] is perhaps one of the latest examples of the Kerch style. An Amazon is represented on a rearing horse in a three-quarter view, riding out of the picture toward us, like her sister, about 150 years or so earlier (see p. 103). Now, however, the foreshortening of horse and rider is successfully accomplished. The several parts are no longer viewed from different points of sight, but from only one, and the whole has become a unified design. The decorative quality is weaker, but the artist has learned the task he had set himself. A combat of Greeks and Amazons, on a pelike in New York,[55a] with colors well preserved, shows the same interest in violent movement. If we translate such pictures into large representations we may realize the power and accomplishment of Greek painting at the time of the great Apelles.

(3) VASES WITH RELIEFS

In the later fourth century vases with reliefs had a short vogue in Attica.[56] Relief decoration on vases was nothing new in Greek ceramics. It had been popular in the early archaic period in various localities, especially in Crete, Boeotia, and Laconia; [57] and even in the fifth and the early fourth century we find occasional examples side by side with the painted ware.[58] Its increased

use in Attica in the late fourth century may be regarded as a
logical development. When once the old two-dimensional decoration was given up and foreshortenings were used to suggest
depth on a flat surface, vase paintings became three-dimensional
representations. By the early fourth century such foreshortenings had, as we have seen, become the general rule and an essentially plastic style had been developed; moreover, increasingly,
minor objects were rendered in applied clay, that is, in relief. The
next step was to adopt this technique first for whole figures, then
for the whole decoration. The figures were applied in red clay—
in barbotine or appliqué technique—against the black-glaze
background and given the same divers shades as the contemporary terra-cotta statuettes. Gilding was popular. Some of these
relief vases are charming creations. One of the most important,
with a group of Eleusinian deities on the shoulder, was found
at Cumae and is now in Leningrad.[59] Another, a hydria from
Lampsakos with the Calydonian boar hunt, is in Istanbul.[60] Two
interesting examples are in New York. On a lekythos [61] is a scene
in appliqué relief of Telephos who has taken refuge on an altar
when discovered by the Greeks; he grasps the child Orestes and
threatens to kill him with his dagger; Klytaimestra extends
both arms to the frightened child. The presence of the queen is
particularly interesting and suggests that the potter is here following the version of the story—perhaps derived from Euripides'
Telephos—in which Telephos took Orestes on Klytaimestra's
advice.[62] A small oinochoe [63] has an attractive scene of Aphrodite
and her retinue, in barbotine technique. The goddess is represented sitting on a rock with a dove perched on her shoulder;
she is extending one arm to a little Eros, who is about to fly
toward her, assisted by a young, shaggy Pan.[64] The Eros is evidently a baby learning to fly. Two older brothers appear behind
Aphrodite, one flying at ease the other sitting by a tree (one
of his wings is in relief, the other is painted on the background
to suggest the turn of his body). It is a pretty scene in the intimate, playful vein of the late fourth century. Considerable
traces of the original colors remain—of the white engobe which
covered the whole relief, of the gilding on the figures and the
tree, and of the blue on the rocky ground.

These Attic relief vases were apparently not produced in
quantity and were short-lived. Comparatively few have survived

and most of them belong to the late fourth and perhaps the early third century. They mark the end of the painted ware. Red-figure had run its course. It had been produced in Attica continuously for two centuries, had enlisted at times great talent, and had been exported far and wide. A change was due. Henceforth the Hellenistic relief ware, inspired by and sometimes directly derived from metal ware, came into vogue and continued its popularity throughout the ancient world until the end of the Roman Empire.[65] The black glaze, however, which had played so prominent a role in black-figured and red-figured paintings was not abandoned. Plain black-glaze vases—chiefly drinking cups, plates, saucers, bowls, and pitchers—continued in use in Attica through the third and second centuries.[66] We have evidence that black-figured Panathenaic amphorae were produced after the fourth century B.C.[67] Black glaze was employed for bands and inside linings on the plain partly glazed household ware, which naturally continued after the demise of red-figure.[68] Above all, the black glaze, even though in a rather deteriorated form, was used on the very relief vases of Hellenistic and Roman times which took the place of the painted ware.

Fig. 34; cf. p. 46. Andokides Painter   Fig. 35; cf. p. 49. Oltos

Fig. 36; cf. p. 47. Psiax

Fig. 37; cf. p. 50. Epiktetos

Fig. 38; cf. p. 52. Hegesiboulos Painter

Figs 39, 40; cf. p. 50. Pheidippos

Fig. 41; cf. p. 58. Gales Painter   Fig. 42; cf. p. 50. Hischylos Painter

Fig. 43; cf. p. 53. Euphronios

Fig. 44; cf. p. 55. Euthymides

Fig. 46; cf. p. 56. Phintias

Fig. 45; cf. p. 57. Sosias Painter

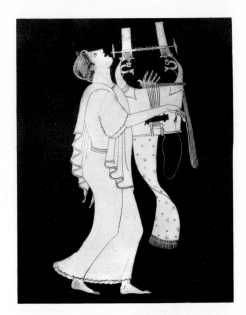

Fig. 47; cf. p. 67.
Kleophrades Painter

Fig. 48; cf. p. 69. Berlin Painter

Fig. 49; cf. p. 72. Myson

Fig. 50; cf. p. 72. Geras Painter

Fig. 51; cf. p. 73. Gallatin Painter

Fig. 52; cf. p. 73. Dutuit Painter   Fig. 53; cf. p. 73. Dutuit Painter

Fig. 54; cf. p. 74. Providence Painter　　　Fig. 55; cf. p. 74. Tithonos Painter

Fig. 56; cf. p. 75. Bowdoin Painter

Fig. 57; cf. p. 78. Panaitios Painter

Fig. 58; cf. p. 86. Thorvaldsen group

Fig. 59; cf. p. 77. Panaitios Painter

Fig. 60; cf. p. 80. Brygos Painter   Fig. 61; cf. pp. 79, 80. Brygos Painter

Fig. 62; cf. p. 87. Briseis Painter

Fig. 63; cf. p. 82. Makron

Fig. 64; cf. p. 84. Douris

Fig. 65; cf. p. 84. Douris

Fig. 66; cf. p. 95. Pan Painter

Fig. 67; cf. p. 95. Pan Painter

Fig. 68; cf. p. 95. Pan Painter

Fig. 69; cf. p. 98. Penthesileia Painter

Fig. 70; cf. p. 98. Penthesileia Painter

Fig. 71; cf. p. 98. Diosphos Painter

Fig. 72; cf. p. 100. Wedding Painter

Fig. 73; cf. p. 98. Penthesileia Painter

Fig. 74; cf. p. 102. Painter of the Woolly Silens

Fig. 75; cf. p. 101. Niobid Painter

Fig. 76; cf. p. 109. Oionokles Painter

Fig. 77; cf. p. 108. Hermonax

Fig. 78; cf. p. 106. Methyse Painter

Fig. 79; cf. p. 111. Sotades Painter

Fig. 80; cf. p. 111. Follower of the Brygos Painter

Fig. 81; cf. p. 113.
Sabouroff Painter

Fig. 82; cf. p. 113. Sabouroff Painter

Fig. 83; cf. p. 114. Vouni Painter

Fig. 84; cf. p. 104. Villa Giulia Painter   Fig. 85; cf. p. 107. Euaichme Painter

Fig. 86; cf. p. 106. Akestorides Painter   Fig. 87; cf. p. 107. Euaion Painter

Fig. 88; cf. p. 124. Mannheim Painter   Fig. 89; cf. p. 119. Achilles Painter

Fig. 90; cf. p. 125. Danae Painter   Fig. 91; cf. p. 122. Phiale Painter

Fig. 92; cf. p. 123. Persephone Painter

Fig. 93; cf. p. 125. Painter of London E 497

Figs. 94, 95; cf. p. 129. Lykaon Painter

Fig. 96; cf. p. 128. Polygnotos

Fig. 97; cf. p. 87.
Foundry Painter

Fig. 98; cf. p. 134.

Fig. 99; cf. p. 105.
Chicago Painter

Fig. 100; cf. p. 131. Athanasia Painter

Fig. 101; cf. p. 133. Eretria Painter   Fig. 102; cf. p. 133. Eretria Painter

Fig. 103; cf. p. 134. Eretria Painter   Fig. 104; cf. p. 136.
Painter of London D 14

Fig. 105; cf. p. 136. Kraipale Painter

Fig. 106; cf. p. 137. Shuvalov Painter

Fig. 107; cf. p. 130.
By or near Coghill Painter

Fig. 108; cf. p. 143.
Manner of Kleophon Painter

Fig. 109; cf. p. 150.
Talos Painter

Fig. 110; cf. p. 146. Aison

Fig. 111; cf. p. 144. Dinos Painter

Fig. 112; cf. p. 145. Polion

Fig. 113; cf. p. 149.
Near the Meidias Painter

Fig. 114; cf. p. 147. Meidias Painter

Fig. 115; cf. p. 148. Meidias Painter

Fig. 116; cf. p. 153. Manner of Woman
Painter

Fig. 117; cf. p. 153

Figs. 118, 119; cf. p. 153. Group R

Fig. 120; cf. p. 151. Pronomos Painter   Fig. 121; cf. p. 159

Fig. 122; cf. p. 151. Suessula Painter

Fig. 123; cf. p. 161

Fig. 124; cf. p. 160   Fig. 125; cf. p. 161

NOTES

INTRODUCTION

1. For a concise account of this evolution from two-dimensional to three-dimensional representation cf. my pamphlet, *Greek Painting* (2d ed.).

2. The recently discovered small wooden panels from near Sikyon [Orlandos, *AA*, 1934, cols. 194 f., and *AJA*, XXXIX (1935), 5; E. P. Blegen, *AJA*, XXXIX (1935), 134] show that panel painting was successfully practised in Greece as early as the third quarter of the sixth century. For fragments of late archaic Greek murals found at Gordion, Phrygia, cf. R. S. Young, *AJA*, LX (1956), 255 ff.

3. On this subject cf. von Mercklin, *RM*, XXXVIII (1923-24), 105 f., note 2.

4. On these cf. my *Craft*, pp. 87 ff.

5. Aristophanes' reference in *Eccl.* 994-996 to "the man who paints lekythoi for the dead" has often been interpreted as a derogatory allusion to the whole craft; but surely it is not the high or low esteem in which the painter is held, but the fact that he paints vases for the dead that is the point here. In a tomb at Capua two superb vases dating from about 490-480 B.C.—the skyphos with Triptolemos by Makron and the kylix with Chrysippos by the Brygos Painter—were found with vases of about 460 B.C.; cf. Beazley's comment *AJA*, XLIX (1945), 158: "The cup and the skyphos must have been treasured for many years before they were placed in the grave. Treasured, it may be, by more than one owner—father and son, father and daughter's husband. Treasured as wonders, not of minor art or industrial art (in the shoddy jargon of today or yesterday), but of art pure and simple: not πάγχρυσα, although there are touches of gold on the Brygos cup; but peak of possessions, κορυφὰ κτεάνων."

6. On dedications by potters cf. Beazley, *Potter*, pp. 21 ff. The fact that some ceramic artists (for instance Hieron and Euthymides) add their father's name to their own has been thought to indicate that they were citizens (Leonard, quoting Pottier, in Pauly-Wissowa, VIII, *s.v.* Hieron, col. 1516); but this is not necessarily the case, for metics had a right to mention their father's name and did so on fifth- and fourth-century gravestones (Wilamowitz, *Aristoteles und Athen*, II, 174 f.).

7. As Miss Marjorie J. Milne reminds me.

8. Kretschmer, *Vaseninschriften*, pp. 73 ff.; Meisterhans, *Grammatik*,[3] p. 223, 5. Dugas, *Mélanges Glotz*, I, 335 ff., argues against the assumption that such names designate aliens. "But the Skythes who signs ὁ Σκύθης (Beazley, p. 75, no. 1) may well have been a Scythian (cf., however, ὁ Μίδας ἐποίησεν, Beazley, p. 897, no. 19). In general Dugas underestimates the power of assimilation of a great cultural environment" (M. J. Milne).

9. The best general compilations of subjects on Attic vases are still those in Walters, *History of Ancient Pottery*, London, 1905, and in the index of S. Reinach, *Répertoire des vases peints*, Paris, 1899-1900.

For mythological and religious subjects cf. Pauly-Wissowa, *Real-Encyclopädie* and *Roscher's Lexikon, passim;* Rumpf, *Die Religion der Griechen (Bilderatlas zur Religionsgeschichte*, no. 13-14), Leipzig, 1928; Deubner, *Attische Feste*, Berlin, 1932; Nilsson, *Greek Popular Religion*, New York, 1940; Jacobsthal in Beazley, *Attic Red-Figure Vase-Painters*, pp. 978 ff., Oxford, 1942.

For athletics cf. E. N. Gardiner, *Greek Athletic Sports and Festivals (Handbook of Archaeology and Antiquities)*, London, 1910, and *Athletics of the Ancient World*, Oxford, 1930; Alexander, *Greek Athletics*, New York, 1925.

For theatrical subjects cf. Bieber, *Die Denkmäler zum Theaterwesen im Altertum*, Berlin and Leipzig, 1920, and *The History of the Greek and Roman Theater*, Princeton, 1939; Séchan, *Études sur la tragédie grecque*, Paris, 1926.

For animals cf. Keller, *Thiere des classischen Altertums*, Innsbruck, 1887, and *Die antike Tierwelt*, Leipzig, 1909–13; Markman, *The Horse in Greek Art*, Baltimore, 1943. Morin-Jean's *Le dessin des animaux en Grèce*, Paris, 1911, contains attractive but often inaccurate drawings.

10. "In literature, however, there were occasional attempts at public control. The freedom of Comedy was limited in 439–437 B.C. by a law meant to curb savage attacks on public figures (cf. Körte in Pauly-Wissowa, XI, *s.v.* Komödie, col. 1233, ll. 57 ff.). Something similar was attempted about 414–412 (cf. Körte, col. 1235, ll. 22 ff.). Kleon tried to muzzle Aristophanes (cf. Körte, col. 1236, ll. 41 ff.). We may remember Phrynichos's experience with his *Sack of Miletos* (Herodotos VI. 21) and the trials of Anaxagoras, Diagoras, Protagoras, to say nothing of Plato's program for literature in the *Republic*" (M. J. Milne).

11. For furniture cf. Ransom, *Studies in Ancient Furniture; Couches and Beds of the Greeks, Etruscans and Romans*, Chicago, 1905; Richter, *Ancient Furniture, Greek, Etruscan and Roman*, Oxford, 1926. For attire cf. Bremer, *Die Haartracht des Mannes in archaisch-griechischer Zeit* (Diss., Giessen, 1911); Erbacher, *Griechisches Schuhwerk* (Diss., Würzburg, 1914); Bieber, *Griechische Kleidung*, Berlin and Leipzig, 1928, and *Entwicklungsgeschichte der griechischen Tracht*, Berlin, 1934; cf. also Daremberg and Saglio, *Dictionnaire*, Paris, 1877–1919, *passim*.

12. Of course in sculpture and on coins and gems representations of separate animals are frequent (cf. Richter, *Animals in Greek Sculpture*, New York, 1930; Imhoof-Blumer and Keller, *Tier- und Pflanzenbilder auf Münzen und Gemmen*, Leipzig, 1889).

13. *The Genteel Tradition at Bay*, p. 64 (applied there to ancient literature, but not, I think, so aptly as to ancient art; for the Greek tragedians surely treated "the dramas within the spirit").

14. For a comprehensive treatment of the subject of ornaments on Greek vases the reader is referred to Jacobsthal, *Ornamente griechischer Vasen*, Berlin, 1927.

15. Plotinus, *Ennead*. I, 6, 1.

16. Cf. Hambidge, *Dynamic Symmetry; the Greek Vase*, New Haven, 1920; Caskey, *Geometry of Greek Vases*, Boston, 1922; I. A. Richter, *Rhythmic Form in Art*, London, 1932.

17. On the development of the kylix from ca. 550–450 B.C. see the excellent analysis by Bloesch, *Formen attischer Schalen von Exekias bis zum Ende des strengen Stils*, Bern—Bümpliz, 1940.

18. Cf., e.g., p. 105 and Richter and Hall, nos. 102, 103. Beazley, however, reminds me that "the small black vases repeat a good deal." The same applies to the coarse "household" pottery—either semi-glazed and thrown or plain and built—which was found in great quantity in the Agora, dating from Geometric to Roman times, with little variation in form or technique; cf., e.g., D. Burr, *Hesperia*, II (1933), 597 ff.; H. A. Thompson, *Hesperia*, III (1934), 469, fig. 122; Talcott, *Hesperia*, IV (1935), 493 ff., and 513, nos. 77–79; R. S. Young, *Hesperia*, Supplement II (1939), p. 199: "Household ware, with very little change in fabric, is found in abundance in Attica throughout antiquity, from the Protogeometric to the Late Roman period; its presence in great quantity over so long a period indicates that it was made locally."

19. By Lindsley F. Hall; many are based on Hambidge, *op. cit.*, and Caskey, *op. cit.* For kylichnis as the Attic term for toilet box rather than pyxis cf. M. J. Milne, *AJA*, XLIII (1939), 247 ff.

20. Cf. Richter and Milne, pp. xii, xiv.

21. The following books and articles will be found especially useful in a study

of Greek inscriptions on vases: Pape, *Wörterbuch der griechischen Eigennamen*, 2 vols., 3d ed., revised by Benseler, Braunschweig, 1884; Fick and Bechtel, *Die griechischen Personennamen*, 2d ed., Göttingen, 1894; Kretschmer, *Die griechischen Vaseninschriften*, Gütersloh, 1894; Meisterhans, *Grammatik der attischen Inschriften*, 3d ed., revised by Eduard Schwyzer, Berlin, 1900; Kirchner, *Prosopographia attica*, 2 vols., Berlin, 1901–3, and *Nachträge zur Prosopographia Attica*, by Sundwall, Helsingfors, 1910 (a revision of Kirchner's *Prosopographia Attica* is in preparation by B. D. Meritt); Bechtel, *Die attischen Frauennamen*, Göttingen, 1902, and *Die historischen Personennamen des Griechischen*, Halle, 1917; C. W. Fränkel, *Satyr- und Bakchennamen auf Vasenbildern*, Halle, 1912; Beazley, "Some Inscriptions on Vases," *AJA*, XXXI (1927), 345–353, XXXIII (1929), 361–367, XXXIX (1935), 475–488, XLV (1941), 593–602, LIV (1950), 310–322, and *Attic Red-figure Vase-Painters*, *passim*, Oxford, 1942; E. Fraenkel in Pauly-Wissowa's *Real-Encyclopädie*, XVI (1935), *s.v.* Namenwesen, cols. 1611–1648. For graffiti and dipinti cf. note 44.

22. εἰκών rather than εἶδος (Kretschmer, *Vaseninschriften*, pp. 84, 137) is Beazley's suggestion, but see now Caskey and Beazley, *AVP*, II, 88, note 1.

23. For the exceptions to this rule cf. Fick, *Personennamen*,² pp. 304–314; for more nearly complete lists cf. Bechtel, *Personennamen*, pp. 564 ff. Names of minor divinities are particularly frequent among hetairai, cf. Bechtel, *Frauennamen*, pp. 69 ff.; M. J. Milne, *AJA*, XLVI (1942), 219 ff.

24. On a psykter by Oltos, Richter and Hall, no. 3.

25. On the kylix by Douris in Munich, no. 2646; Hartwig, *Gr. M.*, p. 258, no. 8; FR, II, 230, pl. 105. The line is probably the beginning of the drinking song preserved in Theognis 939–942, as was noted by Hartwig and Furtwängler:

οὐ δύναμαι φωνῇ λίγ' ἀειδέμεν ὥσπερ ἀηδών· κ.τ.λ.

This is an attractive and reasonable explanation, since the presence of the flute player shows the man is singing. As has been noted, we should emend the Theognis text from the inscription and read:

οὐ δύναμ' οὐ φωνῇ κ.τ.λ.

26. On a Panathenaic amphora; *CIG*, IV, 7860; Gerhard, *Annali*, II (1830), 220; Klein, *Lieblingsinschriften*,² p. 139, no. 11; Kretschmer, *Vaseninschriften*, p. 91.

27. On a pelike in the Vatican; *Mus. Greg.* II (1842 ed.), pl. LXV, 1; Robert, *Bild und Lied*, pp. 81 ff.; Waldhauer, *AA*, 1927, col. 71 ff., figs. 1, 2; Albizzati, pl. 61, no. 413. Albizzati and Kretschmer, *Vaseninschriften*, p. 80, read παρβεβακεν, Robert, *loc. cit.*, παραβεβακεν (which I too seem to see on Albizzati's plate). "If the Doric dialect had been correctly reproduced by the vase painter we should have had παρβεβακε. Apparently he has not only added the Attic ν ephelkystikon (as already pointed out by Kretschmer), but has also given the prepositional prefix in its Attic form. We cannot tell whether the vase painter by πλεον meant πλέων or πλέον. The latter is the Laconian form (see Bechtel, *Gr. Dialekte*, II, 308). Since he does use the Doric α instead of the Attic long, open e in παραβεβακεν, it seems likely that by πλεον he meant πλέον rather than the Attic πλέων" (M. J. Milne).

28. On the same pelike.

29. See our p. 56 and Beazley, p. 22, no. 5 and p. 17, no. 12.

30. On a pelike by Euphronios in Leningrad; *Mon. dell' Inst.*, II (1834–38), pl. XXIV; Kretschmer, *Vaseninschriften*, p. 91; Waldhauer, *op. cit.*, cols. 70 ff., Beilagen 1, 2; Beazley, p. 17, no. 9.

31. About 170 *kalos* names and about 17 *kale* names are known. On kalos names cf. Beazley, pp. 912–947; also D. M. Robinson and Fluck, *A Study of the Greek Love-Names*, 1937.

32. See especially *Charm.* 153 ff.; also Xenophon *Symp.* I. 8 ff.

33. Plato *Charm.* 154 A.

34. Langlotz (*Zeitbestimmung*, pp. 43 ff.) pointed out that occasionally older men figure as favorites and are called kalos. Such exceptions are of course possible; and we have the expression καλὸς κἀγαθός current in Greek literature for "a gentleman." On the other hand, the frequent combination of the word παῖς with καλός would seem to indicate that the vase painters as a rule had boys in mind.

35. Archikles and Glaukytes, and Anakles and Nikosthenes (cf. Beazley, *Potter*, p. 26). As Beazley points out, collaboration in the "making" of a vase seems curious. If one person had designed or decorated it and the other fashioned it, we should expect one to sign with egrapsen, the other with epoiesen, as elsewhere. I doubt whether firing a kiln full of vases would have been described as "making" any one of them. Perhaps one person threw, that is, fashioned the vase, the other turned, that is, finished it; each of these processes—necessarily carried out on different days—is part and parcel of the making of the vase and requires a special skill. But such division of labor in so simple a shape, and especially the recording of it, is, to say the least, unusual.

36. The form used for signatures on Arretine ware is the genitive for the owner of the establishment, the nominative for the workman, but since this is a Latin formula, not the Attic one, it cannot be used as an argument either way.

37. Cf. Hussong, *Zur Technik der attischen Gefässkeramik*, p. 55.

38. See on this subject the illuminating book by Bloesch, *Formen attischer Schalen*, 1940, and Beazley, *Potter*, pp. 25 ff., 36 ff.

39. Usually written ἔγραφσεν on vases, indicating that π was aspirated when followed by σ in the Attic dialect.

40. See Richter and Hall, nos. 52–54, and Hoppin, II, 38 ff.

41. Hoppin, I, 31.

42. As the letters are all separate capital letters and usually painted in a thick pigment that does not allow much individuality, the "style" of the handwriting is usually difficult to determine; see, however, e.g., Richter and Hall, p. 55, note 1.

43. Cf. Beazley, *JHS*, LII (1932), 194 f.

44. Hackl, "Merkantile Inschriften auf attischen Vasen," *Münchener archäologische Studien*, 1909, pp. 5–106; Beazley, "Some Inscriptions on Vases," *AJA*, XXXI (1927), 349 f.; XLV (1941), 597 f. On those found in recent years in the Athenian Agora cf. Talcott, *Hesperia*, V (1936), 346 ff. For the graffiti on vases in the Metropolitan Museum cf. M. J. Milne in Richter and Hall, pp. 221 ff. On a prize graffito in a western alphabet and a west Greek dialect on the foot of an Attic black-figured kylix of about 530 B.C., cf. M. J. Milne, *AJA*, XLIX (1945), 528 ff. On the graffito on a red-figured hydria in Utrecht cf. Jongkees, *Mnemosyne*, 1942, pp. 151 ff. ("Should not προ be read as πρό(χοι) rather than as the preposition πρό, and ον also as a vase name whether ὄνοι or some unknown term?" M. J. Milne). The dipinti, or painted marks, are mostly confined to black-figured vases.

45. Wilamowitz, *Homer. Untersuchungen*, pp. 303 ff.; Kretschmer, *op. cit.*, pp. 104–106; Larfeld, *Griechische Epigraphik*,³ 1914, p. 259.

46. Beazley called my attention to this fact.

47. Hackl, *op. cit.*, pp. 79 ff.; Larfeld, *op. cit.*, pp. 291 ff.; Tod, *BSA*, XVIII (1911–12), 98–132, and XXVIII (1926–27), 141–157.

48. See the excellent recent discussion by Amyx, *University of California Publications in Classical Archaeology*, I, no. 8, 1941, pp. 188 ff., and Beazley, "Some Inscriptions on Vases, IV," *AJA*, XLV (1941), p. 598.

49. Cf. Amyx, *op. cit.*, pp. 179 ff. The inscription δυοβελοκαιμεθιγες on a black-figured amphora has been translated "two obols and you have me" (D. Amyx, *op. cit.*, pp. 186 ff.), and "two obols—and hands off" (Beazley, *ABV*, p. 136).

50. Beazley, *JHS*, LI (1931), 123.

51. Hackl, *op. cit.*, pp. 88 ff.

52. Cf. Talcott, *Hesperia*, V (1936), 346 ff.; Milne and D. von Bothmer, *Hesperia*, XXII (1953), 215 ff.

53. Cf., e.g., Richter and Hall, no. 5. For an Etruscan graffito which may be a dealer's order, on an Attic red-figured vase, cf. Lattes, *Memorie della R. Accademia di Archeologia*, Napoli, II (1913), 103; M. J. Milne, *AJA*, XLIII (1939), 253, note 1.

54. Minto, *NS*, X (1934), 378, fig. 32. Minto describes the inscription as having been painted under the glaze. When I examined it in 1935 it seemed to me painted, in the usual way, on the glaze.

55. Fiesel, *Studi etruschi*, VIII (1934), 435 f.

56. See M. J. Milne in Richter and Hall, p. 224, no. 132.

57. By Milne, *ibid.*

58. See Richter and Hall, no. 118, and the lekythos from Athens described by Körte, *Arch. Ztg.*, XXXVII (1879), 96.

59. See Richter and Hall, no. 157.

60. e.g., the lekythos by Xenophantos in Leningrad (see p. 157).

61. On this whole question cf. Kretschmer, *Vaseninschriften*, pp. 73 ff.

62. Richter, *MM Bulletin*, XXVI (1931), 289 ff.

63. Kretschmer, *Vaseninschriften*, pp. 77 ff.; but *cf.* Richter and Hall, no. 10, and *AJA*, XLIV (1940), 430.

64. Kretschmer, *op. cit.*, pp. 104 ff.; Hackl, *op. cit.*, p. 78.

65. For the old Attic alphabet which we find on Attic vases and in other inscriptions see Roberts, *An Introduction to Greek Epigraphy*, I, 384–385, and Larfeld, *Gr. Epigraphik*,³ Schrifttafel; Meisterhans, *Grammatik*, p. 3.

66. Kretschmer, *op. cit.*, p. 103; Koehler, *AM*, X (1885), 359 ff.

67. Thus the Eretria Painter uses both ⸙ and ⸙ Ɛ and Ⱶ for η (see Richter and Hall, nos. 139, 140).

68. pp. 8 ff. Cf. also Beazley's remarks in his review of *Kouroi* in *Classical Weekly*, LIX (1945), 71 f.

69. For a detailed discussion of the information obtained from these various sources cf. Richter, *Craft*, Richter and Hall, pp. xxxv ff., and Hussong, *Zur Technik der attischen Gefässkeramik* (Diss., Heidelberg, 1928). On most of the important points Dr. Hussong's findings agreed with mine; the few points of disagreement I have discussed in the footnotes of Richter and Hall, pp. xxxv ff. and in my review of his thesis in *AJA*, XXXVI (1932), 84–86. Rieth and Groschopf in *Die Entwicklung der Töpferscheibe* (Leipzig, 1939), discuss the process of throwing throughout the ages including the Greek period; cf. also the general account by Jongkees, *De Gids*, 107 (1943), 1 ff., and my chapter on "Ceramics," *History of Technology*, II, 259 ff.

The representations of potters at work, on vases and plaques, have also been discussed with great insight by Beazley, *Potter*, pp. 5 ff. The most important addition to the list given in my *Craft*, pp. 64 ff., is an Athenian calyx krater from Caltagirone (Libertini, *Mon. Linc.*, XXVIII [1922], 103, fig. 1, pl. I; Cloché, *Les Classes, les métiers, le trafic*, 1931, pl. XIX, 6) with a man working on an incomplete vase (without handles or foot) while a boy makes the wheel revolve. The man's pose—with his left hand on his thigh—suggests that he is bracing himself to keep the position of his right hand constant. He is probably centering the vase, testing by eye and hand how true it is running by letting the vase spin against his hand.

As in my previous writings on technique, I am greatly indebted to Miss Maude Robinson for constant help during my researches and for a revision of my text. I was able to work in her studio, firing my tests in a small kiln under her supervision.

70. Cf. the two chapters in Binns, *The Potter's Craft*, 1922: "The Nature and

Properties of Clay," pp. 29–36, and "The Preparation of the Clay," pp. 37–42.

71. For the different manipulations involved cf. Richter, *Craft*, pp. 7 ff.; Binns, *op. cit.*, pp. 74 ff. For fashioning the outside the ancient Greeks perhaps employed a rib (as do their modern descendants), which affords a greater area of support for raising or forming the clay than the different grips of the fingers.

72. Cf., e.g., the krater 08.258.21 in the Metropolitan Museum. The join is visible underneath the clay ridge where the latter has scaled off (Richter and Hall, pl. 170, no. 135; Richter and Milne, figs. 57, 58).

73. For a possible representation of a three-legged compass on the hydria with a scene of potters at work, cf. Hussong, *op. cit.*, p. 19.

74. Richter, *Craft*, pp. 64 ff.; Hussong, *op. cit.*, pp. 12 ff.; Libertini, *Mon. Linc.*, XXVIII (1922), cols. 101 ff., fig. 1, pl. I; Rieth and Groschopf, *op. cit.*, pp. 60 f.

75. Richter, *Craft*, p. 91; Hussong, *op. cit.*, p. 13 (where further references are cited).

76. Cf. Richter, *Craft*, pp. 84 f.; Hussong, *op. cit.*, p. 14, note 1.

77. Richter, *Craft*, pp. 10 ff.; Binns, *op. cit.*, pp. 99 ff.

78. It is not necessary or practicable to have the shapes of the tools correspond to the desired profiles, as Hussong (*op. cit.*, p. 18) thinks. Cf. Binns, *op. cit.*, pp. 99 ff., fig. 19.

79. Richter, *Craft*, pp. 16 f.

80. *Ibid.*, p. 13, figs. 17, 18.

81. Beazley, pp. 892 ff.

82. Cf., e.g., Buschor, *Münchner Jahrbuch der bildenden Kunst*, XI (1919), I–II, pp. 1 ff.

83. Cf., e.g., Langlotz, *Würzburg*, pl. 118, nos. 436, 437; Richter, *AJA*, XLV (1941), 587 ff.

83a. Cf., e.g., Talcott, *Hesperia*, IV (1935), 513, nos. 77–79; R. S. Young, *Hesperia*, Supplement II (1939), 199; and my note 18.

84. Richter, *Craft*, p. 25, fig. 34.

85. *Berichte der deutschen keramischen Gesellschaft*, XXIII (1942), 408 ff.; *Forschungen und Fortschritte*, XIX (1943), 356 ff. For brief summaries cf. Weickert, *Arch. Anz.*, 1942, cols. 512 ff.; Lane, *Greek Pottery*, pp. 4 ff. Microscopic and X-ray examinations have substantiated Schumann's discoveries; cf. Oberlies and Köppen, *Ber. deutsch. ker. Gesellschaft*, XXX (1953), 102.

86. In Binns and Fraser, *AJA*, XXXIII (1929), 1 ff., where references to the older literature were given.

87. Schumann thought that black magnetic oxide of iron (Fe_3O_4), being magnetic and stable, was preferable to ferrous oxide (FeO), which is nonmagnetic and unstable. Cf. also Farmsworth in Shear, *Hesperia*, IX (1940), 265; but see now Binson, *Antiquaries Journal*, XXXVI (1956), 203, and Farnsworth, *AJA*, LXII (1958), 172.

88. One may ask, if the glaze turned black in a reducing fire, why did the clay fire red? For it too contains red ferric oxide and so is convertible into black by reduction—as we know from the black bucchero ware. To this question Mr. Binns, *AJA*, XXXIII (1929), 6, gave the following answer. He maintained that in the change from ferric to ferrous oxide there takes place a considerable lowering of the point of fusion; "for ferrous oxide contributes to the production of glass, while ferric oxide remains aloof and is simply surrounded by the glassy substance." Hence the reducing fire not only produced the black but also made the glaze insoluble. He therefore conceived the process of firing to have been as follows: "As soon as the kiln attained a visible red color, or at about 600° C., a type of fuel which would produce a dense smoke was used. This was continued until the finishing temperature of about 950° was reached. The cooling was then

allowed to proceed very slowly and with a smoky atmosphere down to about 850°, at which point the air was freely admitted but still with slow cooling. The glaze having become glassy in the fusion, the black iron oxide was locked in and could not change. The body, however, which had also been blackened was, in its porous condition, able to reabsorb the necessary oxygen and to recover its red color." This theory is supported by the fact that whereas it is easy to convert the terra-cotta which turned gray or blackish in the funeral pyre (see p. 35) back into red simply by refiring it under oxidizing conditions up to a temperature of 800° C., black glaze has to be heated to above 950° C. before it changes its color, and then it becomes not red but chestnut brown. The fact that the glaze has been rendered practically insoluble would be a satisfactory explanation of this. Dr. Schumann gave a similar explanation, speaking, however, of black magnetic oxide of iron instead of ferrous oxide. Cf. also Weickert, *Arch. Anz.*, 1942, col. 523. On ferrous oxide and black magnetic oxide of iron, see now Binson, loc. cit., and Farnsworth, loc. cit., in note 87.

89. Richter, "Accidental and Intentional Red Glaze," *BSA*, XLVI (1956), 143 ff.; and "Red-and-Black Glaze," *Het Nederlands Kunsthistorisch Jaarboek*, 1954, pp. 127 ff.

90. The best known are the Euphronios and Exekias kylikes in Munich, nos. 2044 and 2620, and the Sotades cup in London, D 6; for the examples found in the Agora, cf. Talcott and Vanderpool, *Hesperia*, XV (1948), 285 ff. The two firings were tentatively suggested by Schumann in a letter to me. Though the method seems cumbrous, the fact that there are so few specimens in this technique and that the red glaze on these pieces is apt to peel—as it would if applied to fired clay—seemed to bear out its possibility.

91. *AJA*, LXII (1958), 165 ff., in an article entitled "Fifth Century Intentional Red Glaze." It contains important observations also on the black glaze.

92. Cf. Schumann, *Berichte der deutschen keramischen Gesellschaft*, XXIII (1942), 423.

93. Weickert, *Arch. Anz.*, 1942, cols. 523 ff. (reporting findings made by Schumann and sent him by letter).

94. Graphically demonstrated by Binns in op. cit., pl. II, which shows the black glaze on geometric and Mycenaean vases converted into red in an oxidizing fire. Cf. also the interesting remarks by Weickert, cols. 526 ff., on similar phenomena in early, non-Greek wares. They indicate that the three stages in the firing of Attic vases were known from early times.

95. Cf. my *Craft*, pp. 55 ff.

96. Cf., e.g., Richter and Hall, nos. 16 and 98.

97. Reichhold suggested that the design was first made on a surface which had a similar curvature as the vase for which it was intended (in FR, II, 199; cf. also Hussong, *op. cit.*, p. 54); but this would necessitate making two vases instead of one. On preparatory sketches and the materials perhaps used for them cf. Beazley, *Potter*, pp. 38 f.

98. Richter, *Craft*, p. 51.

99. Richter and Hall, no. 80.

100. Cf. Hartwig, *Jb.*, XIV (1899), 164, note 21; Richter, *Craft*, pp. 41 f.; Beazley, *Potter*, p. 39, note 1.

101. See Hussong's excellent illustrations of relief lines enlarged from 6 to 12 times (*op. cit.*, p. 51, fig. 13).

102. Richter, *Craft*, pp. 70 f.; and in *History of Technology*, II, pl. 16. The vase, formerly in the possession of Dr. Scaretti of Rome, is now in the collection of Sig. Ing. Giovanni Torni of Milan.

103. *Ibid.*, p. 74; Beazley, *JHS*, XXVIII (1908), 317 f. What looks like a brush case is here represented as suspended on the wall.

104. Richter, *Craft*, pp. 71 f.

105. *Ibid.*, pp. 72 f.

106. For analyses of these accessory colors see Blümner, *Tech. u. Term.*,[2] II, 80 ff.; Hussong, *op. cit.*, pp. 46 ff.; Weickert, *Arch. Anz.*, 1942, col. 525.

107. See Richter and Hall, nos. 1, 60, 79, 89.

108. For red on white on fillets, etc., cf., e.g., Richter and Hall, nos. 100, 101, 126, 127, 153.

109. Courby, *Les Vases grecs à reliefs*, pp. 117 ff.

110. Beazley, *AWL*, p. 3, and *ABS*, p. 22.

110a. Cf. Crosby, *Hesperia*, XXIV (1955), 76 ff.

111. Tonks, *AJA*, XII (1908), 421; Richter, *Craft*, p. 35; Binns and Fraser, *AJA*, XXXIII (1929), 7.

112. Tonks, *loc. cit.*

113. I answered in *AJA*, XXXVI (1932), 84 ff., Hussong's arguments for two fires. His theory that, though a single fire is general at other times, two fires were in vogue between about 550 and 400 is, I think, exceedingly unlikely. The differences he postulates (*op. cit.*, p. 58, fig. 14) between the incised lines on Corinthian and on Attic wares are not borne out by extensive comparisons; and the *Glasurplatzrisse* ("rifts or crow's-feet in the glaze"), "typische Brandfehler des ersten Brandes," are not mostly confined, as he claims, to the early wares, but are very common also in Athenian red-figure; for instances cf. Richter and Hall.

114. Hussong (*op. cit.*, p. 58) thinks that these dents could have occurred in the second firing. But "the temperature in the Greek firing was never high enough to make the clay flexible" (Binns).

115. e.g., cf. Richter, *Craft*, p. 41, fig. 45.

116. For a case in which clay was added to a vase which was already too dry and to which the clay therefore did not adhere properly see Richter and Hall, p. 35, note 3. There are a few instances of clay applied over the black glaze (cf., e.g., Dragendorff, *Jb.*, XLIII [1928], 332, pls. X, XI); here, too, it must have been added before the firing.

117. Richter, *Craft*, p. 71, fig. 66; Beazley, *Potter*, pp. 11 ff.

118. Richter, *Craft*, p. 72, fig. 67; Beazley, *Potter*, p. 10.

119. I made experiments with clay obtained from one of the potteries outside Athens—a mixed variety, composed of red earth from Chalandri and white earth from Koukouvaones (Richter, *Craft*, p. 40).

120. Hussong (*op. cit.*, p. 33) accepted Reichhold's theory that Athenian vases were put in the kiln in a horizontal position on circular supports and that the *"Lagerringe"*—the round red, or black and red, spots found on the sides of Athenian vases—are due to this practice. But vases so placed would be apt to warp in the fire, and what possible advantage could there be to offset this risk? The kiln can be packed much more economically with the vases standing upright. The representation of the inside of a kiln on a Corinthian pinax (Richter, *Craft*, p. 78, fig. 80) cannot be taken as serious evidence; for at that early period faulty perspective led to many curious renderings.

121. It is to this stacking rather than to a join that I should now attribute such marks as those figured in my *Craft*, p. 19, fig. 25. Cf. Reichhold in FR, I, 156.

122. We may mention as a few examples the kylix Richter and Hall, no. 7, of which the lower outer part is brownish, the rest black; the pelike no. 22, where the band on the inside of the neck is red; the kylix no. 37, which has a red ring on the interior, presumably where the foot of another vase rested on it; and the covered bowl acc. no. 23.43, which is red on the inside.

123. Richter, *Craft*, pp. 76 ff. The oven on the red-figured Athenian lekythos illustrated by Luce, *CV: Providence*, I, pl. 17, i, could hardly be a potter's kiln, for it is not enclosed.

124. Cf. Blümner, *Tech. u. Term.*,[2] II, pp. 23 ff.; Hussong, *op. cit.*, p. 26, notes 1, 2, and the references there cited; S. Loeschcke, *Trierer Zeitschrift*, III (1928), parts 1, 2, pp. 68 f., fig. 1.

125. Cf. especially Mylonas, *Olynthus*, I, pp. 12 ff. (neolithic); Woodward, *JHS*, XLVIII (1928), 186 (Helladic).

126. Cf. Rhomaios, *AM*, XXXIII (1908), 177 ff. (not later than the third century); Cavvadias and Kawerau, *Die Ausgrabungen der Akropolis*, col. 120, pl. Z, 75 (pre-Kimonian); and recently at Corinth and Eretria.

127. Hussong, *op. cit.*, p. 27, fig. 9.

128. He never published this theory; but he discussed it with me and I have some letters on the subject written in 1931. I owe to him also the references to *The National Geographic Magazine* (see note 131) and to the account by his father of a Roman kiln found in England (see note 130).

129. Mylonas, *op. cit.*, p. 16.

130. R. W. Binns, *Worcester Pottery*,[1] p. 186: "Excavations exposed what are believed to be the remains of a Roman pottery kiln; a circular form could be traced outside and a lesser one within, the circles touching, from which point extended a narrow flue 15 feet long, so that from the mouth of this flue to the opposite side of the outer circle was a distance of thirty feet. The smaller circle was raised about three feet and covered with a layer of baked clay, which was quite honey-combed from having had *osiers, or similar wood burnt in the layers;* these had evidently been ᴘ aced for the purpose of binding the clay in its wet state, and the burning of which had destroyed the wood."

131. Cf. Mylonas, *op. cit.*, pp. 17 f., and the picture of an oven in Macedonia in *The National Geographic Magazine*, Dec., 1930, p. 702.

132. In this connection cf. Newhall, *AJA*, XXXV (1931), 6: "No ovens have been found on the site [of a pottery factory in Corinth], probably because they were of clay and have been washed away." But would not the clay have turned into terra cotta during the firing?

133. See, e.g., Richter and Hall, nos. 32, 103.

134. *Ibid.*, nos. 80, 88.

135. *Ibid.*, nos. 13, 16, 32, 33, G R 530.

136. See the illustration of a bad crack on a Corinthian aryballos in Hussong, *op. cit.*, p. 37, fig. 10; also the Italo-Corinthian oinochoe 25.78.106 and the Attic red-figured vase G R 604 in the Metropolitan Museum.

137. See Richter and Hall, no. 66.

138. *Ibid.*, no. 71.

139. *Ibid.*, nos. 35, 68, 93.

140. *Ibid.*, no. 80.

141. *Ibid.*, nos. 10, 147. On reduction cf. p. 28, note 94; also Richter, "The Technique of Bucchero Ware," *Studi etruschi*, X (1936), and the references there cited.

142. See, e.g., Richter and Hall, no. 118.

143. *Ibid.*, no. 120.

144. *Ibid.*, nos. 17, 100.

145. *Ibid.*, no. 107.

146. Richter, *Craft*, pp. 59 ff.

147. *Ibid.*, pp. 64 ff.; Beazley, *Potter*, pp. 5 ff.

148. *Rhet.* II. 4. 21.

149. Quoted from Hesiod, *Works and Days*, 25.

I. EARLY STYLE

1. Beazley, *ABS,* pp. 24 ff.
2. Beazley, *op. cit.,* pp. 24 f.
3. There is occasionally an earlier example of this, for instance on the François vase.
4. Cf. also Pfuhl, fig. 325 (Epiktetos).
5. Cf., e.g., Pfuhl, fig. 351.
6. Naturally there are exceptions; for instance, the clavicles and ankles were sometimes drawn in diluted glaze (e.g., by Euthymides), and, as we saw, early artists occasionally used the glaze full strength for most or all anatomical markings (e.g., the Goluchow Painter, Beazley, *V. Pol.,* pl. III; the Hegesiboulos Painter, Richter and Hall, pls. 9, 10; and the Hischylos Painter, fig. 42).
7. Euripides, *Herakles Mainomenos,* 131 f.
8. Langlotz, *Zeitbestimmung,* pp. 28 ff. Herodotos' famous story (V. 87 f.) of how the Ionic chiton came to supersede the peplos in Athens is an aetiological legend, as Wilamowitz (*Aristoteles und Athen,* II, 280 ff.) has shown.
9. Langlotz (*op. cit.,* pp. 17–38 *passim*) was the first properly to utilize this observation for the dating of sixth-century sculpture and vases. He did not distinguish, however, between the simplified renderings of stacked folds observable occasionally on vases and sculptures of the third quarter of the sixth century and the more complicated ones current in the late sixth century. Hence his late dating of the sculptures of Temple C of Selinus. I have discussed this question more fully in my forthcoming *Archaic Greek Art.*
10. VIII. 19–20 (tr. Marchant).
11. Cf. my recent articles on "Polychromy in Greek Sculpture," *AJA,* XLVIII (1944), 321 ff.; "Terracotta Plaques from Early Attic Tombs," *MM Bulletin,* new series, I (1942), 80 ff.; and the references there cited.
12. Overbeck, *Schriftquellen,* nos. 375 ff.; A. Reinach, *Recueil Milliet,* pp. 64 ff.
13. *N.H.* XXXV. 56 (probably derived from Xenokrates, cf. Jex-Blake and Sellers, pp. xxviii, xxix): Hic catagrapha invenit, hoc est obliquas imagines, et varie formare voltus, respicientes suspicientesve vel despicientes. Articulis membra distinxit, venas protulit, praeterque in vestibus rugas et sinus invenit (reading "vestibus" with Traube). The translation given above is that of Jex-Blake and Sellers, with slight changes; cf. also their note on *catagrapha* (= foreshortening?).
14. See Kirchner, *Imagines inscriptionum Atticarum,* p. 10, no. 10, pl. 5.
15. Richter, *Kouroi,* pp. 154 f.
16. Richter, *Archaic Attic Gravestones,* 1944, p. 69, note 42.
17. The steady development of this stylized rendering in Greek sculpture shows that the scheme must have been invented by Greek artists, not taken by them from the Persians, as had been claimed. I have discussed this question at length in an article on "Greeks in Persia," *AJA,* L (1946), 15 ff.
18. In this reëxamination of the evidence supplied by kalos names I want to acknowledge specially the help given me by Marjorie J. Milne.
19. Hoppin, *Bf.,* p. 358.
20. Cf. the stemma in Kirchner, *Prosopographia Attica,* I, 62 f.
21. Beazley, *CV,* pl. I, 5; Langlotz, *Zeitbestimmung,* pp. 58 ff.; and Beazley, p. 55, no. 8. That Stesagoras, the brother of Miltiades, cannot be referred to in the kalos inscriptions with that name, as some had thought, has been pointed out by Langlotz (*op. cit.,* pp. 60 f.) and others. Stesagoras died before the cups with that name could have been painted.

22. Beazley, p. 925. For an alabastron in New York with the inscription, Ιππαρχος καλος ναι, "Hipparchos is handsome, yes", cf. *MM. Handbook,*[6] p. 140, and Richter and Milne, fig. 109; Beazley, p. 69, no. 27.

23. Hipparchos, the son of Peisistratos (514), seems too old to come into consideration, though Langlotz (*op. cit.,* pp. 54 ff.) makes out a good case for the bon vivant tyrant, then middle-aged.

24. Androtion, frag. 5; Aristotle *Ath. Pol.* 22. 4 (Hipparchos is there also described as ἡγεμών and προστάτης of the tyrants' friends); cf. also Lykourgos, *Against Leokrates,* 117; Wilamowitz, *Aristoteles und Athen,* I, 114 f. He was the first man to be ostracized (Kleisthenes is said to have introduced ostracism to get rid of him). Ostraka with his name have been found in the Athenian Agora.

25. Beazley, p. 934.

26. The kylix E 18 in the British Museum. Beazley, p. 40, no. 69.

27. In Syracuse. Hoppin, I, 464.

28. Beazley, p. 123, no. 29.

29. Aristotle, *loc. cit.;* Langlotz, *Zeitbestimmung,* pp. 41 f.

30. Beazley, p. 930.

31. *Ibid.,* p. 924.

32. Herodotos IX. 75; Thucydides I. 100. 3, IV. 102. 2. In the excavations of the Athenian Agora the base of a statue was found with a dedicatory inscription by "Leagros, the son of Glaukon"; cf. Meritt, *Hesperia,* V (1936), 359; Raubitschek, *Hesperia,* VIII (1939), 155 ff.

33. Katterfeld (*Metopen,* p. 74) and Langlotz (*op. cit.,* pp. 48 ff.) use as additional evidence the eighth letter of Themistokles (Hercher, *Epist. Gr.,* p. 747), where Leagros, son of Glaukon, is called συνέφηβος and ἡλικιώτης of Themistokles. But this is a late (second century A.D.) and unreliable source, and the term συνέφηβος is an anachronism, for the ἐφηβεία was an institution created in the second half of the fourth century B.C. (Wilamowitz, *op. cit.,* pp. 189 ff.). Furthermore Themistokles was archon in 493, when the office was still elective, and as he was the first person in his family to take part in politics it is unlikely that he was then still a very young man.

34. Beazley, p. 934.

35. Pfuhl, fig. 484; Casson, *Cat. of the Acrop. Mus.,* II, 306 ff., no. 57; Graef and Langlotz, *Akropolis,* II, 93 f., no. 1037, pl. 80.

35a. On such well-groups, cf. especially *Hesperia,* IV (1935), 476 ff., V, 333 ff. (Talcott); VI, 257 ff. (Pease); XV, 265 ff. (Vanderpool); XXII, 59 ff. (Boulter).

36. Beazley, *ABS,* p. 24.

37. Broneer, *Hesperia,* VI (1937), 469 ff.

37a. That little-master cups, however, continued in use until about 500 B.C. is shown by representations of them on vases; cf., e.g., Graef and Langlotz, *Akropolis,* II, pl. VI, no. 166; Haspels, *Bf. Lekythoi,* pl. 23, no. 3.

38. G 1. FR, pl. 3; Hoppin, I, 41; Pfuhl, fig. 313; Pfuhl, *Masterpieces,* fig. 27; Pottier, *CV,* pls. 25, 26, no. 2; Buschor, *Gr. V.,* fig. 141; Beazley, p. 2, no. 2.

39. F 203. Hoppin, I, 39; Seltman, *AV,* pl. 9 b; Beazley, p. 2, no. 11.

40. V 650. Hoppin, I, 36; Pfuhl, figs. 262, 263; Marconi Bovio, *CV,* pls. 1, 2; Beazley, p. 3, no. 12.

41. 2159. Hoppin, I, 33; Pfuhl, fig. 314; Swindler, *AP,* figs. 294, 301; Neugebauer, *Führer,* II, pl. 42; FR, pl. 133; Beazley, p. 1, no. 1.

42. Beazley, pp. 1 ff., 948.

43. The black-figured vases now attributed to the Andokides Painter used to be listed as works by the Lysippides Painter (Beazley, *ABS,* pp. 25, 38–41).

44. 99.538. Beazley, *VA,* p. 4; Pfuhl, figs. 316, 266; Seltman, *AV,* pl. 10; Beazley, p. 2, no. 10.

45. F 204. Buschor, *Gr. V.*, fig. 155; Beazley, p. 2, no. 6.

46. Faina 64. Buschor, *Gr. V.*, fig. 154; Beazley, p. 2, no. 4.

47. 5399. Dohan, *Museum Journal*, V (1914), 31 ff.; Hoppin, II, 203; Pfuhl, fig. 318; Beazley, p. 8, no. 3.

48. Richter, *AJA*, XXXVIII (1934), 547 ff., and XLIII (1939), 645 f.; Beazley, p. 7.

49. 242. Hoppin, II, 397; Richter, *AJA*, XXXVIII (1934), 550, fig. 3; Beazley, p. 8, no. 4.

50. Hoppin, II, 403; Richter, *AJA*, XXXVIII (1934), 548, fig. 1; Beazley, p. 8, no. 5.

51. H. R. W. Smith, *Menon Painter;* Beazley, pp. 7 ff., 948.

52. 11008. Hoppin, I, 34; Pfuhl, figs. 317 and 264; Mélida, *CV*, pl. 23, no. 1, pls. 24, 25, pl. 26, no. 1; Beazley, p. 8, no. 2.

53. 2302. FR, I, 151, 266; Smith, *Menon Painter*, pp. 47, 53, pl. 5; Beazley, p. 7, no. 1.

54. 14.146.1. Smith, *Menon Painter*, pp. 9, 12, 13, pls. 2, 3; Richter and Hall, no. 1, pl. 1, pl. 2, no. 1, pl. 179; Richter, *Greek Painting*,[2] p. 9; Beazley, p. 9, no. 9.

55. P U 322. Pellegrini. *VPU*, pp. 56, 57; Beazley, p. 8, no. 6.

56. 2587. Smith, *Menon Painter*, pl. 1, p. 3; Beazley, p. 8, no. 8.

57. 98 b. Richter, *AJA*, XXXVIII (1934), 553, fig. 9.

58. Richter, *AJA*, XLV (1941), 587 ff.; Beazley, p. 948.

59. Richter, *AJA*, XXXVIII (1934), 551, fig. 8; Beazley, p. 11, no. 31.

60. British Museum B 589, 590, 591. Berlin, no. 2099. Smith, *Menon Painter*, pl. 4, p. 35; Beazley, p. 10, nos. 26–29.

61. Formerly in the collection of Monsieur Jameson in Paris (Chabouillet, *Le Cabinet Fould*, pl. 17, no. 1395; Beazley, p. 11, no. 30), now in that of Mr. Käppeli in Meggen, Switzerland (Beazley, *ABV*, p. 294, no. 21).

62. 2603. Hoppin, II, 398 f.; Richter, *AJA*, XXXVIII (1934), 553, fig. 10; Beazley, p. 11.

63. 14.146.2. Hoppin, II, 401; Richter and Hall, no. 2, pls. 8, 2, 179; Beazley, p. 11.

64. Cf. Richter and Hall, p. 15.

65. Richter, *Greek Painting*,[2] p. 9.

66. Beazley, p. 12.

67. Czartoryski, nos. 61, 62. Beazley, *V. Pol.*, pl. 3; Beazley, p. 12, nos. 1, 2.

68. Beazley, pp. 34 ff., 949.

69. 2264. Hoppin, II, 249; von Lücken, *GV*, pls. 8, 9; Beazley, p. 38, no. 48.

70. R C 6848. Hoppin, II, 251; Pfuhl, figs. 359, 360; Seltman, *AV*, pl. 11; Beazley, p. 38, no. 50.

71. E 258. Beazley, *VA*, p. 9; Hoppin, I, 449; Beazley, p. 34, no. 2.

72. E 437. Hoppin, II, 293; Pfuhl, fig. 361; Pfuhl, *Masterpieces*, fig. 36; Swindler, *AP*, fig. 279; Beazley, p. 35, no. 5.

73. G 2. Hoppin, II, 301; Pfuhl, fig. 362; Buschor, *Gr. V.*, fig. 153; Beazley, p. 34, no. 4.

74. 10.210.18. Beazley, *VA*, p. 8; Richter and Hall, no. 3, pls. 4, 173; Beazley, p. 35, no. 6.

75. *Pyth.* IX. 123–125 (tr. Sandys).

76. Beazley, pp. 44 ff., 949.

77. Villa Giulia. Beazley, p. 51, no. 86.

78. Acr. 6. Graef and Langlotz, *Akropolis*, II, pl. 2; Beazley, p. 51, no. 84.

79. Beazley, p. 925.

80. Beazley, *VA*, p. 18.

81. E 24. Beazley, *VA*, p. 15, fig. 8; Hoppin, I, 309; Pfuhl, fig. 327; Beazley, p. 48, no. 50.

82. Beazley, *VA*, p. 15, fig. 7; Hoppin, I, 301; D. M. Robinson, *CV*, II, pl. I, no. 3; Beazley, p. 48, no. 49.

83. Hoppin, I, 306, 314, 315, 317, 324, 325, 330; Pfuhl, figs. 324–329; Pfuhl, *Masterpieces*, figs. 30, 31; Seltman, *AV*, pl. 13 a, b; Beazley, p. 50, nos. 75 ff.

84. 79. Hoppin, I, 306; Beazley, *BSR*, XI (1929), pl. 4, no. 4; Beazley, p. 50, no. 76.

85. 41.162.112. Pease, *CV*, Gallatin Coll., pl. 47, no. 4; Beazley, p. 49, no. 61. We may compare the warrior on a cup in Naples, "a slight work by Epiktetos in his later phase" (Beazley, *Potter*, p. 28, pl. 8).

86. Kraiker, *AM*, LV (1930), 167 ff.; Beazley, p. 54, 950.

87. E 6. Hoppin, II, 351; Kraiker, *AM*, LV (1930), pl. 9, no. 1, pl. 10, and Beilage 58; Beazley, p. 55, no. 10.

88. 41.162.8. Kraiker, *op. cit.*, pl. 9, no. 2, and Beilage 54, nos. 2, 3; Pease, *CV*, Gallatin Coll., pl. 46, no. 1; Beazley, p. 54, no. 6.

89. Beazley, pp. 57, 950.

90. 2588. Hoppin, *Bf.*, p. 465; FR, III, 240 f.; Beazley, p. 57, no. 1.

91. 22.139.81. Beazley, p. 57, no. 4.

92. Beazley, pp. 53 f. The New York box by him (20.253) has a squatting satyr and the inscription "Lysikles is handsome" (Richter and Hall, no. 4, pls. 9, 178; Beazley, p. 54, no. 4).

93. Beazley, pp. 59 ff., 950.

94. Acr. 166. Graef and Langlotz, *Akropolis*, II, pl. 6, no. 166; Beazley, *Potter*, pp. 8 ff.; Beazley, p. 62, no. 60.

95. 09.221.47. Richter and Hall, no. 5, pls. 3, 179; Beazley, p. 61, no. 44.

96. Beazley, pp. 68 f., 950.

97. C A 487. Hoppin, II, 273; Beazley, p. 68, no. 2.

98. London B 668, Athens 15002, Louvre C A 1921. Pfuhl, fig. 355; Demangel, *Mon. Piot*, XXVI (1923), 68 ff., 86 ff., pl. 3; Pfuhl, *Masterpieces*, fig. 35; Beazley, p. 69, nos. 19, 20, 25.

99. Acr. A P 422. Pease, *Hesperia*, IV (1935), 291; Beazley, p. 70.

100. Beazley, pp. 86 ff., 950.

101. G 139–140. Hoppin, I, 47; Beazley, p. 87, no. 1.

102. Hoppin, I, 45; Beazley, *JHS*, LIII (1933), 69 f., pl. 6; Beazley, p. 87, no. 3.

103. 18.145.28. Richter and Hall, no. 38, pl. 36; Beazley, p. 87, no. 9.

104. Beazley, pp. 84 ff.

105. 2279. Hoppin, II, 335; Pfuhl, fig. 417; Pfuhl, *Masterpieces*, fig. 50; FR, III, 20; Neugebauer, *Führer*, II, pl. 49, no. 1; Beazley, p. 81.

106. Beazley, pp. 73 ff., 950.

107. Villa Giulia 20760. Hoppin, II, 412–413; Pfuhl, fig. 334; Pfuhl, *Masterpieces*, fig. 33; Swindler, *AP*, fig. 285; Buschor, *Gr. V.*, fig. 156; Beazley, p. 74, no. 13.

108. 4041, 1. FR, II, 182, fig. 62; Hoppin, II, 411; Beazley, p. 74, no. 8.

109. Acr. bf. 2557, 2586. Rizzo, *Mon. Piot*, XX (1913), 118, pl. VIII, 2; Hoppin, *Bf.*, 327, 328; Graef and Langlotz, *Akropolis*, I, pls. 106, 110; Beazley, pp. 75 f., nos. 1, 2.

110. Acr. bf. 2556. Rizzo, *Mon. Piot*, XX (1913), 117; Hoppin, *Bf.*, 329; Graef and Langlotz, *Akropolis*, I, pl. 106; Beazley, p. 76.

111. 07.286.47. FR, pl. 93, 2, and II, 179; Hoppin, II, 11; Pfuhl, figs. 340–341; Richter and Hall, no. 10, pls. 9 f., 179; Beazley, p. 77; D. von Bothmer, *AJA*, LXII (1958), 173.

112. FR, II, 181, fig. 61; Hoppin, II, 9; Beazley, p. 77.

113. Beazley, pp. 90, 950.

114. 07.286.50. Richter and Hall, no. 9, pl. 8; Beazley, p. 90, no. 2.

115. 2269. Licht, *Sittengeschichte Griechenlands*, II, 12; Beazley, p. 90, no. 1.

116. D. M. Robinson, *CV*, II, pls. 5, 6; Beazley, p. 90, no. 3.

117. Beazley, pp. 71 ff., 950.
118. Faina 62. Philippart, *Collections de céramique grecque en Italie*, II, pl. XI, 1; Beazley, p. 71, no. 4.
119. Hoppin, I, 150, 169, II, 15–18; Beazley, pp. 77 f., 950.
120. Hoppin, I, 185–189; Beazley, pp. 79 f., 950.
121. Beazley, pp. 95 ff., 951.
122. *Ibid.*, pp. 98 ff., 951.
123. *Ibid.*, pp. 107 ff., 951.
124. *Ibid.*, pp. 113 ff., 951. Several characteristic examples are in New York.
125. *Ibid.*, pp. 15 ff., 948; Beazley, *Potter*, p. 34.
126. G 103. FR, pl. 92, pl. 93, 1; Hoppin, I, 397; Pfuhl, figs. 392–393; Swindler, *AP*, figs. 245, 314; Seltman, *AV*, pl. 16; Buschor, *Gr. V.*, fig. 160; Beazley, p. 15, no. 1.
127. 644. FR, pl. 63; Hoppin, I, 405; Pfuhl, fig. 394; Buschor, *Gr. V.*, fig. 159; Beazley, p. 17, no. 12.
128. 2620. Hoppin, I, 391; Pfuhl, fig. 391; Swindler, *AP*, fig. 290; Seltman, *AV*, pl. 18; Buschor, *Gr. V.*, fig. 158; Beazley, p. 18, no. 14.
129. Acr. 176. Hoppin, I, 379; Graef and Langlotz, *Akropolis*, II, pl. 8 (Athens); Johnson, *Art Bulletin*, XXI (1939), 266, fig. 7 (Chicago); Beazley, p. 18, no. 15.
130. G 110. Pottier, pl. 105; Beazley, p. 16, no. 3; Villard, *Mon. Piot*, XLV (1951), 1 ff. (with new fragments joined).
131. Richter, *Sc. Sc.*, fig. 181.
132. 1465. FR, pls. 61, 62; Pfuhl, fig. 395; Pfuhl, *Masterpieces*, fig. 47; Seltman, *AV*, pl. 17; Beazley, p. 16, no. 5.
133. Cf. Beazley, under "Love Names."
134. Beazley, pp. 24 ff., 949.
135. 2307. FR, pl. 14, I, 63, 70, figs. 3 and 5; Hoppin, *Euth. F.*, pl. I; Hoppin, I, 433; Pfuhl, figs. 364, 365; Pfuhl, *Masterpieces*, figs. 38, 39; Richter, *MM Bulletin*, new series, III (1944–45), pp. 166 ff.; Beazley, *Potter*, p. 20; Beazley, p. 24, no. 1.
136. 2308. FR, pl. 81; Hoppin, *Euth. F.*, pl. 2; Hoppin, I, 435; Pfuhl, fig. 366; Pfuhl, *Masterpieces*, fig. 40; Buschor, *Gr. V.*, fig. 163; Beazley, p. 25, no. 4.
137. Inv. 70. Hoppin, *Euth. F.*, pl. 6; Hoppin, I, 431; Beazley, p. 26, no. 10.
138. Hoppin, *Euth. F.*, pls. 4 and 5, p. 19, fig. 3; Hoppin, I, 436; Pfuhl, fig. 367; Beazley, p. 25, no. 9.
139. B c 10. Hoppin, I, 438; Beazley, p. 26, no. 16.
140. D. Levi, *CV*, pl. 7, B 2; Beazley, *CF*, pl. Y, 9 and 23, 24; Beazley, p. 26, no. 17.
141. The name of a sculptor Pollias occurs in Attic inscriptions of the archaic period (*IG*, I², nos. 504, 505). It has been plausibly conjectured that he was Euthymides' father (cf. Robert, Pauly-Wissowa, VI, *s.v.* Euthymides, col. 1512). Single consonants are still written for double occasionally even on vases by Douris and Makron.
142. P 4683 and P 4744. Talcott, *Hesperia*, V (1936), 60 ff. and 68; Beazley, p. 26, no. 15.
143. 2309. FR, pl. 33 and I, 173; Hoppin, *Euth. F.*, pl. III; Pfuhl, figs. 368, 369; Pfuhl, *Masterpieces*, figs. 41–42; Seltman, *AV*, pl. 19; Buschor, *Gr. V.*, fig. 164; Beazley, p. 25, no. 3.
144. Beazley, *V. Pol.*, pls. 4–6; Seltman, *AV*, pl. 20; Buschor, *Gr. V.*, fig. 166; Beazley, p. 25, no. 7.
145. G 31 and S 1317. Hoppin, *Euth. F.*, p. 88; Beazley, p. 25, no. 8.
146. Beazley, p. 934.
147. *Ibid.*, pp. 21 ff., 949.
148. *Ibid.*, p. 24, *a.*
149. *Ibid.*, p. 24, *β, γ.*

150. R C 6843. FR, pl. 91, II, 167; Hoppin, *Euth. F.*, pl. 26; Hoppin, II, 357; Pfuhl, fig. 381; Seltman, *AV*, pl. 14; Beazley, p. 22, no. 2.

151. E 159. FR, II, 67, 66, fig. 27; Hoppin, *Euth. F.*, pl. 27, and fig. 18; Hoppin, II, 360 f.; Pfuhl, fig. 382; Beazley, p. 22, no. 7.

152. Hoppin, *Euth. F.*, fig. 17; Hoppin, II, 355; Pfuhl, fig. 384; Beazley, p. 23, no. 11.

153. 2590. FR, pl. 32; Hoppin, II, 363; Beazley, p. 23, no. 9.

154. 2421. FR, pl. 71; Hoppin, *Euth. F.*, pl. 28; Pfuhl, fig. 385; Beazley, p. 22, no. 5. For the inscription cf. Kretschmer, *Griechische Vaseninschriften*, p. 87, no. 3; Beazley, *Potter*, p. 19, and *Classical Weekly*, LVII (1943), p. 102.

155. Beazley, pp. 20 f., 948.

156. E 438. Hoppin, II, 419; Beazley, p. 20, no. 3.

157. A 717. Hoppin, II, 417; Pfuhl, fig. 388; Buschor, *Gr. V.*, figs. 161, 162; Beazley, p. 20, no. 1.

158. Beazley, pp. 21, 949.

159. 2278. Hoppin, II, 423; Pfuhl, fig. 418; Pfuhl, *Masterpieces*, fig. 51; Swindler, *AP*, figs. 310, 315; Neugebauer, *Führer*, II, pl. 48; FR, pl. 123; Buschor, *Gr. V.*, fig. 167; Beazley, p. 21, no. 1.

160. Acr. 556. Graef and Langlotz, *Akropolis*, II, pl. 42; Beazley, p. 21, no. 2.

161. 2315. Hoppin, II, 426; FR, III, p. 13, fig. 6; Beazley, p. 21.

162. Agora P 5157. Talcott, *Hesperia*, V (1936), 347, fig. 15; Beazley, *Potter*, p. 20; Milne and D. von Bothmer, *Hesperia*, XXII (1953), 218.

163. Beazley, pp. 27 f.

164. Oest. Mus. 333. FR, pl. 72; Pfuhl, fig. 370; Pfuhl, *Masterpieces*, fig. 43; Beazley, p. 27, no. 1.

165. Beazley, pp. 28 f., 949.

166. G 45. Pottier, pls. 92, 93; Beazley, p. 28, no. 4.

167. Beazley, p. 30.

168. 2423. FR, pl. 82; Hoppin, II, 121; Beazley, p. 30, no. 1.

169. Torlonia Gallery. FR, II, 114; Hoppin, II, 123; Richter and Milne, p. 11; Beazley, p. 30, no. 2.

170. 21.88.2. Richter and Milne, figs. 81, 82; Richter and Hall, no. 11, pls. 11, 172; Beazley, p. 30.

171. Beazley, pp. 30 f.

172. 13.195. Hoppin, I, 463; Caskey and Beazley, *AVP*, pl. 4; Beazley, p. 30, no. 1.

173. 26967. Hoppin, I, 465; Schefold, *Die Bildnisse der antiken Dichter Redner und Denker*, 1943, 50 f.; Beazley, p. 31, no. 2.

II. RIPE ARCHAIC STYLE

1. Langlotz, *Zeitbestimmung*, p. 85. Occasionally the jaw line was continued past the neck line much earlier, cf. Beazley, *JHS*, XLIX (1929), 269: "Sakonides, in his outline heads, continues the lower line of the jaw far past the line of the neck; the Hermogenes painter a short distance only; in the other heads the jaw-line stops at the neck-line."

2. Langlotz, *op. cit.*, pp. 100 ff. For an enlarged view of the coin, useful for comparison, see my *Sc. Sc.*,² fig. 160; and for illustrations of the Tyrannicides, *ibid.*, figs. 565–574; Buschor, "Die Tyrannen-Mörder," *Sitzungsberichte der bayerischen Akademie der Wissenschaften, phil. hist. Abteilung* (1940), Heft 5, 3–31.

3. Staïs, *AM*, XVIII (1893), 63, pl. 5, 2.

4. Langlotz, *op. cit.*, pp. 38–40.

5. Graef and Langlotz, *Akropolis*, I, pp. xi ff.; Langlotz, *Zeitbestimmung*, pp. 98 ff.; Dinsmoor, *AJA*, XXXVIII (1934), 416 ff.

6. Beazley, *Kl.*; Beazley, pp. 120 ff., 952.

7. Cab. Méd. 535, 699, and other fragments. Hoppin, II, 137, 139; Pfuhl, fig. 371; Beazley, *Kl.*, pl. 8, pl. 10, no. 1, pls. 1–12, pl. 15, nos. 1–2, pl. 30, no. 5; p. 17 = discussion of inscription; Beazley, p. 128, no. 91.

8. Richter, *AJA*, XL (1936), 112 f.; Beazley, *Potter*, p. 42.

9. 2170. Hoppin, I, 303; Pfuhl, fig. 330; Richter, *loc. cit.*; Beazley, p. 123, no. 25.

10. The faint and fragmentary inscriptions on a neck amphora in Vienna were once read as signatures by Epiktetos: *Epi . . e . . . egr . ph . . . .* and *Ep. . . . . . . e . . . .*, and the scenes were attributed to the early Epiktetos (Schneider, *Archäologisch-epigraphische Mitteilungen aus Oesterreich*, V, 139, pl. 4; Hoppin, I, 334 f.; von Lücken, *GV*, pls. 83, 84). Dr. den Tex, however, informed me (in Athens in 1935) that these letters had recently been reëxamined by Dr. Wilhelm and other epigraphists and were considered to be meaningless. (I have not had the opportunity to examine the inscriptions myself.) The decoration—a boxer and a youth with a strigil—is "in the manner of the Kleophrades Painter, in his earliest period" (Beazley, p. 129, 1); or perhaps a very early work by the artist himself, before his style was formed (cf. Richter, *AJA*, XL (1936), 112 ff., fig. 15).

11. See note 6.

12. 07.286.79, with chariot; 16.71 with pankration. Cf. Beazley, *ABV*, p. 404.

13. 507. FR, pl. 103, II, 226, fig. 109; Pfuhl, fig. 377; Langlotz, *Würzburg*, no. 507, pl. 175; Beazley, p. 120, no. 1.

14. Pfuhl, 376; Beazley, *Kl.*, pl. I; Beazley, p. 120, no. 2.

15. 2305. Pfuhl, figs. 372–373; Swindler, *AP*, fig. 299; Beazley, *Kl.*, pl. 7; Beazley, p. 121, no. 3.

16. See note 10.

17. 1068. Flot, *CV*, pl. 13, 7–8, pl. 15, 4, pl. 16; Richter, *AJA*, XL (1936), 100 ff.; Beazley, p. 125, no. 58.

18. Louvre G 57. Pottier, *CV*, pl. 58, 2, 5, 8 and pl. 59, 2–3; Beazley, p. 125, no. 57.

19. A fragment from the Agora P 7241. Beazley, p. 125, no. 59.

20. Richter, *AJA*, XL (1936), 101–103; Beazley, p. 123, no. 28.

21. R C 4196. Pfuhl, fig. 375; Beazley, *Kl.*, pl. 16; Buschor, *Gr. V.*, fig. 195; Beazley, p. 123, no. 31.

22. 08.258.58. Beazley, *Kl.*, pl. 19; Richter and Hall, no. 12, pls. 12, 13, 170; Beazley, p. 123, no. 32.

23. See note 7 and Cab. Méd. 536, etc. FR, I, 264; Beazley, *Kl.*, pl. 9, pl. 10, no. 2, pls. 13, 14, pl. 15, nos. 8–12; Beazley, p. 128, no. 92.

24. 2344. FR, pls. 44, 45; Pfuhl, figs. 379, 380; Pfuhl, *Masterpieces*, figs. 44, 45; Swindler, *AP*, fig. 316; Beazley, *Kl.*, pls. 3, 5, 6; Beazley, p. 121, no. 5.

25. 13.233. Beazley, *Kl.*, pl. 29, 3–4; Richter and Hall, no. 13, pls. 14, 15, 169; Beazley, p. 122, no. 11.

26. E 270. Walters, *CV*, pl. 8, 2; Beazley, p. 122, no. 13.

27. 2422. FR, pl. 34; Pfuhl, fig. 378; Beazley, *Kl.*, pl. 27; Seltman, *AV*, pl. 21 a; Beazley, p. 126, no. 66.

28. 26040. Pfuhl, fig. 332; Giglioli, *CV*, pl. 6 and pl. 7, nos. 2–3; Beazley, p. 125, no. 56.

29. 149. Blinkenberg and Johansen, *CV*, pl. 133; Beazley, p. 123, no. 24.

30. Beazley, *JHS*, XXX (1910), 38 ff.

31. *Ibid.*, p. 47.

32. 2160. FR, pl. 159, 2, III, 255, fig. 121; von Lücken, *GV*, pls. 52, 53; Pfuhl, fig. 473; Beazley, *Berl.*, pls. 1–5, 22, no. 2; Neugebauer, *Führer*, II, pl. 43; Seltman, *AV*, pl. 23; Beazley, p. 131, no. 1.

33. Beazley, *Berl.;* Beazley, pp. 131 ff., 952. On black-figured Panathenaic amphorae by the Berlin Painter cf. Beazley, *AJA,* XLVII (1943), 449; *ABV,* pp. 407 f.

34. E 468. Beazley, *Berl.,* pls. 29–31; Beazley, p. 138, no. 102.

35. Beazley, *Berl.,* pls. 25, 26; Buschor, *Gr. V.,* fig. 191; Beazley, p. 140, no. 129.

36. 2311. Beazley, *Berl.,* pl. 6; Beazley, p. 132, no. 8.

37. 07.286.69. Richter and Hall, no. 16, pls. 18, 169; Beazley, p. 135, no. 56.

38. 10.210.19. Richter and Hall, no. 14, pls. 16, 172; Richter, *Greek Painting,*[2] p. 9; Beazley, p. 140, no. 132.

39. 22.139.32. Richter and Hall, no. 15, pls. 17, 177; Beazley, *Potter,* p. 31; Beazley, p. 142, no. 179.

40. Cf. 56.171.38. Beazley, p. 131, no. 3; D. von Bothmer, *MM Bull.,* March 1957, p. 176.

41. 41.162.17. Pease, *CV,* Gallatin Coll., p. 51, no. 2; Beazley, p. 135, no. 65.

42. 21.88.163. Beazley, p. 141, no. 162.

43. 41.162.139. Pease, *CV,* Gallatin Coll., p. 58, no. 5; Beazley, p. 142, no. 174.

44. Beazley, *JHS,* XLII (1922), 70 ff.

45. D. M. Robinson, *CV,* II, pl. 24, no. 1, pl. 25; Beazley, p. 147, no. 5.

46. Beazley, pp. 147 ff., 952.

47. On the Nikoxenos Painter cf. Beazley, *BSA,* XIX (1912–13), 243 ff., and *ABV,* p. 395.

48. 06.1021.99. Richter and Hall, no. 17, pls. 19, 169; Beazley, p. 147, no. 3.

49. XIII. 226–231 (tr. A. S. Way).

50. Beazley, pp. 153 ff., 953 f.

51. 124. Blinkenberg and Johansen, *CV,* pl. 134; Beazley, p. 155, no. 27.

52. For a detailed analysis of the style of the Eucharides Painter cf. Beazley, *BSA,* XVIII (1911–12), 228 ff.; XIX (1912–13), 245 ff.

53. On the black-figured Panathenaics by the Eucharides Painter cf. besides Beazley, pp. 157, 953, Beazley, *AJA,* XLVIII (1943), 446.

54. 07.286.78. Richter and Hall, no. 19, pls. 21, 22, 169; Beazley, p. 154, no. 9.

55. Acr. 806. Graef and Langlotz, *Akropolis,* II, pl. 72; Beazley, p. 169, no. 12.

56. Beazley, pp. 169 ff., 954.

57. G 197. FR, pl. 113 and II, 277, fig. 99; Beazley, p. 171, no. 47.

58. E 458. Beazley, *VA,* p. 49; Beazley, p. 171, no. 46.

59. 3982. D. Levi, *CV,* pl. 25, no. 1, pl. 26; Beazley, p. 172, no. 48.

60. 07.286.73. Richter and Hall, no. 20, pls. 23, 170; Beazley, p. 170, no. 15.

61. Beazley, pp. 174 ff., 954; Amyx, *AJA,* XLIX (1945), 508 ff.

62. Louvre G 234. Pfuhl, fig. 493; Beazley, p. 175, no. 11.

63. G R 578. Richter and Hall, no. 22, pls. 22, 173; Beazley, p. 175, no. 14.

64. 56. Beazley, *JHS,* XXXVI (1916), pl. 7, 2 and p. 133; Beazley, *VA,* p. 56; Beazley, p. 181, no. 67.

65. Beazley, pp. 177 ff., 954.

66. 12.229.13. Richter and Hall, no. 24, pl. 33; Beazley, p. 181, no. 71.

67. For a list of diskoi with owls cf. Beazley, *JHS,* XXVIII (1908), 316.

68. Inv. 3293. Blinkenberg and Johansen, *CV,* pl. 135; Beazley, p. 166, no. 29.

69. 21.88.1. Richter and Hall, no. 27, pl. 24; Beazley, p. 167, no. 32.

70. 20.244 and 11.212.7. Richter and Hall, nos. 25, 26, pls. 25–27, 169, 172; Beazley, p. 165, no. 8, p. 167, no. 37.

71. Beazley, pp. 192 ff.

72. *Ibid.,* pp. 195 ff., 954.

73. 125. Ussing, *To graeske Vaser,* pl. I, p. 7; Blinkenberg and Johansen, *CV,* pl. 130; Beazley, p. 193, no. 1.

74. 866. Hoppin, II, 442 f.; Giglioli, *CV,* pls. I and II, nos. 1–2; Beazley, p. 198, no. 39.

75. Beazley, p. 163, pp. 163 f., 185 ff., 190 f.

76. *Ibid.*, p. 163.

77. 41.162.101. Pease, *CV*, Gallatin Coll., pl. 51, no. 1; Beazley, p. 163, no. 3.

78. 56.171.53. Beazley, p. 191, no. 13; von Bothmer, *MM Bull.*, *March* 1957, p. 175.

79. Beazley, pp. 205 f., 955; Caskey and Beazley, *AVP*, II, 41 ff.

80. Petit Palais 315. Beazley, *JHS*, XXXIII (1913), 106; Plaoutine, *CV*, pl. 19, nos. 1–6, pl. 20, no. 3; Beazley, p. 205, no. 11.

81. 13.227.16. Richter and Hall, no. 28, pls. 28, 175; Beazley, p. 206, no. 15.

82. 41.162.27. Gallatin, *CV*, pl. 18, no. 1; Beazley, p. 206, no. 18.

83. 13.188. Beazley, *JHS*, XXXIII (1913), pl. 11, p. 110; Beazley, p. 205, no. 2.

84. Beazley, pp. 206 f.

85. 03.816. Beazley, p. 206, no. 1.

86. 27.122.6. Richter and Hall, no. 29, pls. 29, 175; Beazley, p. 207, no. 14.

87. 25.78.2. Richter and Hall, no. 30, pls. 29, 175; Beazley, p. 207, no. 13.

88. 00.340. Beazley, *VA*, p. 68; Beazley, p. 207, no. 10.

89. Beazley, pp. 431 ff., 968; Caskey and Beazley, *AVP*, II, 41 ff.

90. 15.005. Luce, *CV*, pl. 18; Beazley, p. 431, no. 1.

91. Beazley in his *Att. V.* (pp. 132 ff.) placed the Providence Painter in the Ripe Archaic period, in his *Attic Red-Figure Vase-Painters* (pp. 431 ff.) he has put him in the Early Free period.

92. 07.286.67. Beazley, *VA*, p. 75, fig. 44; Richter and Hall, no. 31, pls. 30, 175; Beazley, p. 435, no. 69.

93. 41.162.18. Pease, *CV*, Gallatin Coll., pl. 58, no. 4; Beazley, p. 434, no. 57.

94. 06.1021.114. Richter and Hall, no. 32, pls. 31, 169; Beazley, p. 432, no. 29.

95. 41.162.117. Gallatin, *CV*, pl. 26, no. 8; Beazley, p. 435, no. 79.

96. Beazley, pp. 470 ff., 960; Haspels, *Bf. Lekythoi*, pp. 157 ff. Haspels envisages the possibility that the Bowdoin Painter is the Athena Painter (see p. 75) in a late stage.

97. Nos. 112 and 133 in Beazley's list. The pyxis in Bowdoin with an archer, after which the artist was originally named, is now attributed by Beazley to the Heraion Painter, cf. Beazley, p. 119, no. 10.

98. 06.1021.90. Richter and Hall, no. 34, pls. 33, 175; Beazley, p. 473, no. 83.

99. Haspels, *Bf. Lekythoi*, pp. 94 ff. and 232 ff.; Beazley, p. 203.

100. Haspels, *op. cit.*, pp. 94 ff. and 225 ff.; Beazley, p. 203 f.

101. Haspels, *op. cit.*, pp. 141 ff. and 254 ff. (See also my note 96.)

102. *Ibid.*, pp. 130 ff.

103. *Ibid.*, pp. 141 ff., 249 ff.

104. 06.1070. Fairbanks, *AWL*, I, pl. 4; Richter, *MM Handbook*,[6] p. 129, fig. 85; Haspels, *op. cit.*, p. 235, no. 71; Beazley, p. 203, no. 2.

105. 41.162.178. Pease, *CV*, Gallatin Coll., pl. 39, no. 2.

106. 25.70.2. *MM Bulletin*, XX (1925), 300, fig. 4; Haspels, *op. cit.*, p. 233, no. 15.

107. 34.11.6.

108. 06.1021.49 and 17.230.9. Alexander, *Athletics*, p. 25; Haspels, *op. cit.*, pp. 250 f., nos. 22, 43.

109. 41.162.29, 30, 34, 35. Pease, *CV*, Gallatin Coll., pl. 44, nos. 1, 2, pl. 45, nos. 1, 2; Haspels, *op. cit.*, pp. 225 f., nos. 3, 5, 6, 10.

110. 23.160.87. Richter, *MM Bulletin*, XXV (1930), 136 f.; Haspels, *op. cit.*, p. 228, no. 43.

111. Beazley, *Potter*, p. 36; Beazley, pp. 209 ff., 955; Caskey and Beazley, *AVP*, II, 23 ff.

112. *Ibid.*, pp. 209 f., 955.

113. 10.179. Beazley, *VA*, p. 82; Pfuhl, fig. 414; Beazley, p. 212, no. 1.

114. G 104. FR, pls. 5, 141; Hoppin, I, 399; Pfuhl, fig. 398; Pfuhl, *Masterpieces*, fig. 48; Swindler, *AP*, pl. 9; Buschor, *Gr. V.*, fig. 169; Beazley, p. 214, no. 10.

115. E 44. FR, pl. 23; Hoppin, I, 389; Pfuhl, figs. 401, 402; Pfuhl, *Masterpieces*, fig. 49; Beazley, p. 214, no. 11.

116. 95.27. Hoppin, I, 387; Pfuhl, figs. 409–411; Beazley, p. 215, no. 31.

117. Hoppin, I, 395 (with restorations); Beazley, p. 215, no. 27.

118. Beazley, p. 215, no. 25.

119. 12.231.2. Hoppin, I, 393; Pfuhl, fig. 400; Richter and Hall, no. 39, pls. 37, 38, 39; Beazley, p. 215, no. 28.

120. For other possibilities—Philoktetes, Hylas, Oionos—cf. Richter and Hall, p. 60, note 2.

121. 2322. Neugebauer, *Führer*, II, pl. 55, no. 2; Beazley, p. 216, no. 33.

122. D. M. Robinson, *CV*, II, pls. 8, 9; Beazley, *VA*, p. 85; Beazley, p. 214, no. 12.

123. Beazley, pp. 245 ff., 956.

124. *Ibid.*, p. 245.

125. G 152. FR, pl. 25; Hoppin, I, 118; Pfuhl, figs. 419–420, 428; Pfuhl, *Masterpieces*, fig. 52; Swindler, *AP*, fig. 311; Buschor, *Gr. V.*, fig. 173; Beazley, p. 245, no. 1.

126. 2645. FR, pl. 49, I, 250; Buschor, *Gr. V.*, fig. 175; Beazley, p. 246, no. 2.

127. 479. FR, pl. 50, I, 250; Hoppin, I, 121; Pfuhl, figs. 421–423; Pfuhl, *Masterpieces*, figs. 53, 54; Langlotz, *Würzburg*, no. 479, pls. 145–149, 164; Seltman, *AV*, pl. 26; Buschor, *Gr. V.*, figs. 176, 177; Beazley, p. 248, no. 27.

128. E 65. FR, pl. 47, no. 1; Hoppin, I, 110; Pfuhl, fig. 424; Seltman, *AV*, pl. 25; Beazley, p. 247, no. 13.

129. 95.36. Beazley, *VA*, p. 90, fig. 57; Pfuhl, fig. 433; Pfuhl, *Masterpieces*, fig. 55; Caskey and Beazley, *AVP*, pl. 6; Beazley, p. 254, no. 136.

130. 12.234.5. Beazley, *VA*, p. 92 and *JHS*, XLIX (1929), 57, fig. 9; Richter and Hall, no. 43, pls. 43, 178; Beazley, p. 254, no. 137.

131. 29.131.4. Richter and Hall, no. 42, pls. 42, 178; Richter, *Greek Painting*,[2] p. 11; Beazley, p. 253, no. 132.

132. 28.57.12. Richter and Hall, no. 40, pls. 40, 175; Beazley, p. 255, no. 156.

133. 09.221.43. Richter and Hall, no. 41, pls. 41, 175; Beazley, p. 255, no. 155.

134. 16.174.43. Richter and Hall, no. 44, pls. 44, 180; Beazley, p. 251, no. 75.

135. Beazley, *Att. V.*, pp. 183 f.

136. As I pointed out in Richter and Hall, p. 69. In Beazley's new list in *Attic Red-figure Vase-Painters*, they are also assigned to the Brygos Painter himself; see his remarks on p. 245.

137. 13.189. Caskey and Beazley, *AVP*, pl. 10, no. 29, p. 25; Beazley, p. 256, no. 161.

138. 318. Beazley, *CV*, pl. 38, no. 11; Beazley, p. 256, no. 162.

139. 25.189.1. Richter and Hall, no. 48, pls. 46, 175; Beazley, p. 256, no. 160.

140. On Nikai with *akroteria* cf. Wade-Gery, *JHS*, LIII (1933), 99 ff. A Nike holding an *akroterion* appears also on coins of Kyzikos, Knidos, Syracuse, etc., which were probably struck in celebration of specific victories; cf. Brett, "The Aphlaston, Symbol of Naval Victory," *Transactions of the International Numismatic Congress*, London, June 30–July 6, 1936, pp. 23 ff.

141. G R 577. Richter and Hall, no. 49, pls. 47, 180; Beazley, p. 253, no. 117. For other typical "late Brygan" pictures in New York see Richter and Hall, nos. 26, 47, 50, and Beazley, p. 255, no. 152.

142. Beazley, p. 301.

143. *Ibid.*, pp. 301 ff., 958.

144. 13.186. FR, pl. 85; Hoppin, II, p. 53; Pfuhl, figs. 435–436; Seltman, *AV*, pl. 28 b; Beazley, p. 301, no. 1.

145. Acr. 560. Graef and Langlotz, *Akropolis*, II, pl. 43; Beazley, p. 314, no. 239.

146. G 146. Hoppin, II, p. 81; Beazley, p. 301, no. 2.

147. E 140. FR, pl. 161, III, 259; Hoppin, II, p. 61; Pfuhl, fig. 437; Seltman, *AV*, pl. 28 a; Beazley, p. 301, no. 3.

148. 2290 (and frgt. in Villa Giulia). Hoppin, II, 41; Pfuhl, fig. 438; Pfuhl, *Masterpieces*, fig. 58; Swindler, *AP*, fig. 313; Neugebauer, *Führer*, II, pl. 51; Buschor, *Gr. V.*, fig. 174; Beazley, p. 304, no. 37.

149. G R 1120. Beazley, *VA*, p. 101; Pfuhl, fig. 439; Richter and Hall, no. 56, pls. 57, 180; Beazley, p. 314, no. 229.

150. 20.246. Richter and Hall, no. 53, pls. 50, 53, 54, 180; Beazley, p. 306, no. 83.

151. 12.231.1 and 08.258.57, both signed by Hieron. Hoppin, II, 68 f. and 66 f.; Richter and Hall, no. 53, pls. 49, 51, 180, and no. 54, pls. 50, 55, 56; Beazley, pp. 307, 310, nos. 102 and 144.

152. 06.1152. Richter and Hall, no. 55, pls. 57, 59, 60, 180; Beazley, p. 304, no. 42.

153. Herodotos II. 134 f. See Richter and Hall, p. 75, note 1.

154. Beazley, pp. 279 ff., 957, 968.

155. A 718. FR, pl. 74, no. 1; Hoppin, I, 233; Pfuhl, fig. 453; Pfuhl, *Masterpieces*, fig. 60; Mayence, *CV*, pls. 5, 6; Beazley, p. 292, no. 197.

156. 15375. Herbig, *AA*, 1928, col. 571; Papaspyridi and Kyparissis, *Arch. Delt.*, 1927–28, pls. 4–5, suppl. plate, pp. 94, 102; Beazley, p. 293, no. 210.

157. 2286. Hoppin, I, 217; Pfuhl, fig. 465; Beazley, *Potter*, pp. 39 ff.; Beazley, p. 241, no. 27.

158. Beazley, pp. 239 ff., 956. The only example by the Triptolemos Painter in New York is the athlete on the fragmentary kylix 14.105.7.

159. G 187. Pottier, *CV*, pl. 20, nos. 3, 6; Beazley, p. 239, no. 2.

160. Beazley, pp. 297 f.

161. Beazley, *JHS*, XXXIX (1919), 84 ff.; Beazley, p. 279.

162. Oest. Mus. 324. FR, pl. 53; Hoppin, I, 266 f.; von Lücken, *GV*, pls. 100, 101; Pfuhl, figs. 455, 456; Pfuhl, *Masterpieces*, figs. 61–63; Beazley, p. 280, no. 6.

163. 00.338. Hoppin, I, 229; Pfuhl, figs. 451, 452; Beazley, p. 280, no. 8.

164. G 115. Hoppin, I, 245; Pfuhl, fig. 466; Pfuhl, *Masterpieces*, fig. 64; Beazley, p. 285, no. 70.

165. E 768. FR, pl. 48; Hoppin, I, 242; Walters, *CV*, pl. 105; Buschor, *Gr. V.*, figs. 183, 184; Beazley, p. 292, no. 201.

166. 52.11.4. *MM Bull.*, 1952, pp. 100 f. Though the subject—a conversation scene—is usual, the execution is extraordinarily fine.

167. 23.160.54. Richter and Hall, no. 59, pls. 61, 63, 64, 181; Richter, *Greek Painting*,[2] p. 12; Beazley, p. 289, no. 152.

168. 00.343. Pfuhl, fig. 470; Beazley, p. 288, no. 118.

169. 2647. Buschor, *Jb.*, XXXI (1916), pl. 3, pp. 84, 85; Beazley, p. 287, no. 112.

170. Beazley, pp. 219 ff., 955; Caskey and Beazley, *AVP*, II, 33 ff.

171. G 105. Hoppin, I, 401; Pfuhl, fig. 404; Beazley, p. 219, no. 1.

172. 89. Hoppin, I, 403; Beazley, p. 222, no. 56.

173. Beazley, *Potter*, p. 36; Beazley, p. 209.

174. D. K. Hill, *AJA*, XLIX (1945), 503 ff.; Beazley, pp. 226 ff., 955.

175. 48. Harald Hofmann, *AA*, 1904, col. 53; Beazley, p. 227, no. 17.

176. Faina, 48. Philippart, *Collections de céramique grecque en Italie*, II, pl. 12, 1; Beazley, p. 227, no. 2.

177. 16.174.71. Richter and Hall, no. 36, pls. 35, 179.

178. 14.105.9. Richter and Hall, no. 37, pl. 36; Beazley, p. 227, no. 8.

179. Beazley, pp. 230 ff., 955 f.

180. 2325. FR, pl. 162, III, 264; Neugebauer, *Führer*, II, pl. 54, no. 2; Beazley, p. 230, no. 1.

181. G R 575. Richter and Hall, no. 61, pls. 62, 181; Beazley, p. 233, no. 72.

182. 16.174.42. Richter and Hall, no. 62, pls. 65, 181; Beazley, p. 232, no. 41.

183. G R 567. Beazley, p. 233, no. 59.

184. 41.162.1. Gallatin, *CV*, pls. 10–12; Beazley, p. 299, no. 1.

185. Beazley, p. 299.

186. 41.162.6. Pease, *CV*, Gallatin Coll., pl. 47, no. 5, pl. 49, no. 2; Pfuhl, fig. 412 (restored); Beazley, p. 300, no. 2.

187. Beazley, pp. 300, 957.

188. *Ibid.*, pp. 263 ff., 956.

189. 2294. FR, pl. 135; Neugebauer, *Führer*, II, pl. 53; Beazley, p. 263, no. 1.

190. 2640. FR, pl. 86, II, 132; Buschor, *Gr. V.*, fig. 179; Beazley, p. 264, no. 20.

191. 31.19.2. Dohan, *Museum Journal*, XXIII (1932), 33 ff.; Beazley, p. 264, no. 21.

192. G R 1075.

193. 07.156.8. Beazley, p. 264, no. 5.

194. E 76. Hartwig, *Gr. M.*, pls. 41, 42, no. 1; Beazley, p. 266, no. 1.

195. Beazley, pp. 266 ff., 956 f.

196. 27.74. Richter and Hall, no. 51, pls. 47, 48, 180; Beazley, p. 267, no. 10.

197. According to a recent interpretation by Professor Bieber, the young men are the members of a chorus, probably a tragic chorus, being trained for some public performance, cf. *AJA*, XLV (1941), 529 ff.

198. 1900.518. Beazley, p. 267, no. 8.

198a. 53.11.4. *MM Bull.*, Oct. 1954, pp. 62 f.

199. Beazley, pp. 274 ff., 957.

200. 573. Gerhard, *Trinkschalen*, pls. A, B; Cook, *Zeus*, III, pl. 3; Beazley, p. 274, no. 1.

201. Beazley, pp. 271 f., 957.

202. 2296. von Lücken, *GV*, pl. 90, ho. 2, pls. 45, 46; Beazley, p. 271, no. 1.

III. EARLY FREE STYLE

1. Overbeck, *Schriftquellen*, pp. 187 ff.; A. Reinach, *Recueil Milliet*, I, 86 ff.

2. *De architect.* VII. praef. 11: Agatharchus Athenis Aeschylo docente tragoediam scaenam fecit et de ea commentarium reliquit. Ex eo moniti Democritus et Anaxagoras de eadem re scripserunt, quemadmodum oporteat ad aciem oculorum radiorumque extentionem certo loco centro constituto lineas ratione naturali respondere, uti de incerta re certae imagines aedificiorum in scaenarum picturis redderent speciem et, quae in directis planisque frontibus sint figurata, alia abscendentia, alia prominentia esse videantur (ed. Rose, 1899).

3. The translation is based on that of Professor M. H. Morgan (1926), with a few changes. Certo loco centro is, I imagine, "the station point." De incerta re, M. J. Milne suggests, should be interpreted as "a visual impression difficult to grasp mentally"; the reading incertae imagines proposed by Grander (*Journal of the Royal Institute of British Architects*, XXXVIII, 1930–31, 367 and pp. xix f. of vol. I of his edition of Vitruvius in the Loeb Series), while ingenious, rests on too slight a foundation to carry conviction ("a flourish not unlike the symbol for *m*" on the *e* in *re* which led Mr. Granger to suggest "that the scribe of H found *in* before him and read it as *m*"). For a discussion of the whole passage and of Vitruvius I. 2. 2, which must be taken in conjunction with it, cf. my article on Perspective in *Scritti in onore di Bartolomeo Nogara*, 1937, pp. 381 ff.

4. FR, pls. 6, 55.

5. Cf., e.g., Philippart, *CAB*.

6. Beazley, p. 924.

7. Studniczka, *Jb.*, II (1887), 162; Kirchner in Pauly-Wissowa, VII, *s.v.* Glaukon, col. 1402, no. 4; Kirchner, *Prosopographia Attica*, no. 3027.

8. Beazley, *Panm.;* Beazley, pp. 361 ff., 959.

9. 2417. FR, pl. 16, I, 77; Pfuhl, fig. 771; Beazley, p. 365, no. 55.

10. Beazley, *Panm.*, pl. 17, no. 2; Beazley, p. 366, no. 61.

11. 10.185. FR, pl. 115; Beazley, *VA*, p. 113; Pfuhl, figs. 475, 476, 783; Beazley, *Panm.*, pls. 1–4; Seltman, *AV*, pl. 24 a; Buschor, *Gr. V.*, fig. 199; Beazley, p. 361, no. 1.

12. 9683. Beazley, *Panm.*, pls. 7–10, 11, no. 1; Beazley, p. 364, no. 41.

13. 16.72. Beazley, *Panm.*, pl. 25, no. 3; Richter and Hall, no. 64, pls. 67, 68, 170; Beazley, p. 362, no. 8.

14. 20.245. Beazley, *Panm.*, pl. 28, no. 2; Richter and Hall, no. 66, pls. 70, 72, 169; Beazley, p. 363, no. 23. Cf. the remarks on the Greek kithara by Gombosi in "New Light on Ancient Greek Music," a paper read at the International Congress of Musicology held at New York, Sept. 11–16, 1939.

15. See p. 69, fig. 48; Beazley, *Berl.*, pl. 21; Beazley, p. 131, no. 3.

16. 23.160.55. Beazley, *Panm.*, pl. 18, 2; Richter and Hall, no. 65, pls. 69, 177; Beazley, p. 367, no. 76.

17. 10.184. Beazley, *Panm.*, pl. 18, no. 1; FR, pl. 159, no. 1; Beazley, p. 364, no. 32.

18. G R 585. Richter and Hall, no. 67, pls. 69, 178; Beazley, p. 367, no. 84.

19. V 778 (2554). Beazley, *Panm.*, pls. 31, 32, 27, no. 2; Bovio Marconi, *CV*, pl. 34; Beazley, p. 361, no. 2.

20. Cf. on these Beazley, *JHS*, XXXII (1912), 363 ff.

21. Beazley, pp. 370 ff.

22. 9.17. Lamb, *CV*, pl. 33, no. 2, pl. 34, no. 4; Beazley, p. 371, no. 21.

23. 06.1021.152. Richter and Hall, no. 69, pl. 72; Beazley, p. 370, no. 11. 41.162.86. Pease, *CV*, Gallatin Coll., pl. 57, no. 1; Beazley, p. 371, no. 20.

24. Beazley, pp. 373 ff., 959.

25. Nos. 34 and 59 in Beazley's list.

26. FR, II, 307, fig. 102; Richter, *Craft*, p. 71; Beazley, *Potter*, pp. 11 ff.; Beazley, p. 376, no. 61.

27. 41.162.60. Gallatin, *CV*, pl. 23, 3–4; Beazley, p. 373, no. 5.

28. Beazley, pp. 377 ff., 959, 968.

29. Gabrici, *Vasi greci inediti dei Musei di Palermo e Agrigento*, fig. 9; Beazley, p. 380, no. 45.

30. E 171. Walters, *CV*, pl. 75, no. 3, pl. 76, no. 2; Beazley, p. 381, no. 63.

31. 15.27. Richter and Hall, no. 70, pls. 73, 170; Beazley, p. 378, no. 9.

32. Cf. Beazley, *Panm.*, p. 13, note 18; Richter and Hall, p. 61. On the hydria in the Louvre G 50 (Pottier, II, pl. 94) the "Egyptians" are depicted as Greeks, but the subject is not certain.

33. Beazley, pp. 384 ff., 959.

34. 2322. Pfuhl, fig. 514; Swindler, *AP*, fig. 363; FR, pl. 138, no. 1; Beazley, p. 384, no. 4.

35. E 284. Hoppin, II, 376, 377; Walters, *CV*, pl. 17, no. 3; Beazley, p. 384, no. 7.

36. 25.28. Richter and Hall, no. 71, pls. 74, 172; Beazley, p. 386, no. 39.

37. I. 33 ff.

38. 06.1021.144. Richter and Hall, no. 72, pls. 75, 173; Beazley, p. 385, no. 9.

39. 41.162.69. Gallatin, *CV*, pl. 23, 1–2; Beazley, p. 385, no. 22.

40. Beazley, pp. 582 ff., 962.

41. 2688. FR, pls. 6, 56, nos. 1–3, I, 31; Pfuhl, fig. 501; Pfuhl, *Masterpieces*, fig. 71; Swindler, *AP*, pl. 11, fig. 373; Seltman, *AV*, pl. 31 a; Diepolder, *P*, pls. 13–15, 12, no. 2; Buschor, *Gr. V.*, fig. 203; Beazley, p. 582, no. 1.

42. 2689. FR, pl. 55, I, 279; Pfuhl, fig. 502; Pfuhl, *Masterpieces*, fig. 72; Diepolder, *P*, pls. 16, 17, no. 1, pl. 18; Beazley, p. 583, no. 2.

43. 07.286.36. Diepolder, *P*, pl. 11, no. 2, pl. 12, no. 1; Richter and Hall, pl. 77; Beazley, p. 588, no. 112.

44. The alternative suggested by H. R. W. Smith in *AJA*, XLI (1937), 342, of Eros and a youth is accepted by many (cf. Rumpf, *M. u. Z.*, p. 101).

45. 28.167. Diepolder, *P*, pl. 19; Richter and Hall, no. 74, pls. 76, 178; Richter, *Greek Painting*,[2] p. 14; Beazley, p. 588, no. 114.

46. G R 597. Richter and Hall, no. 75, pls. 78, 181; Beazley, p. 587, no. 98.

47. 06.1079. Richter and Hall, no. 77, pls. 79, 178; Beazley, p. 588, no. 105.

48. 41.162.9. Gallatin, *CV*, pls. 19–20; Diepolder, *P*, pl. 31, no. 1; Beazley, p. 584, no. 25.

49. 22.139.29. Richter and Hall, no. 76, pls. 78, 178; Beazley, p. 589, no. 5.

50. Beazley, pp. 574 ff., 962; Diepolder, *Der Pistoxenos Maler*, 1954.

51. Hoppin, II, 373; Pfuhl, fig. 471; Pfuhl, *Masterpieces*, figs. 66 and 67; Swindler, *AP*, fig. 320; FR, pl. 163, no. 1; Seltman, *AV*, pl. 29; Diepolder, *P*, pl. 4; Buschor, *Gr. V.*, figs. 181, 182; Beazley, p. 576, no. 16.

52. Hoppin, II, 175; Beazley, p. 576, no. 18.

53. Nos. 1, 2, 4 in Beazley's list.

54. Acr. 439. Hoppin, I, 381; Pfuhl, fig. 416; Pfuhl, *Masterpieces*, fig. 69; Graef and Langlotz, *Akropolis*, II, pls. 36, 35, no. 2; Seltman, *AV*, pl. 30 a; Diepolder, *P*, pls. 5, 17, nos. 2, 3; Buschor, *Gr. V.*, fig. 196; Beazley, p. 575, no. 2.

55. D 2. Pfuhl, fig. 498; Pfuhl, *Masterpieces*, fig. 70; Swindler, *AP*, fig. 286; Diepolder, *P*, pl. 6; Buschor, *Gr. V.*, fig. 197; Beazley, p. 575, no. 3.

56. 07.286.63. Beazley, p. 575, no 10.

57. *Ibid.*, pp. 589 ff., 962.

58. 39.11.8. Richter, *AJA*, XLIV (1940), 182, fig. 7, p. 183; Beazley, p. 606, no. 21. The interpretation of the scene as the Birth of Aphrodite is Beazley's.

59. 06.1021.167. Richter and Hall, no. 78, pls. 80, 181; Beazley, p. 597, no. 4.

60. 143. Kraiker, *Die rotfiguren attischen Vasen*, pl. 25; Beazley, p. 591, no. 43.

61. 26.60.79. Richter and Hall, no. 79, pl. 81; Beazley, p. 589, no. 1.

62. pp. 581 f. On collaboration of vase painters in general cf. Beazley, *Potter*, pp. 27 ff.

63. Beazley, pp. 418 ff.; Webster, *N*.

64. G 341. FR, pls. 108, 165, II, 244, 251; Pfuhl, fig. 492; Pfuhl, *Masterpieces*, fig. 77; Swindler, *AP*, figs. 319, 349, 351, 352, 363; Seltman, *AV*, pl. 33; Webster, *N*, pls. 2–5; Buschor, *Gr. V.*, fig. 215; Beazley, p. 419, no. 20.

65. 42.11.43. Arndt in *Br. Br.*, pls. 763–765; Richter, *MM Bulletin*, new series, I (1942–1943), 206 ff.

66. 41.162.98. Pease, *CV*, Gallatin Coll., pl. 56, no. 1; Beazley, p. 423, no. 65.

67. G R 579. Richter and Hall, no. 97, pls. 100, 169; Beazley, p. 422, no. 50.

68. 07.286.66. Richter and Hall, no. 127, pls. 126, 170; Richter, *Greek Painting*,[2]

68a. 56.171.44 and 51. D. von Bothmer, *MM Bull.*, March 1957, pp. 175, 177.

69. Beazley, pp. 412 ff., 427 ff., 960. For illustrations cf. especially Löwy, *Polygnot*.

70. 07.286.84. FR, pls. 116, 117; Pfuhl, fig. 506; Swindler, *AP*, fig. 350; Richter and Hall, no. 98, pls. 97, 98, 171; Richter, *Gk. Painting*,[4] p. 13; Beazley, p. 427, no. 1.

71. Beazley, p. 427.

72. 07.286.86. FR, pls. 118, 119; Pfuhl, fig. 507; Swindler, *AP*, figs. 325, 326; Richter and Hall, no. 99, pls. 99, 170; Richter, *Greek Painting*,[2] p. 13; Beazley, p. 429, no. 3.

73. Beazley, pp. 401 ff., 959 f.

74. 909. FR, pls. 17, 18; Giglioli, *CV*, pls. 21, 22; Beazley, p. 401, no. 1.

75. E 492; Beazley, *VA*, p. 153; Beazley, p. 402, no. 15.

76. 208. Beazley, *RM*, XXVII (1912), pl. 10, 2 and Beilage to p. 286, no. 1; Beazley, p. 401, no. 3.

77. 24.97.96. Richter and Hall, no. 100, pls. 101, 171; Beazley, p. 402, no. 16.

78. 06.1021.176. Richter and Hall, no. 101, pls. 102, 173; Beazley, p. 402, no. 28.

79. 06.1021.134. Fairbanks, *AWL*, I, 158, no. 4 a; Beazley, p. 407, no. 1.

80. For a detailed analysis of this painter's style cf. Beazley, *RM*, XXVII (1912), 291 ff.

81. Beazley, pp. 407 ff., 960.

82. Frickenhaus, *Berliner Winckelmannsprogramm*, LXXII (1912), pl. IV; Beazley, p. 407, no. 1.

83. 06.1021.190, 06.1021.192. Richter and Hall, nos. 102, 103, pls. 104, 105, 172; Beazley, p. 409, nos. 26, 27.

84. 17.230.23. Beazley, p. 408, no. 17.

85. Beazley, pp. 410 f.

86. 07.286.85. Richter and Hall, no. 109, pls. 109, 110, 171; Beazley, p. 410, no. 1.

87. Beazley, pp. 521 ff., 537, bottom.

88. 22.139.72. Richter and Hall, no. 106, pls. 107, pl. 181; Beazley, p. 521, no. 1.

89. Caskey, *Catalogue of Sculpture*, no. 17.

90. Beazley, pp. 523 ff.

91. 17.230.10. Richter and Hall, no. 105, pls. 106, 181; Beazley, p. 524, no. 25.

92. Beazley, pp. 526 ff., 961.

93. G 401. Pottier, pl. 141; Beazley, p. 526, no. 5.

94. 06.1021.177. Richter and Hall, no. 107, pls. 107, 181; Beazley, p. 531, no. 95.

95. Beazley, pp. 525 f.

96. 06.1101. Richter and Milne, fig. 131; Beazley, p. 525, no. 3.

97. Beazley, pp. 524 f.

98. 01.8097. *Jb.*, XVII (1902), pl. 2; Beazley, p. 524, no. 2.

99. 41.162.5. Pease, *CV*, Gallatin Coll., pl. 50, no. 2; Beazley, p. 524, no. 3.

100. Beazley, pp. 542 ff.

101. 98.931. Hoppin, II, 49; Pfuhl, fig. 447; Beazley, p. 542, no. 2.

102. 95.28. Hoppin, II, 47; Pfuhl, fig. 449; Beazley, p. 542, no. 1. Fragments in the Villa Giulia and Florence belong to this cup.

103. H. R. W. Smith, *CV*, University of California, p. 41; Beazley, pp. 538 f.

104. C A 2183. Pottier, *Mon. Piot*, XIII (1906), 149 ff., pls. 13, 14; Beazley, *BSA*, XXIX (1927–28), 206 f.; Beazley, p. 538, no. 1.

105. E 66. FR, I, 244, pl. 47, no. 2; Beazley, p. 538, no. 4.

106. 98.932. Hoppin, II, 51; Caskey and Beazley, *AVP*, p. 15, fig. 13 (shape); Beazley, p. 550, no. 1.

107. Beazley, pp. 550 ff.

108. 1708. Heydemann, *Gr. V.*, pl. I, 2; Beazley, p. 552, no. 31.

109. F. P. Johnson, *AJA*, XLIX (1945), 491 ff.; Beazley, pp. 317 ff., 958.

110. 2413. FR, pl. 137, III, 95; Beazley, p. 318, no. 18.

111. 41.162.19. Gallatin, *CV*, pl. 16, no. 2, pl. 17; Beazley, p. 321, no. 77.

112. 26.60.77. Richter and Hall, no. 85, pls. 89, 175; Beazley, p. 321, no. 83.

113. Beazley, pp. 437 ff., 960.

114. 09.221.41 and 41.162.21. Richter and Hall, no. 33, pls. 32, 169; Gallatin, *CV*, pl. 15; Beazley, p. 437, nos. 5 and 1.

115. 41.162.15. Gallatin, *CV*, pl. 16, 1; Swindler, *AJA*, XXVIII (1924), 282 f.; Beazley, p. 439, no. 34.

116. Beazley, pp. 441 f., 960.

117. 41.162.134. Pease, *CV*, Gallatin Coll., pl. 52, no. 1; Beazley, p. 442, no. 9.

118. Beazley, pp. 328 ff.
119. 41.162.155. Gallatin, *CV*, pl. 18, no. 2; Beazley, p. 329, no. 13.
120. Beazley, pp. 443 ff.
121. 41.162.56. Gallatin, *CV*, pl. 13; Beazley, p. 443, no. 4.
122. 07.286.44. Fairbanks, *AWL*, II, pl. 32, 1; Beazley, p. 446, no. 54.
123. 06.1021.115, G R 592, 41.162.131. Richter and Hall, nos. 94, 95, pls. 95, 169; Pease, *CV*, Gallatin Coll., pl. 54, no. 2.
124. Beazley, pp. 35 ff.
125. 06.1021.151. Richter and Milne, fig. 8; Richter and Hall, no. 91, pls. 93, 169; Beazley, p. 352, no. 10.
126. 26.60.80. Richter and Milne, fig. 125; Richter and Hall, no. 92, pls. 93, 177; Beazley, p. 353, no. 24.
127. 41.162.10. Pease, *CV*, Gallatin Coll., pl. 57, no. 2; Beazley, p. 351, no. 4.
128. Beazley, p. 351.
129. 41.162.33. Gallatin, *CV*, pl. 29, nos. 1, 2; Beazley, p. 568, no. 4.
130. Beazley, p. 568.
131. *Ibid.*, pp. 330 ff., 958.
132. G 161. FR, pl. 104; Swindler, *AP*, figs. 328, 329; Buschor, *Gr. V.*, fig. 201; Beazley, p. 330, no. 1.
133. Beazley, pp. 346 ff.
134. 07.286.74. Richter and Hall, no. 87, pls. 90, 91, and 170; Beazley, p. 346, no. 1.
135. 34.11.7. Richter and Hall, no. 88, pls. 90, 170; Beazley, p. 347, no. 22.
136. Beazley, pp. 335 ff.
137. 29.131.7. Richter and Hall, no. 80, pls. 82, 88, 170; Beazley, p. 336, no. 2. Formerly attributed to the Painter of the Brussels oinochoai.
138. 1170. Zschietzschmann, *AM*, LIII (1928), Beilagen 16–17, no. 96; Swindler, *AP*, fig. 322; Beazley, p. 336, no. 11.
139. 07.286.70. Richter and Hall, no. 81, pls. 83, 84, 173; Beazley, p. 336, no. 13.
140. Beazley, pp. 356 ff., 958.
141. Inv. 30035. Beazley, *VA*, p. 137; Licht, *Sittengeschichte*, I, 283; Beazley, p. 358, no. 46.
142. 41.162.16. Gallatin, *CV*, pl. 22; Beazley, p. 356, no. 1.
143. Beazley, pp. 326 ff., 958.
144. Tillyard, *The Hope Vases*, pl. 8, no. 84; Beazley, p. 327, no. 25.
145. 17.230.37. Richter and Hall, no. 82, pls. 85, 86, 173; Beazley, p. 326, no. 1; Caskey and Beazley, *AVP*, II, 12.
146. 18.74.1 and 41.162.20. Richter and Hall, no. 83, pls. 87, 173; Gallatin, *CV*, pl. 14; Beazley, p. 326, nos. 2, 8; D. von Bothmer, *MM Bull.*, March 1957, p. 175.
147. Beazley, pp. 450 ff., 960.
148. D 5, 6, 7. Hoppin, II, 429, 430; Pfuhl, figs. 526, 527, 528; Pfuhl, *Masterpieces*, figs. 82–84; Swindler, *AP*, fig. 288; Seltman, *AV*, pl. 32 b, c; Beazley, p. 450, nos. 2, 1, 3.
149. On the spelling of this name cf. Beazley, *AJA*, XXXIX (1935), 483.
150. E 804. FR, pl. 136, no. 2; Walters, *CV*, pls. 26, 27; Beazley, p. 452, no. 15. Two other such magnified knuckle bones (*astragaloi*) are in the Villa Giulia Museum (decorated by the Syriskos Painter, see p. 72) and in New York (Richter, *MM Bulletin*, XXXVI [1941], 122 f.). A fragment of a third has recently been found in the Athenian Agora.
151. Nos. 7–13 in Beazley's list.
152. Czartoryski Coll. Hoppin, II, 432; Beazley, *V. Pol.*, pls. 15, 16, Bulas, *CV*, pl. 35; Seltman, *AV*, pl. 32 a; Peredolski, *AM*, LIII (1928), pp. 9 ff.; Beazley, p. 451, nos. 6, 12.

153. Beazley, pp. 457 f.

154. 38.11.2. Richter, *MM Bulletin*, XXXIII (1938), 225 ff., figs. 1–4; *AJA*, XLIII (1939), 6 ff., figs. 4, 5. Plaoutine's ingenious suggestion (*CV*, Petit Palais, p. 56) that the two objects right and left of the hare are plants, perhaps sea onions, to frighten away the wolf (cf. Aelianus, *De natura animalium*, I, 36) cannot, I am afraid, be accepted; for the two objects are in relief, part and parcel of the shape, and are clearly intended for the two little protuberances of the fetlock above a cow's hoof with grooves for hair. Moreover the long legs of the animal near the cave suggest a dog rather than a wolf. Dogs are used for rounding up cattle as well as sheep.

155. Beazley, pp. 516 ff.; Smith, *L*.

156. Bicknell, *JHS*, XLI (1921), pls. 13, 14, p. 222; Smith, *L*, pls. 10, 33 c–d; Beazley, p. 517, no. 15.

157. D. M. Robinson, *CV*, II, pl. 40, no. 2, pls. 41, 42; Smith, *L*, pl. 15, pl. 23 b, pl. 34 a; Beazley, p. 517, no. 25.

158. E 106. Watzinger, *Griechische Vasen in Tübingen*, pl. 28; D. M. Robinson and Freeman, *AJA*, XL (1936), 221; Smith, *L*, pl. 23 a; Beazley, p. 517, no. 26.

159. Beazley, p. 519; Smith, *L*, pp. 17 f.

160. 191. Smith, *L*, pls. 27, 33 a; Beazley, p. 519, no. 2.

161. Beazley, pp. 556 ff., 962.

162. 2402. Furtwängler, *Sabouroff Collection*, pl. 68, no. 1; Beazley, p. 558, no. 47.

163. 26.60.78. Richter and Hall, no. 104, pls. 103, 175; Beazley, p. 560, no. 80.

164. Herodotos II. 135; Athenaios XIII. 596 d. However, Archedike is a fairly common Attic name.

165. 2685. FR, pl. 65; Beazley, p. 556, no. 14.

166. Beazley, *AWL*, p. 17, pl. 3, no. 1; Buschor, *Grab*, p. 30 f.; Beazley, p. 561, no. 95.

167. 07.286.40. Fairbanks, *AWL*, II, pl. 38, nos. 2, 3; Pfuhl, fig. 539; Pfuhl, *Masterpieces*, fig. 90; Beazley, p. 561, no. 107.

168. 21.88.17. *MM Bull.*, XVIII (1923), 193, figs. 3, 4; Beazley, p. 561, no. 111.

169. 06.1021.132. Fairbanks, *AWL*, II, pl. I, no. 11; Beazley, p. 563, no. 142.

170. 39.11.1. Richter, *AJA*, XLIV (1940), 186; Beazley, p. 566. The new attribution is by Beazley (in a letter).

170a. Cf. D. von Bothmer, *Amazons in Greek Art*, p. 202. He points out that white lines indicate that the Amazon is lying on a rock.

171. 56.171.41. D. von Bothmer, *MM Bull.*, March 1957, p. 178.

172. 35.11.5. Beazley, p. 580, no. 1.

173. V 453. Gjerstadt, *Swedish Cyprus Expedition*, III, pl. 86, 1–2; Beazley, p. 580, no. 2.

174. Beazley, pp. 467 f., 960.

175. 41.162.102. Gallatin, *CV*, pl. 27, 7 and 9.

176. Beazley, pp. 494 ff., 968.

177. 01.8122. Beazley, p. 500, no. 184.

178. 35.54 and 06.1021.126. Richter and Hall, no. 93, pls. 95, 175; Beazley, pp. 496, 499, nos. 56 and 165.

179. Beazley, pp. 503 ff., 961. Nos. 41, 55, and 68 in Beazley's list are in New York.

180. Beazley, pp. 508 ff., 961, 968. Nos. 9, 56, 58, 62, 92 in Beazley's list are in New York.

181. Welter, *Aus der Karlsruher Vasensammlung*, pl. 14, no. 32 a; Beazley, p. 508, no. 2.

182. Beazley, pp. 482 f.

183. 24.97.37. Beazley, *JHS*, XLVII (1927), 231, fig. 6; Beazley, p. 482, no. 1.

IV. FREE STYLE

1. Hartwig, *Mon. Piot*, X (1903), pl. 8; *Oest. Jh.*, XII (1897), 166; Richter, *Ancient Furniture*, fig. 223; Beazley, p. 666, no. 8.

2. Cf. instances cited by Buschor in FR, III, 128 f.

3. 2357. Pfuhl, fig. 577; Zahn in FR, pl. 171, 2; Beazley, p. 748, no. 6. The date is later than 430, and so the theory advanced by Riezler (*Der Parthenon und die Vasenmalerei*, p. 18) and Pfuhl, p. 574, that the vase was made before the frieze was erected, i.e., before 438, does not hold.

4. A. H. Smith, *Sculptures of the Parthenon*, pl. 69.

5. D. M. Robinson, *AJA*, XXXVIII (1934), 45 ff. (for the whole subject of copies on vases from the Parthenon sculptures see the references cited in his notes 9, 10, and *CV*, III, pl. IX).

6. Hahland, *M*, pl. 6 a.

7. No. 2418. Hirschfeld, *Berliner Winckelmannsprogramm*, XXXII (1872), 3 ff., pl. I; Richter, *Sc. Sc.*, fig. 587.

8. Beazley, pp. 634 ff.

9. Beazley, *VA*, p. 163; FR, pl. 167, no. 2, III, 293, fig. 137; Buschor, *Gr. V.*, fig. 217; Beazley, p. 634, no. 1.

10. Beazley, *AJA*, XLVII (1943), 448 f.

11. 07.286.81. FR, II, 264, fig. 94 a; Pfuhl, fig. 496; Pfuhl, *Masterpieces*, fig. 78; Swindler, *AP*, fig. 318; Richter and Hall, no. 118, pls. 118, 119, 171; Beazley, p. 637, no. 49.

12. 12.236.2 and 25.189.2. Richter and Hall, nos. 119, 120, pls. 117, 120, 169; Beazley, p. 635, no. 19 and p. 648. 25.189.2, according to Beazley, may belong to "the late-school of the Berlin Painter." It certainly shows the close connection between the Berlin and the Achilles Painters.

13. 12.236.1. Richter and Hall, no. 121, pls. 120, 121, 169; Beazley, p. 635, no. 20.

14. Cab. Méd. 372. Pfuhl, fig. 521; Swindler, *AP*, fig. 338; FR, pl. 167, no. 1, III, 290, fig. 136; Beazley, p. 634, no. 4.

15. Cab. Méd. 357. FR, pl. 77, no. 1, II, 92, fig. 47; Pfuhl, fig. 523; Swindler, *AP*, fig. 330; Beazley, p. 634, no. 2.

16. T 1052. Aurigemma *S*,[1] 163–165 = *S*,[2] 197–199; Beazley, p. 637, no. 42.

17. 30.4.1. Beazley, *Museum Journal*, XXXIII (1932), 4 ff.; Seltman, *AV*, pl. 34 a; Beazley, p. 636, no. 38.

18. 17.230.13. Richter and Hall, no. 113, pls. 114, 176; Beazley, p. 640, no. 86.

19. E 385. Beazley, *JHS*, XXXIV (1914), 188, fig. 8 a; Beazley, p. 637, no. 41.

20. G 444. Beazley, *JHS*, XXXIV (1914), 190, fig. 9; Beazley, p. 639, no. 74.

21. Beazley, pp. 640 ff.; Beazley, *AWL*, pp. 13 ff.; Riezler, *WAL*; Fairbanks, *AWL*, I and II.

22. No. 1818. Riezler, *WAL*, pl. 36; Pfuhl, fig. 543; Pfuhl, *Masterpieces*, fig. 94; Swindler, *AP*, fig. 333; FR, III, 113, fig. 56; Beazley, p. 643, no. 135.

23. FR, III, 303, Beazley, *AWL*, pl. 3, 2; Buschor, *Grab*, pp. 35–37, 57; Beazley, p. 642, no. 130; Lullies, *Eine Sammlung griechischer Kleinkunst*, no. 80.

24. 08.258.17. Fairbanks, *AWL*, II, pl. 35, no. 1; Richter and Hall, no. 114, pls. 114, 176; Beazley, p. 644, no. 154.

25. 08.258.18. Fairbanks, *AWL*, II, pl. 35, no. 2; Swindler, *AP*, pl. 10 c; Richter and Hall, no. 115, pls. 115, 176; Beazley, p. 644, no. 153.

26. No. 377. Robinson and Harcum, *Catalogue*, pl. 65, p. 185; Beazley, p. 644, no. 155.

27. Beazley, p. 644, no. 156.

28. 06.1171. Fairbanks, *AWL*, I, pl. 10, no. 1. Richter and Hall, no. 116, pls. 115, 176; Beazley, p. 644, no. 152.

29. 08.258.16. Richter, *MM Bulletin*, IV (1909), 102; Beazley, p. 645, no. 176.

30. 07.286.42. Fairbanks, *AWL*, II, pl. 39; Pfuhl, fig. 536; Richter and Hall, no. 117, pls. 116, 176; Buschor, *Grab*, p. 39; Beazley, p. 645, no. 178.

31. For a detailed analysis of the Achilles Painter's style cf. Beazley, *JHS*, XXXIV (1914), 207 ff.

32. Beazley, pp. 807 ff.

33. 12.229.10. Beazley, *AWL*, p. 19, pl. VI, 1; Beazley, p. 809, no. 20.

34. 15.165. Richter, *MM Bulletin*, XI (1916), 128, fig. 5; Buschor *ALP*, p. 181; Beazley, p. 808, no. 6.

35. 09.221.44. Fairbanks, *AWL*, II, pl. 4; Beazley, p. 782, no. 71.

36. G R 608. Fairbanks, *AWL*, II, pl. VI, no. 9; Beazley, p. 783, no. 81.

37. 23.160.38, 23.160.39. Richter, *MM Bulletin*, XX (1925), 48, figs. 1, 2.

38. Beazley, pp. 653 ff., 963.

39. 97.371. Beazley, *VA*, p. 167; Caskey and Beazley, *AVP*, pl. 29, no. 62, p. 55; Beazley, p. 658, no. 108.

40. Czartoryski, no. 42. Pfuhl, fig. 571; Pfuhl, *Masterpieces*, fig. 103; Beazley, *V. Pol.*, pl. 23; Bulas, *CV*, pl. 26; Beazley, p. 656, no. 53.

41. 17.230.35. Richter and Hall, no. 122, pls. 122, 176; Beazley, p. 656, no. 66.

42. 41.162.142. Pease, *CV*, Gallatin Coll., pl. 55, no. 1; Beazley, p. 653, no. 9.

43. 08.258.23. Richter and Hall, no. 123, pls. 121, 176; Beazley, p. 657, no. 82.

44. 98.883. Beazley, *VA*, p. 168; Caskey and Beazley, *AVP*, pl. 29, no. 63, fig. 40; FR, III, 135; Bieber, *HT*, p. 80, fig. 108; Beazley, p. 655, no. 38.

45. 13.11. Beazley, *VA*, p. 169; Beazley, p. 657, no. 83.

46. E 185. Walters, *CV*, pl. 80, no. 4; Beazley, p. 656, no. 55.

47. H 498. Pfuhl, fig. 511; Beazley, p. 656, no. 59.

48. 2798. Pfuhl, fig. 784; Buschor, *ALP*, pp. 1 ff., pl. I, no. 1, pl. III; Beazley, *AWL*, p. 18, pl. 5; Beazley, p. 658, no. 102.

49. 2797. Buschor, *ALP*, pp. 1 ff., pl. I, no. 2, pl. II; Beazley, *AWL*, pp. 17 f., pl. I, no. 2; Beazley, p. 658, no. 101.

50. Beazley, pp. 651 ff.

51. 08.258.27. Richter and Hall, no. 125, pls. 123, 178; Beazley, p. 653, no. 14.

52. 28.57.23. Pfuhl, fig. 556; Richter and Hall, no. 124, pls. 124, 123, 171; Beazley, p. 651, no. 1.

53. 385 f. (tr. Evelyn White).

54. Cf., e.g., the column krater in Bologna, Laurinsich, *CV*, pl. 25, and the krater in Berlin, no. 3275, Hartwig, *RM*, XII (1897), pls. IV, V.

55. Beazley, pp. 650 f., 963.

56. 56.171.44. D. von Bothmer, *MM Bull.*, March 1957, p. 178.

57. von Mercklin, *RM*, XXXVIII–XXXIX (1923–24), 106 ff.; Beazley, pp. 661 f.

58. Cg 61. Hoffmann, pl. I, fig. 1; Beazley, p. 661, no. 8.

59. 06.1021.189. FR, III, 287, fig. 135; Richter and Hall, no. 108, pls. 108, 177; Beazley, p. 661, no. 9.

60. Gow, *JHS*, XLVIII (1928), 149, fig. 7; FR, pl. 168, no. 1, III, 296, fig. 140; Beazley, p. 661, no. 7.

61. Cf. Gow, *loc. cit.*; Schoppa, *Darstellung der Perser*; Smith, *Menon Painter*, p. 14, note 12; Beazley, *CV*, Oxford, p. 2, no. 5; Richter and Hall, pp. 14, 56; Seyrig, *Syria*, XVIII (1937), 4 ff. For a representation of a Greek fighting a Persian, dated about 480–470 B.C., in New York, cf. Richter and Hall, no. 35, pl. 34.

62. Beazley, pp. 666 f.

63. 03.792. Hartwig, *Mon. Piot*, X (1903), pl. 8; Beazley, p. 666, no. 8.

64. 23.160.80. Richter and Hall, no. 110, pls. 103, 111, 171; Beazley, p. 666, no. 1.

65. 697. von Lücken, *GV*, pl. 114; Beazley, p. 666, no. 2.

66. Beazley, p. 668.

67. 24.97.30. Richter and Hall, no. 131, pls. 130, 171; Beazley, p. 668, no. 2.

68. E 497. Jacobsthal, *MM Studies*, V (1934–36), 131; Beazley, p. 668, no. 1.

69. Beazley, p. 667.

70. G 424. FR, III, 308, fig. 148; Pottier, *CV*, pl. 23, nos. 4–6; Beazley, p. 667, no. 3.

71. 21.88.4. Richter and Hall, no. 111, pls. 112, 173; Beazley, p. 667, no. 2.

72. Beazley, pp. 671 ff.

73. 2401. Dütschke, *Jb.*, XXVII (1912), 133; von Lücken, *GV*, pl. 22; Beazley, p. 671, no. 1.

74. Beazley, pp. 668 ff.

75. 1772. von Lücken, *GV*, pl. 113; Beazley, p. 668, no. 1.

76. Beazley, pp. 670 f.

77. FR, pl. 169, III, 302, fig. 144; Beazley, p. 671, no. 1.

78. 34.155. Richter and Hall, no. 129, pls. 116, 176; Beazley, p. 671, no. 4.

79. Beazley, pp. 674 f., 963.

80. T 435. Jacobsthal, *Die Melischen Reliefs*, p. 193; Beazley, p. 674, no. 1.

81. 22.139.11. Richter and Hall, no. 132, pls. 131, 171; Beazley, p. 674, no. 5.

82. 06.1021.187. Richter and Hall, no. 133, pls. 132, 177. Beazley, p. 665, no. 1 (below).

83. 41.162.113. Pease, *CV*, Gallatin Coll., pl. 55, no. 2; Beazley, p. 665, no. 1 (above).

84. Beazley, pp. 677 ff.

85. A 134. Hoppin, II, 375; Mayence, *CV*, pl. 7, no. 2; Beazley, p. 677, no. 1.

86. 96.7–16.5. Hoppin, II, 378, 379; Pfuhl, fig. 520; Walters, *CV*, pl. 25, 2; FR, III, 43, fig. 19; Beazley, p. 677, no. 2.

87. 23507. Hoppin, II, 381; Swindler, *AP*, fig. 355; Beazley, p. 680, no. 47.

88. Inv. 73. Blawatski, *AA*, 1927, Beilagen 3–4 at p. 75, p. 78; Beazley, p 679, no. 31.

89. 2385. Beazley, p. 698, no. 58.

90. E 280. Klein, *Jb.*, XXXIII (1918), 17; Swindler, *AP*, fig. 361; Walters, *CV*, pl. 16, no. 1, pl. 12, no. 3; Seltman, *AV*, pl. 35 b; Beazley, p. 679, no. 32.

91. 45.11.1. Libertini. *Bollettino d'arte*, XXVII (1933), 554 ff. (ill.); Hampe, *AM*, LX–LXI (1935–36), 298, no. 43, pl. 100; Catterall in Pauly-Wissowa, XIX (1938), *s.v.* Perseus, col. 981; M. J. Milne, *MM Bulletin*, new series, IV (1945–46), 126 ff.; Beazley, p. 680, no. 49. Miss Milne, *loc. cit.*, discusses the significance of the rays round Perseus' head.

92. 21.88.73. Richter and Hall, no. 126, pls. 125, 129, 171; Beazley, p. 678, no. 16.

93. Beazley, pp. 690 ff.

94. E 379. Beazley, *VA*, p. 173; Beazley, p. 690, no. 3.

95. 06.1021.116. Richter and Hall, no. 130, pls. 128, 129, 169; Beazley, p. 690, no. 1.

96. Buschor, *Gr. V.*, p. 207.

97. Beazley, *V. Pol.*, pls. 24, 25; Bulas, *CV*, pl. 24; Seltman, *AV*, pl. 36 b; Beazley, p. 691, no. 6.

98. 34.79. Caskey, *AJA*, XXXVIII (1934), pls. 26, 27; Caskey, *JHS*, LIV (1924), 201 f., pl. 11; Beazley, p. 690, no. 2; Caskey and Beazley, *AVP*, II, no. 111.

99. 00.346. Beazley, *VA*, p. 174, figs. 107, 107 bis; Pfuhl, fig. 515; Beazley, p. 691, no. 7; Caskey and Beazley, *AVP*, II, no. 110.

100. Beazley, pp. 703 ff.

101. Inv. 3172. von Lücken, *GV*, pl. 58; Pfuhl, fig. 554; Pfuhl, *Masterpieces*, fig. 100; Swindler, *AP*, fig. 369; Neugebauer, *Führer*, II, pl. 59; FR, III, 109, fig. 52; Buschor, *Gr. V.*, fig. 226; Beazley, p. 703, no. 1.

102. 17.230.15. Richter and Hall, no. 138, pls. 140, 141, 172; Beazley, p. 704, no. 12.

103. Beazley, pp. 692 ff.

104. Tillyard, *The Hope Vases*, no. 138, pl. 23; Beazley, p. 692, no. 13. Now in the possession of the Trustees of the Christie estate.

105. Beazley, pp. 684 f.

106. Gerhard, *Auserlesene Vasenbilder*, pl. 189; Beazley, p. 684, no. 1.

107. Beazley, pp. 686 f.

108. T 617. Aurigemma *S*,[1] pp. 195–199, 193 middle = *S*,[2] pp. 223–227 and 221 middle; Beazley, p. 686, no. 1.

109. E 271. Pfuhl, fig. 555; Walters, *CV*, pl. 11, no. 1, pl. 12, no. 2; Swindler, *AP*, fig. 340; FR, pl. 139; Beazley, p. 687, no. 9.

110. Beazley, p. 688.

111. Studniczka, *Jb.*, XXXI (1916), 211, fig. 26; Tillyard, *The Hope Vases*, pl. 17, no. 116, pl. 18; Beazley, p. 688, no. 1.

112. 24.97.25. Richter and Hall, no. 128, pls. 127, 171; Beazley, p. 688.

113. Beazley, pp. 704 ff.

114. Beazley, pp. 709 ff., 963.

115. 06.1021.173. Richter and Hall, no. 134, pls. 133, 134, 170; Beazley, p. 711, no. 54.

116. 08.258.21. Jacobsthal, *MM Studies*, V (1934–36), 125 ff.; P. Friedländer, *AA*, 1935, cols. 20 ff.; Richter and Hall, no. 135, pls. 135–137, 170; Beazley, p. 717, no. 1.

117. 1026. von Lücken, *GV*, pls. 111, 112; Jacobsthal, *MM Studies*, V (1934–36), pp. 132, 133; Beazley, p. 717, no. 2.

118. Beazley, pp. 718 f.

119. 20.187. Tillyard, *op. cit.*, pl. 14, no. 104; Beazley, p. 718, no. 2.

120. L 63. Benndorf, *Griechische und sicilische Vasenbilder*, pl. 31, 1; Beazley, p. 719, no. 8.

121. 12.229.14. Richter and Hall, no. 136, pls. 138, 145.

122. Beazley, pp. 721 f.

123. 1831. FR, pl. 142, III, 124, fig. 57; Beazley, p. 721, no. 2.

124. 2588. von Lücken, *GV*, pls. 16, 17; Pfuhl, fig. 559; Pfuhl, *Masterpieces*, figs. 98 and 99; Swindler, *AP*, fig. 365; Neugebauer, *Führer*, II, pl. 60, no. 1; FR, pl. 138, no. 2; Beazley, p. 721, no. 1.

125. 2589. von Lücken, *GV*, pls. 18, 19; Pfuhl, fig. 567; Swindler, *AP*, 341; FR, pl. 125; Beazley, p. 721, no. 7.

126. Beazley, pp. 766 ff.

127. 4.12. Lamb, *CV*, pl. 37, no. 2; Beazley, p. 766, no. 2.

128. 07.286.65. Richter and Hall, no. 137, pls. 139, 170; Beazley, p. 766, no. 9.

129. 41.162.137, 41.162.141. Gallatin, *CV*, pl. 24, nos. 1–3; Beazley, p. 768, nos. 35, 47.

130. Inv. 3275. Hartwig, *RM*, XII (1897), pls. 4, 5; Beazley, p. 766, no. 1.

131. Beazley, pp. 724 ff., 964.

132. 1629. *Eph.*, 1897, pls. 9, 10; Pfuhl, fig. 561; Beazley and Ashmole, *Greek Sculpture and Painting*, fig. 108; Beazley, p. 726, no. 27.

133. Cab. Méd. 851. Hoppin, I, 299; Beazley, p. 727, no. 33.

134. T 544. Hauser, *Jb.*, XI (1896), 193, fig. 40; Beazley, p. 729, no. 72.

135. E 774. FR, pl. 57, no. 3; Beazley, p. 726, no. 25.

136. 2471. Pfuhl, fig. 560; Pfuhl, *Masterpieces*, fig. 105; Neugebauer, *Führer*, II, pl. 64, no. 1; Beazley, p. 724, no. 1.

137. Beazley, *VA*, p. 179, fig. 110 bis, *CV*, pl. 40, 3–5; Beazley, p. 725, no. 8.

138. 08.258.22. FR, pl. 120, 1; Pfuhl, fig. 566; Richter and Hall, no. 140, pls. 142, 177; Beazley, p. 725, no. 9.

139. 30.11.8. Richter and Hall, no. 141, pls. 142, 176; Beazley, p. 724, no. 4.

139a. 56.171.58. D. von Bothmer, *MM Bull.*, March 1957, p. 79.

140. Beazley, p. 725, no. 6.

141. 31.11.13. Richter and Hall, no. 139, pls. 143, 144, 176; Beazley, *AWL*, pl. 7, no. 1; Beazley, p. 725, no. 7; Richter, *Greek Painting*,[2] p. 16.

142. 95.48. Caskey and Beazley, *AVP*, pl. 30 and suppl. pl. 4, no. 43; Beazley, p. 724, no. 2.

143. Beazley, p. 725, no. 11. Illustrated in part *AJA*, L (1946), 134, fig. 11.

144. S. Karouzou, *AJA*, L (1946), 122; Beazley, p. 725, no. 10.

145. *BCH*, 1934, pl. 6; Beazley, p. 725, no. 16.

146. Beazley, pp. 733 ff., 964.

147. 12.229.12. Beazley, *VA*, p. 180; Richter and Hall, no. 143, pl. 145; Beazley, p. 733, no. 2.

148. 666.64. *L'Antiquité Classique*, IV, pl. 31; Beazley, p. 733, no. 3.

149. Beazley, p. 734, no. 7.

150. T 617. Aurigemma *S*,[1] p. 193, right, above = *S*,[2] p. 221, right, above; Beazley, p. 733, no. 1.

151. Beazley, pp. 739 ff., 964.

152. P U 273. Pfuhl, fig. 563; Mayence, *CV*, pls. 19–22; Beazley, p. 739, no. 1.

153. Nos. 2537, 2538. *Mon. dell' Inst.*, X (1874–78), pl. 39 (no. 2537); FR, pl. 140; Neugebauer, *Führer*, II, pl. 65, no. 1 (no. 2538); Beazley, p. 739, nos. 2, 5.

154. 19.192.46. Richter and Hall, no. 142, pl. 145; Beazley, p. 740, no. 8.

155. E 94. Hartwig, *Gr. M.*, p. 138; Gardiner, *Athl.*, fig. 156; Beazley, p. 740, no. 15.

156. 37.11.19. Richter, *MM Bulletin*, XXXIV (1939), 231 f., fig. 2, and *Greek Painting*,[2] p. 15.

157. Beazley, p. 737.

158. 40.11.2. Richter, *AJA*, XLIV (1940), 428 ff.; Beazley, p. 737.

159. Beazley, p. 738.

160. 00.352. Beazley, p. 738, no. 1; Caskey and Beazley, *AVP*, II, no. 112, with discussion of subject and name of second Maenad.

161. E 389. Panofka, *Pourt.*, pl. 5; Beazley, p. 738, no. 2.

162. Beazley, pp. 742 ff.

163. 16.73. Richter and Hall, no. 144, pls. 147, 174; Beazley, p. 743, no. 5.

164. 07.286.35. Richter and Hall, no. 145, pls. 146, 174; Beazley, p. 742, no. 1.

165. On the Greek harp see Herbig, *AM*, LIV (1929), 164.

166. 19.192.86. Richter and Hall, no. 146, pls. 148, 172; Beazley, p. 745, no. 59.

167. Beazley, pp. 753 ff., 964.

168. 855. Peredolski, *RM*, XLII (1927), Beilage 30, no. 1; Beazley, p. 754, no. 20.

169. C A 1587. *Enc. phot.*, III, 30 b; Beazley, p. 756, no. 53.

170. 08.258.24. Richter and Hall, no. 149, pls. 150, 177; Beazley, p. 754, no. 27.

171. 41.162.89. Gallatin, *CV*, pl. 24, no. 8; Beazley, p. 755, no. 47.

172. Beazley, pp. 732 f.

173. Ny Carlsberg I N 2783. Bruhn, *From the Collections of the Ny Carlsberg Glyptothek*, II (1938), 134, 135, fig. 19; Beazley, p. 732, no. 2.

174. 24.97.24. Richter and Hall, no. 152, pls. 150, 177; Beazley, p. 733, no. 13.

175. Beazley, p. 758.

176. 06.1021.175. Richter and Hall, no. 150, pls. 150, 177; Beazley, p. 758, no. 2.

177. Beazley, pp. 763 f.

178. 10.210.11. Fairbanks, *AWL*, II, pl. 33, no. 19 a; Beazley, p. 764, no. 31.

179. Beazley, p. 752.
180. 99.539. Hoppin, II, 477; Swindler, *AP*, fig. 282; Beazley, p. 752.

V. LATE FIFTH-CENTURY STYLE

1. Overbeck, *Schriftquellen*, pp. 310 f.; A. Reinach, *Recueil Milliet*, pp. 184 ff.
2. Reinach, *op. cit.*, pp. 188 ff.
3. *Ibid.*, pp. 220 ff.
4. Pliny *N.H.* XXXV. 61: Ab hoc (Apollodoro) artis fores apertas Zeuxis Heracleotes intravit.
5. *Ibid. N.H.* XXXV. 60: . . . primus species exprimere instituit.
6. Hesychius, Σκιά· σκίασις, ἐπιφάνεια τοῦ χρώματος ἀντίμορφος. Σκιαγραφίαν· τὴν σκηνογραφίαν οὕτω λέγουσιν. ἐλέγετο δέ τις καὶ 'Απολλόδωρος ζωγράφος σκιαγράφος ἀντὶ τοῦ σκηνογράφος, "Shadow: shading, that is, mimicking form through color. Shadow painting a name for scene painting. A painter Apollodoros was called shadow painter, that is, scene painter."
7. Plutarch *De glor. Ath.* 346 a: 'Απολλόδωρος ὁ ζωγράφος, ἀνθρώπων πρῶτος ἐξευρὼν φθορὰν καὶ ἀπόχρωσιν σκιᾶς.
8. Cf., e.g., Bulle, *Eph.*, 1937 (100th anniversary volume), pp. 473 ff.; Dinsmoor, *Hesperia*, IX (1940), 48, fig. 18; Buschor in FR, pl. 148, p. 165, figs. 78–80 (South Italian); Hahland, *M*, pls. 3, 11 b, 16 a; Bieber, *HT*, pp. 58 ff. (South Italian); Richter, *Greek Painting*[2], pp. 18 ff.
9. Cf., e.g., the figures on the calyx krater in Athens (Hahland, *M*, pl. 4), dated about 390 B.C., and the statuettes of Muses on the hydria, Richter and Hall, no. 162, pl. 160.
10. Cf., e.g., *Republic*, 523, 598, 602; *Parmenides*, 165; *Laws*, 663. For a general account of Plato's views on art cf. Schuhl, *Platon et l'art de son temps*.
11. There is an extensive literature on perspective in ancient art; cf. especially Wickhoff, *Wiener Genesis*, 1895, p. 57; Delbrück, *Beiträge zur Linienperspektive* (Diss., Bonn, 1899); Riegl, *Spätrömische Kunstindustrie*, 1901, p. 18; Pfuhl, *Jb.*, XXV (1910), 12 ff., XXVII (1912), 227 ff.; Grüneisen, *Mél. d'arch.*, XXXI (1911), 393 ff.; Schöne, *Jb.*, XXVII (1912), 19 ff.; Panofsky, "Die Perspektive als 'symbolische Form,'" *Bibliothek Warburg: Vorträge*, 1924–25, pp. 258 ff.; Swindler, *AP*, p. 225; Bulle, *Berliner Winckelmannsprogramm*, XCIV (1934), 16, 26, 34, note 70; Richter, *Actes du XIV*[e] *congrès international d'histoire de l'art*, 1936, Résumés, pp. 174 f., "Perspective, Ancient, Mediaeval and Renaissance" in *Scritii in onore di Bartolomeo Nogara*, 1937, pp. 381 ff., and *Greek Painting*[4]; Schweitzer, *Vom Sinn der Perspektive*, 1953.
12. For a recent analysis of the development of perspective in the Renaissance—a much debated subject—see A. Wieleitner, "Zur Erfindung der verschiedenen Distanzkonstruktionen in der malerischen Perspektive," in *Repertorium für Kunstwissenschaft*, XLII (1920), 249 ff.; also Panofsky, *op. cit.*, pp. 277 ff.; H. Brockhaus' edition of *De sculptura* by Pomponius Gauricus, Leipzig, 1896, pp. 32–58; Ivins, "The Rationalization of Sight," *Metropolitan Museum Papers*, no. 8, 1938.
13. For recent lists of these see Diepolder, *Attische Grabreliefs*, p. 64; Binneboessel, *Urkundenreliefs* (Diss., Leipzig, 1932); Speier, *RM*, LXVII (1932), 90 ff.
14. On this subject see especially Hahland, *M*, pp. 6 ff.
15. One of the latest found is by the Shuvalov Painter. See Hahland, *M*, p. 18, note 10; Rhomaios, *Deltion*, XII (1929), 201, fig. 9.
16. Hauser, *RM*, XIX (1904), 163 ff., pl. 6; E. Robinson, *Bulletin Museum Fine Arts*, III (1905), 27 ff.; Hahland, *M*, p. 6, pls. 6, 24.

17. Brueckner, *Der Friedhof am Eridanos,* p. 62; Conze, *Die attischen Grabreliefs,* II, 254.

18. 102: τὸν Προνόμου πώγων' ἔχων, "wearing the beard of Pronomos." A scholiast adds that this is the flute player.

19. As the father of a flute player named [Oi]niades (*IG,* II, 1234). The Theban flute player was the son of an Oiniades (*Anth. Plan.* 28).

20. Cf. Pausanias IX. 12. 5–6.

21. Douris in Athenaios IV. 184 d.

22. Pausanias IV. 27. 7.

23. We must remember, however, that there was apparently a musical family in Thebes continuing for several generations in which the name Pronomos appears more than once (cf. *IG,* II, 1292). That the musician on the Naples vase has no beard whereas Aristophanes' Pronomos was bearded can easily be explained by the license which vase painters took in such matters (Hahland, *M,* p. 17, note 9). Besides, as Beazley suggests, he might have been beardless at the time the vase was painted and acquired a beard by the time of the *Ekklesiazousai.*

24. Beazley, pp. 784 ff., 968.

25. 810. Beazley, *VA,* p. 181; Beazley, p. 784, no. 6.

26. 2361. FR, pl. 29; Pfuhl, fig. 767; Beazley, p. 785, no. 27.

27. 2415. FR, pl. 35; Pfuhl, figs. 558, 774; Pfuhl, *Masterpieces,* fig. 102; Buschor, *Gr. V.,* fig. 228; Beazley, p. 784, no. 2.

28. Beazley, p. 968.

29. 22.139.89. Beazley, p. 787, no. 49.

30. Beazley, pp. 789 ff., 965.

31. 2402. Hahland, *M,* pl. 12 a; Beazley, p. 790, no. 3.

32. 300. Hahland, *M,* pl. 8 b; Beazley, p. 790, no. 7.

33. 2419. FR, pls. 36, 37; Pfuhl, fig. 582; Swindler, *AP,* fig. 332; Hahland, *M,* pl. 2; Buschor, *Gr. V.,* figs. 242, 243; Beazley, p. 789, no. 2.

34. 1937.983. Beazley, *AJA,* XLIII (1939), 618 ff.; Beazley, p. 790, no. 11.

35. Hahland, *M,* pl. 5; Buschor, *Gr. V.,* fig. 252; Beazley, p. 790, no. 6.

36. 24.97.38. Beazley, p. 791, no. 16.

37. Beazley, p. 794 f.

38. 06.1021.185. Richter and Hall, no. 158, pls. 157, 172; Beazley, p. 794, no. 5.

38a. GR 593. Richter and Hall, no. 153, pls. 152, 173; Beazley, p. 795, no. 4.

39. Beazley, p. 797 f.

40. 27.122.8. Richter and Hall, no. 154, pls. 153, 154, 171; Buschor, *Gr. V.,* fig. 244; Richter, *Greek Painting,*[2] p. 16; Beazley, p. 797, no. 2.

41. 25.78.66. Messerschmidt, *RM,* XLVII (1932), 130, 146 b; Richter and Hall, no. 155, pls. 155, 171; Bieber, *HT,* p. 6, fig. 9; Beazley, p. 797, no. 7.

42. Cf. Dionysios of Halikarnassos VII.72.10.

43. On this whole subject cf. Richter and Hall, p. 196, notes 2–8; Bieber, *loc cit.*

44. T 127. Aurigemma, *S,*[1] p. 207 middle and pp. 209–211 = *S,*[2] p. 245, middle and pp. 247–249; Beazley, p. 797, no. 1.

45. 06.1021.174. Richter and Hall, no. 156, pls. 156, 178; Beazley, p. 798, no. 17.

46. F. P. Johnson, *AJA,* XLII (1938), 357, no. 26; Beazley, p. 797, no. 8.

47. Beazley, pp. 798 ff., 965.

48. 11265. Hoppin, I, 15; Pfuhl, fig. 576; Pfuhl, *Masterpieces,* fig. 107; Swindler, *AP,* fig. 345; Dugas, *Aison,* fig. 9; FR, III, 48; Beazley, p. 800, no. 20.

49. R C 239. Dugas, *Aison,* fig. 11; Swindler, *AP,* figs. 297, 327; Beazley, p. 799, no. 11.

50. 27.122.9. Beazley, *JHS,* XLIX (1929), 73, fig. 25; Richter and Hall, no. 151, pl. 151; Beazley, p. 800, no. 19.

51. 19.192.44. Richter and Hall, no. 157.

52. Beazley, pp. 803 ff., 965.

53. 2633. Neugebauer, *Führer,* II, pl. 66; Beazley, p. 805, no. 21.

54. Beazley, pp. 801 ff.

55. 23.324. Tillyard, *The Hope Vases,* pl. 23, no. 140; Luce, *CV,* pl. 23, no. 1; Beazley, p. 801, no. 1.

56. Nicole, *Meid.;* Ducati, *Midia;* Hahland, *M* and *Studien;* Beazley, pp. 831 ff., 965.

57. E 224. FR, pls. 8, 9; Hoppin, II, 179–181; Pfuhl, fig. 593; Pfuhl, *Masterpieces,* fig. 109; Swindler, *AP,* fig. 344; Walters, *CV,* pls. 91, 92; Seltman, *AV,* pl. 37; Buschor, *Gr. V.,* figs. 250, 251; Beazley, p. 831, no. 1.

58. 37.11.23. Richter, *AJA,* XLIV (1939), 1 ff., and *Greek Painting,*[2] p. 17; Beazley, p. 832, no. 6.

59. Jatta 1538. Jatta, *RM,* III (1888), pl. 9; Nicole, *op. cit.,* pl. 7, no. 4; Beazley, p. 832, no. 9.

60. 81947, 81948. Nicole, *op. cit.,* pl. 3, nos. 1, 2; Pfuhl, fig. 594; Ducati, *op. cit.,* pp. 100, 101; D. Levi, *CV,* pls. 60–65; Beazley, p. 832, nos. 3, 4.

61. G R. 1243. Richter and Hall, no. 159, pls. 158, 177; Beazley, p. 832, no. 7.

62. Stg. 311. Nicole, *op. cit.;* Beazley, p. 833, no. 12.

63. 11.213.2. Richter and Hall, no. 160, pls. 159, 176; Beazley, p. 838, no. 46.

64. 09.221.40. Richter and Hall, no. 161, pls. 159, 178; Beazley, p. 840, no. 86.

65. 06.1021.196. Richter and Hall, no. 164, pls. 161, 177; Beazley, p. 837, no. 42.

65a. Cf. Smith, *CV,* San Francisco, pp. 47 f.; S. Karouzou, *AJA,* L (1946), 122 ff.

66. 1460. FR, pl. 67, II, 35; Nicole, *op. cit.,* p. 117; Pfuhl, fig. 583; Pfuhl, *Masterpieces,* fig. 108; Swindler, *AP,* fig. 342; Buschor, *Gr. V.,* fig. 245; Beazley, p. 793.

67. 259. Nicole, *op. cit.,* pl. 2, no. 2; FR, pl. 30; Pfuhl, fig. 595; Beazley, p. 834.

68. Beazley, pp. 841 ff.

69. 2531. Hoppin, I, 50; Pfuhl, fig. 587; Swindler, *AP,* fig. 346; FR, pl. 127; Neugebauer, *Führer,* II, pl. 65, no. 2; Beazley, p. 841, no. 1.

70. 00.344. FR, pl. 128; Hoppin, I, 52; Beazley, p. 842, no. 2.

71. Marconi, *Atti Soc. Magna Grecia,* 1931, p. 73; Beazley, p. 842, no. 4.

72. 00.345. Pfuhl, fig. 586; FR, pl. 129; Seltman, *AV,* pl. 4 b; Beazley, p. 842, no. 3.

73. 2706. FR, III, 41; Beazley, p. 842, no. 5.

74. Acr. 594 and Pnyx 349; Graef and Langlotz, *Akropolis,* II, pl. 45; Beazley, p. 831, nos. 1, 2.

75. Beazley, pp. 847 ff.

76. 98.7–16.6. Hoppin, II, 219; Beazley, p. 847, no. 1.

77. 41.162.4. Gallatin, *CV,* pl. 25, nos. 5, 6; Beazley, p. 847, no. 9.

78. Jatta 1501. FR, pls. 38, 39, I, 197; Pfuhl, fig. 574; Swindler, *AP,* fig. 376; Buschor, *Gr. V.,* fig. 255; Beazley, p. 845, no. 1.

79. Beazley, pp. 845.f.

80. 12.229.15. Beazley, p. 846, no. 2.

81. 3240. Bieber, *Th.,* pp. 91, 94; Pfuhl, fig. 575; Bieber, *HT,* pp. 14 and 34; Buschor, *Gr. V.,* fig. 257; Beazley, p. 849, no. 1.

82. Beazley, p. 849, 965.

83. Beazley, pp. 852 f.

84. FR, pls. 96, 97; Pfuhl, fig. 584; Swindler, *AP,* fig. 468; Buschor, *Gr. V.,* fig. 258; Beazley, p. 852, no. 6.

85. 44.11.12, 44.11.13. Gabrici, *Mon. Linc.,* XXII (1913), 682, fig. 234, nos. 1, 3; Richter, *MM Bull.,* new series, III (1944–45), 168 ff.; Beazley, p. 852, nos. 2, 4.

86. 17.46.1. Richter and Hall, no. 165, pls. 162, 169; Beazley, p. 852, no. 1.

87. Gebauer and Johannes, *AA,* 1937, p. 194, fig. 13, no. 3; Beazley, p. 852.

88. Beazley, pp. 854 ff., 859 ff., 966.

89. Inv. 953. Hoppin, *Bf.*, p. 467; Blinkenberg and Johansen, *CV*, pl. 162, no. 2, p. 125; Beazley, p. 854, no. 1.
90. E 770. Hoppin, II, 173; Beazley, p. 854.
91. Beazley, *AWL*, p. 25.
92. 06.1169. Fairbanks, *AWL*, II, pl. 27, 2; Buschor, *ALP*, p. 187; Beazley, p. 820, no. 3.
93. 07.286.45. Fairbanks, *AWL*, II, pl. 26; Buschor, *ALP*, p. 20; Beazley, p. 828, no. 8.
94. 06.1021.135. Sambon, *Coll. Canessa*, p. 70, no. 243; Buschor, *ALP*, p. 186; Beazley, p. 829, no. 19.
95. 41.162.12. Gallatin, *CV*, pl. 28, no. 1.
96. 41.162.11. *Ibid.*, pl. 28, no. 2.

VI. THE FOURTH CENTURY

1. Cf. Ducati, *Saggio*, and especially Schefold, *U*, pp. 154–156.
2. Cf. Overbeck, *Schriftquellen*, pp. 330 ff., 334 ff.; A. Reinach, *Recueil Milliet*, pp. 250 ff., 268 ff.; Swindler, *AP*, pp. 265 ff.
3. *N.H.* XXXV. 65. 95.
4. Schefold, *U*, p. 105.
5. Binneboessel, *Studien zu den attischen Urkundenreliefs*, 1932, and the references there cited.
6. On this subject cf. especially Hahland, *M*, pp. 6 ff.; Schefold, *U*, pp. 62 ff.
7. P. Herrmann, "Das Gräberfeld von Marion auf Cypern," *Berliner Winckelmannsprogramm*, XLVIII (1888), 34–36; Hahland, *M*, p. 7.
8. Hauser, *Neu-att. Reliefs*, pp. 161 f.
9. Brauchitsch, *Preisamphoren*, p. 80, fig. 11; Smets, "Groupes chronologiques des amphores panathénaïques inscrites," *L'Antiquité classique*, V (1936), 96 ff.
10. Brauchitsch, *op. cit.*, pp. 51 ff.; Smets, *op. cit.*, 97 ff.; Beazley, *AJA*, XLVII (1943), 455 ff.
11. D. M. Robinson, *AJA*, XXXIII (1929), p. 66, fig. 14.
12. For this evidence cf. Schefold, *U*, pp. 63 ff.
13. *Cat. Musée d'Alexandrie: La Necropoli di Sciatbi*, pls. XLVII, XLVIII.
14. Cf. Beazley, *JHS*, LIX (1939), 26, 35, and *passim;* Hahland, *M;* and Schefold, *KV* and *U.*
15. Beazley, p. 870.
16. 06.1021.140. Nicole, *Meid.*, p. 109; Ducati, *Midia*, p. 117; FR, III, 52; Richter and Hall, no. 163, pl. 161; Beazley, p. 870, no. 2.
17. 33 A. FR, III, 53; Hahland, *M*, pl. 17 a; Beazley, p. 870, no. 1.
18. *C R* 1869, pl. 4, nos. 6–7; Beazley, p. 870, no. 3.
19. Swindler, *AJA*, XX (1916), 343, nos. 22–24; Beazley, p. 870, no. 4.
20. Beazley, pp. 870 ff., 966.
21. 158. *Mon. dell' Inst.*, IV (1844–48), pl. 43; Curtius, *Jb.*, XLIII (1928), 288; Beazley, p. 870, no. 1.
22. 522. Langlotz, *Würzburg*, pl. 191; Beazley, p. 871, no. 8.
23. Beazley, p. 874.
24. Hoppin, II, 475; Beazley, pp. 874 f., nos. 1, 2.
25. Beazley, pp. 876 ff., 966.
26. Hahland, *M*, pl. 16 a.

27. Beazley, p. 866.

28. *Ibid.*, p. 867.

29. *Ibid.*, p. 868.

30. *Ibid.*, pp. 880 ff., 966.

31. Hahland, *M*, pp. 20 f.

32. Jena 390. Hahland, *M*, pl. 22 c; Beazley, p. 880, no. 1. For the Greek harp see our p. 137.

33. Inv. 3768. Schefold, *KV*, pl. 3 b; Schefold, *U*, figs. 27–28; Beazley, p. 883, no. 72.

34. Beazley, pp. 885 f., 967.

35. *Ibid.*, pp. 886 f.

36. *Ibid.*, pp. 888 f.

37. *Ibid.*, p. 891.

38. 08.258.20. Richter and Hall, no. 166, pls. 162, 163, 173.

39. 21.88.162. *Ibid.*, no. 167, pls. 163, 172.

40. Cf. Richter and Hall, p. 212, notes 2–4.

41. E 231. Schefold, *KV*, pl. I, no. 1 a.

42. E 432. *Ibid.*, pl. I, no. 1 b.

43. 06.1021.184. Richter and Hall, no. 168, pls. 167, 172.

44. 24.97.5. *Ibid.*, no. 171, pl. 166; Schefold, *KV*, pl. 11.

45. Schefold, *KV*, pl. 21.

46. St. 1807. *C R* 1861, pls. 3–4; Beazley, p. 804, no. 5.

47. St. 1791. FR, II, 36 ff., pl. 68; Schefold, *KV*, pls. 13, 14.

48. 25.190. Richter and Hall, no. 169, pls. 164, 177; Schefold, *KV*, pl. 10; Brendel, *AJA*, XLIX (1945), 519 ff.

49. 06.1021.181. Richter and Hall, no. 170, pls. 165, 178; Schefold, *KV*, pl. 9.

50. Cf. Schefold, *Untersuchungen*, pp. 146 ff.

51. Hauser, *Oest. Jh.*, XII (1909), 90 ff.; Metzger, *Repr. du IV siècle*, pp. 92 ff., pl. VII.

52. 22.139.26. Richter and Hall, no. 173, pl. 168.

52a. 26.60.75. Schefold, *U*, no. 191, fig. 3, pl. 11.

53. 16878. Schefold, *KV*, pl. 15 a.

54. 15592. *Materyali*, XXXV (1916), pls. 1–4; Schefold, *KV*, pls. 19, 20.

55. Schefold, *KV*, pl. 24 a; Buschor, *Gr. V.*, fig. 269.

55a. 06.1021.195. Schefold, *U*, no. 547, pl. 38.

56. Cf. the lists of examples given by Courby, *Les Vases grecs à reliefs*, pp. 123 ff.; Ducati, *Saggio*, pp. 107 ff.; and *Storia*, pp. 520 ff.

57. Cf. Courby, *op. cit.*, pp. 40 ff.

58. Cf., e.g., Courby, *op. cit.*, pp. 117 ff.; Schefold, *U*, figs. 41, 42.

59. Gabrici, *Mon. Linc.*, XXII (1913), 696 ff., pls. C–CII.

60. Reinach, *Mon. Piot*, X (1903), pls. 6, 7.

61. 28.57.9. Ht. 5⅜ in. (13.7 cm.).

62. Cf. Höfer in *Roscher's Lexikon*, s.v. Klytaim(n)estra, col. 1234, and s.v. Orestes, cols. 958 ff.; J. Schmidt, *ibid.*, s.v. Telephos, cols. 288 f. For a list of representations cf. Schmidt, *op. cit.*, cols. 304 ff.

63. 44.11.10. Ht. 5¼ in (13.4 cm.); Richter, *MM Bull.*, III (1944–45), 170 ff.

64. For Pan and Eros in Hellenistic art cf. Wernicke in *Roscher's Lexikon*, s.v. Pan, cols. 1456 ff.

65. Thompson, *Hesperia*, III (1934), 451 ff.

66. *Ibid.*, pp. 429 ff.

67. S. Dow, *Hesperia*, V (1936), 50 ff.

68. Talcott, *Hesperia*, IV (1935), 493 ff., and V (1936), 342 ff.

GENERAL INDEX

Accidents, 34–35
Acheloos Painter, 37
Achilles and Patroklos, 134
Achilles and Penthesileia, 69, 97, 113–114, 127
Achilles Painter, 16, 66, 117, 118–121, 124, 127, 143, 191 n. 12, 192 n. 31; circle of, 123; follower of, 124; pupil of, 122
Adonia, 161
Adrastos, 146
Aeschylus, 2, 6, 91
Agatharchos of Samos, 90, 139
Agora, Athenian, base of statue found in, 175 n. 32; bowl found in, 57; fragmentary cylinder found in, 55; vases with graffiti, from, 20
Agrigento Painter, 96–97
Aigina, sculptures from temple at, 64
Aigisthos Painter, 110
Aischines (kalos), 114
Aischines Painter, 114
Aison, 146
Ajax, 113
Akestorides (kalos), 109
Akestorides Painter, 106–107
Akropolis, dedicatory offerings found on the, 6; inscribed base from the, 42; maidens from the, 46; mounting charioteer from the, 64; pits on the, 22; potsherds from the, 65; votive plaque from the, 45
Aktaion, death of, 95, 129
Alabastron, 13, 114; group of, 51
Alexander, Christine, vi
Alkaios (kalos), 121
Alkimachos (kalos), 105, 110, 129, 135
Alkimachos Painter, 110
Alkimedes (kalos), son of Aischylides, 121
Alkmeon (kalos), 81
Alphabet, Attic, 169 n. 65
Altamura Painter, 101
Alxenor stele, 64
Amasis, 36, 66
Amazonomachy, 101, 102, 103–104, 113, 124
Ambrosios Painter, 53
Amphiaraos, 32
Amphora, 11, 12, 15, 25, 45, 65, 94, 152, 157, 164

Amphora, neck, 11, 45, 65
Amphora, Nolan, 65, 73, 94
Amphora, Panathenaic, 11, 19, 22, 36, 65, 66–67, 68, 156, 164, 167 n. 26
Amphora, pointed, 11, 65
Amphoriskos, 133
Amymone Painter, 108
Anakreon, 7, 8, 22, 44, 58
Analysis, technical and stylistic, 36–42, 59–63, 90–92, 115–116, 139–141, 154–155
Anatomical details, 37–39, 60–62, 91–92, 115–116, 141, 155
Anaxagoras, 91, 116, 166 n. 10
Andokides (potter), 44, 46, 47, 50
Andokides (kalos), 43–44
Andokides Painter, 18, 19, 43–44, 46, 47, 48, 49, 50, 175 n. 43
Androtion, 175 n. 24
Animals, 166 n. 9
Antenor, 42
Anthesteria, 134, 135, 148
Antias (kalos), 57
Antimenes Painter, 37
Antiphanes (kalos), 83
Antiphon Painter, 85–86
Apelles, 5, 154, 162
Apollodoros, 5, 51–52, 139, 140
Archedike, 112, 190 n. 164
Archinos (kalos), 73
Archons, 22, 156, 175 n. 33
Arethusa, 64
Aristagoras (kalos), 84
Aristarchos (kalos), 85
Aristeides of Thebes, 154
Aristion stele, 43
Aristogeiton, 64
Aristophanes, 6, 20, 22, 142, 165 n. 5, 166 n. 10, 197 n. 23
Aristophanes (painter), 19, 149
Aristotle, 35, 175 nn. 24 and 29
Aryballos, 13, 114
Astragalos. See Knuckle-bone vase
Athanasia, 132
Athanasia Painter, 131–132
Athena Painter, 75, 182 n. 96
Athenaios, 190 n. 164, 197 n. 21
Athenodotos (kalos), 77, 84

Athens 1943, Painter of, 126
Athens, potters' quarter in, 5; Stoa Poikile at, 89; Theseion at, 89; see also: Agora, Athenian; Akropolis; Erechtheion; Kerameikos, Athenian; Nike Balustrade; Parthenon
Athletics, 165 n. 9
Axiopeithes (kalos), 120, 121, 129

BARBOTINE TECHNIQUE, 163
Base, inscribed, from the Akropolis, 42, 43; from Athenian Agora, 175 n. 32
Beazley, J. D., vi, 3, 50, 52, 69, 77, 83, 86, 100, 107, 118, 127, 147, 149, 152, 166 n. 18, 167 n. 22, 169 n. 68, 182 n. 97, 187 n. 58, 191 n. 12, 197 n. 23
Berlin Painter, 3, 16, 66, 68–70, 73, 74, 78, 95, 108, 109, 118, 120, 124, 127, 181 n. 33, 186 n. 15, 191 n. 12; pupils of, 109
Berlin 2268, Painter of, 53
Berlin Hydria, Painter of the, 102
Bieber, Margarete, 185 n. 197
"Bilingual" vases, 47, 49, 50
Binns, Charles F., 27, 28, 33, 34, 170 n. 89, 171 n. 94, 172 n. 114
Black-figure, 75–76
Black-Thyrsos Painter, 158
Bologna 228, Painter of, 110
Bologna 279, Painter of, 102
Bologna 417, Painter of, 100
Bosanquet Painter, 121, 122
Boston, three-sided relief, 64, 106
Bowdoin Painter, 74–75, 182 nn. 96 and 97
Bowdoin-Eye Painter, 53
Bowl, 57, 164, 172 n. 22; libation, 122
Box. See pyxis
Briseis Painter, 87, 88
Brown-Egg Painter, 159
Brussels Oinochoai, Painter of, 189 n. 137
Brussels R330, Painter of, 100
Brygos, 6, 19, 78
Brygos Painter, 3, 16, 62, 66, 76, 78–81, 88, 106, 165 n. 5, 183 n. 136, 183 n. 141; circle of, 87; manner of, 79
Building, in fashioning of vase, 26
Buildings, Periklean, 22; post-Periklean, 22
Buschor, E., 128

CARLSRUHE PAINTER, 114
Cartellino Painter, 83
Cassel Painter, 126–127
Centauromachies, 101, 130, 157
Cerberus Painter, 44
Chairestratos (kalos), 84
Chairias (kalos), 56
Chairis (kalos), 105
Charioteer, mounting, from the Akropolis, 64
Chelis (potter), 49, 53
Chelis Painter, 53
Chicago Painter, 105–106
Choes, 148, 149
Christie Painter, 130
Chronological Data, 16, 43–45, 64–65, 93, 117, 141–142, 156
Chronology, 22–23, 156
Chrysis Painter, 144, 146
Clay, 23, 26, 27, 31, 32, 33, 34, 35; applied, gilded, 63, 92, 116, 155, 161, 163; coils of, 25; fired, 32; preparation of, 24; sedimentary, 24; residual, 24
Cleveland Painter, 109
Clinic Painter, 108
Coghill Painter, 130
Collaboration of two painters, 53, 100, 119, 135
Colmar Painter, 45, 85, 86
Comparisons with painting and sculpture, 42–43, 64, 93, 117, 141, 155
Copenhagen Painter, 72–73
Cow's hoof, cup in form of, 111
Cups, Megarian and Pergamene, 171 n. 94; see also kylix
Cylinder, fragmentary, found in Athenian Agora, 55

DANAE PAINTER, 116, 125; associate of, 126
Danae legend, 110–111
Decoration of the vase, 27–31
Deepdene Painter, 110
Deiniades (potter), 56
Delphi, Lesche at, 89, 131
Delphi, Temple of Apollo, 43
Demokritos, 91, 116
Dexileos, burial plot of, 117, 141–142, 156; death of, 22
Diagoras, 166 n. 10
Dikaios (kalos), 57
Dikaios Painter, 57

Dinos, 144
Dinos Painter, 142, 143–144, 151, 157
Diogenes (kalos), 84
Diogenes Painter, 73
Diokles (kalos), 74
Dionysiac scene, 106, 161
Dionysios of Halikarnassos, 197 n. 42
Diosphos Painter, 75
Diphilos (kalos), 81, 121
Diphilos (kalos), son of Melanopos, 121
Dipinti, 19
Disney Painter, 137
"Document" reliefs, 141, 155
Dokimasia Painter, 88
Double disk, 98
Douris (potter), 83
Douris, 5, 17, 18, 19, 56, 64, 76, 83–85,
    106, 167 n. 25, 178 n. 141
Douris of Samos, 197 n. 21
Dromippos (kalos), son of Dromokleides,
    121
Dutuit Painter, 73
Dwarf Painter, 124

EARLY STYLE, 36–58
Edinburgh Oinochoe, Painter of the,
    137
Egrapsen, 17–18; see also signatures of
    painters (with egrapsen), and under
    artists' names
Eleusis Painter, 45, 77
Elpenor, 129
Emotion, rendering of, 4, 61, 89, 129,
    152
Epeleios (kalos), 53, 121
Epeleios Painter, 53
Ephesos drums, figures on the, 43
Epicharis (kale), 148
Epidauros, akroteria and pediments, 155
Epidromos (kalos), 52, 53
Epidromos Painter, 52
Epigenes (potter), 19, 133
Epiktetos, 5, 17, 18, 19, 44, 48, 49–50, 51,
    65, 66, 174 n. 4, 177 n. 85, 180 n. 10
Epiktetos II, 3, 66; see also under Kleo-
    phrades Painter
Epilykos (kalos), 52
Epoiesen, 16–17; see also signatures of
    potters (with epoiesen) and under
    potters' names
Erbach Painter, 158
Erechtheion, frieze of, 141

Eretria Painter, 117, 132–135, 142, 146,
    148, 169 n. 67
Erothemis (kalos), 85
Ethiop Painter, 113
Euaichme Painter, 107
Euaion (kalos), 107, 123, 129
Euaion Painter, 3, 107
Eualkides (kalos), 57
Eucharides (kalos), 71
Eucharides Painter, 71, 181 nn. 52 and
    53
Euemporos, 150
Euergides (potter), 51
Euergides Painter, 51
Eumares, father of Antenor, 42
Eumaros, 42
Euphronios (potter), 54, 76–77, 85, 99
Euphronios, 5, 15, 17, 19, 53–55, 56,
    57, 77, 167 n. 30, 171 n. 94
Eupolis Painter, 126
Eupompos of Sikyon, 154
Euripides, 163, 174 n. 7
Euthymides, 15, 19, 36, 45, 53, 55–56, 67,
    165 n. 6, 174 n. 6; companion of,
    58; father of, 178 n. 141
Euxitheos (potter), 49
[Euxi]theos (potter), 54
Exekias, 36, 45, 171 n. 94
Expression, contrast in, 110

FAT BOY GROUP, 159
Firing, 31–34
Foreshortening, 2, 5, 38, 42, 43, 48, 49,
    50, 51, 52, 54, 55, 56, 60, 61, 89, 90,
    101, 104, 128, 129, 139, 151, 162,
    163; see also perspective, two di-
    mensional, third dimension, spatial
    relations
Forgery, 87
Foundry Painter, 87
François vase, 21, 133, 174 n. 3
Fraser, A. D., 28
Furniture, 166 n. 11

GALES (potter), 44, 58
Gales Painter, 58
Gallatin Painter, 73
Ganymede, 95–96
Ganymedes (kalos), 148
Gaurion (potter), 152
Geneva Painter, 102
Geras Painter, 72
Glaukon (kalos), 45, 74, 93, 99

Glaukon, son of Leagros, 16, 22, 45, 93;
    see also Leagros, son of Glaukon
Glaze, black, 27–29
Goluchow Painter, 46, 48, 49, 174 n. 6
Gombosi, O., 186 n. 14
Graffiti, 19–21, 169 n. 53
Granger, F., 185 n. 3

HACKL, R., 19
Haimon Painter, 75
Hall, Lindsley F., vi, 166 n. 19
Handles, attachment of, 26–27
Harmodios, 64
Harrow Painter, 72
Haspels, C. H. E., 182 n. 96
Hegesiboulos (potter), 52
Hegesiboulos Painter, 52, 174 n. 6
Hektor Painter, 130
Hephaistos, return of, 133
Heraion Painter, 182 n. 97
Herakles and Busiris, 96–97; in the
    garden of the Hesperides, 147, 159,
    160; strangling the serpents, 97
Herdsman, 111–112
Hermaios (potter), 53
Hermaios Painter, 53
Hermogenes (kalos), 84
Hermogenes Painter, 179 n. 1
Hermonax, 19, 108–109
Heroes, names given to, 14
Herodotos, 166 n. 10, 174 n. 8, 175 n. 32
    184 n. 153, 190 n. 164
Hesiod, 173 n. 149
Hesychius, 196 n. 6
Hieron (potter), 17, 18, 19, 81, 108, 165 n.
    6, 184 n. 151
Hilaron (kalos), 109
Hilinos (potter), 47
Hipparchos, beauty of a, 44; death of,
    36; son of Peisistratos, 44
Hipparchos (kalos), 50, 175, nn. 22–24
Hippodamas (kalos), 83, 84
Hippokrates, 45
Hippokrates (kalos), 47
Hippon (kalos), 74
Hischylos (potter), 50
Hischylos Painter, 50–51, 174 n. 6
Historical background, 36, 59, 89, 115,
    139, 154
Homeric heroes, 48
Homeric "Hymn to Demeter," 123, 124
Household pottery, 166 n. 18
Hussong, 169 n. 69, 172 nn. 113, 114, 120

Hydria, 12, 25, 45, 46, 65, 142, 156; with
    potters at work, 170 n. 73
Hygiainon (kalos), 121
Hylas, 183 n. 120
Hypsis, 57

IKAROS PAINTER, 114
Ilioupersis, 89, 101
Inscription Painter, 114
Inscriptions, 6, 14–21, 22, 42, 50, 57, 63,
    99, 142, 145; meaningless, 19, 180 n.
    10; technique of, 4, 21, 36; see also
    kale names, kalos names, signatures
Isthmodoros (kalos), 107

JAMESON, M., 176 n. 61
Jason, 110
Jena Painter, 158–159; group of, 159
Jug, see oinochoe

KACHRYLION (potter), 45, 49, 54
Kadmos Painter, 146, 160
Kale names, 15, 46, 81, 83, 148, 167 n. 31
Kalliades (potter), 83
Kallias (kalos), 109, 133
Kallikles (kalos), 74, 109
Kalliope Painter, 135
Kalos names, 3, 15–16, 19, 20; see also
    under individual names
Kalpis, 45, 55, 57
Kantharos, 13
Karystios (kalos), 47
Kassandra, 113
Kerameikos, Athenian, 19, 22; fragment
    of bell krater found in, in style of
    Suessula Painter, 142, 151, 156; stele
    in, 114
Kerch Vases, 154, 155, 156, 158, 159–162
Kiln, 33–34, 35
Kimon of Kleonai, 42
Kiss Painter, 45, 52–53
Kleinias (kalos), the son of Pedieus, 121
Kleio Painter, 126
Kleisthenes, 45, 175 n. 24
Kleitias, 21, 36
Kleomales (kalos), 52
Kleomales Painter, 52
Kleon, 166 n. 10
Kleophon (kalos), 143
Kleophon Painter, 142, 143, 144
Kleophrades (potter), 18, 19, 83
Kleophrades Painter, 3, 5, 6, 18, 44, 58,
    66–68, 69, 84, 106, 133; in manner
    of, 180 n. 10

Klügmann Painter, 137–138
Klytaimestra, 163
Knidian Aphrodite, 155, 161
Knuckle-bone vase, 73
Korkyra, document relief of, 155
Kraipale Painter, 136
Krater, 12, 94, 142; cost of, 20
Krater, bell, 11
Krater, calyx, 11, 45, 65, 156, 169 n. 19
Krater, column, 11, 45, 65, 94; handles of, 27
Krater, volute, 11, 45, 65
Kritias, 16
Kodros Painter, 117, 135
Kyathos, 13
Kylichnis, 13, 166 n. 19; see also pyxis
Kylix, 11, 13, 17, 32, 33, 45, 48, 49, 65, 76, 93, 94, 152, 156, 157, 164, 166 n. 17

LACHES (kalos), 85
Lamb's head, cup in form of, 110
Lapiths and centaurs, 102–103
Leagros, 15, 16, 45, 93; see also Glaukon, son of Leagros
Leagros, son of Glaukon, 45, 175 nn. 32 and 33
Leagros (kalos), 45, 53, 54, 55, 65, 77
Lebes, 11, 12; see also Nuptial vase
Lebes gamikos. See Nuptial vase
Lekanis, 13, 142, 156
Lekythos, 13, 73, 93, 94, 139, 142, 152, 156; cost of, 20; sepulchral, 152–153; white-ground, 152–153, 155
Leningrad Painter, 96
Lewis Painter (Polygnotos), 3, 18, 112, 127, 132
Lichas (kalos), 108, 121
Little-Master cup, 17, 45, 48, 175 n. 37a
London 106, Painter of, 152
London D14, Painter of, 136
London E100, Painter of, 110
London E342, Painter of, 109
London E497, Painter of, 125, 126
Loutrophoros, 13
Louvre CA 1694, Painter of, 107
Louvre Centauromachy, Painter of, 130
Ludovisi three-sided relief, 64
Lydos, 36, 133
Lykaon Painter, 3, 128–129
Lykos (kalos), 85
Lykourgos, 175 n. 24
Lyons kore, 43

Lysias, 6, 145
Lysikles (kalos), 177 n. 92
Lysippian statues, 155
Lysippides (kalos), 46, 175 n. 43
Lysippides Painter, 175 n. 43
Lysippos, 2, 155
Lysis (kalos), 85, 99
Lysis, Laches, and Lykos group, 85

MAGNONCOURT PAINTER, 86
Makron, 16, 17, 19, 62, 64, 65, 66, 76, 81–83, 108, 165 n. 5, 178 n. 141, 184 n. 148; pupil of, 108; school of, 107
Mannheim Painter, 124–125
Marathon mound, 64
Marlay Painter, 132
"Maussolos" of Halikarnassos, 162
Medon, father of Hieron, 108
Megakles, 45
Megakles (kalos), 45, 55, 56, 143
Megakles (potter), 99
Meidias Painter, 3, 19, 117, 134, 142, 146–148, 149; manner of, 141, 148–149, 156
Melanippos, 131–132
Melas (kalos), 55
Meleager Painter, 157
Meletos (kalos), 121
Meletos Painter. See Achilles Painter
Melitta (kale), 83
Memnon (kalos), 44, 49
Menander, 2
Menelaos Painter, 126
Menon (kalos), 47, 84
Menon Painter. See Psiax
Methyse Painter, 3, 106
Mikion (potter), 19, 149
Mikon, 5, 89, 94, 100, 115
Milne, Marjorie J., vi, 165 nn. 7 and 8, 166 n. 10, 167 n. 27, 174 n. 18, 185 n. 3
Miltiades, 16, 44, 174 n. 21
Miltiades (kalos), 44
Mina Painter, 152
Minto, A., 169 n. 54
Mnesilla (kale), 46
Molding, 26
Molon, archonship of, 155
Mouret Painter, 152
Mourners, 7, 113, 114, 121, 122, 134, 141, 152, 153
Mousaios, 147

Munich 2335, Painter of, 121–122
Munich 2363, Painter of, 113
Munich 2660, Painter of, 107
Munich 2661, Painter of, 107
Munich 2662, Painter of, 107
Musical scenes, 7, 49, 125, 128, 129, 136, 137, 145, 147
Myron's Athena, 101, 117
Myrrhiniske (kale), 148
Myson (potter), 71
Myson, 16, 17, 71, 94
Mythological subjects, 165 n. 9; see also under subjects

NAMES. See inscriptions
Naples Painter, 130
Nauklea (kale), 83
Nausikaa Painter (Polygnotos), 18, 97, 127
Nearchos, 36
Nekyia, 89, 130, 131
Nekyia Painter, 130–131
Neoptolemos, departure of, 128
New York, statue from South Italy, in, 101
New York Centauromachy, Painter of, 157
Nike Balustrade, 141, 146
Nikias of Athens, 154
Nikias Painter, 150
Nikomas (kalos), 128
Nikon (kalos), 146
Nikon Painter, 93, 109
Nikophile (kale), 81
Nikosthenes (potter), 50, 53
Nikosthenes Painter, 53
Nikoxenos (kalos), 70
Nikoxenos Painter, 70–71, 181 n. 47
Niobid Painter, 100, 101, 104, 127; school of, 151; manner of, 101
Nuptial vase, lebes gamikos, 13, 112, 130, 136, 137, 150

ODYSSEUS AND ELPENOR, 129
Offerings, dedicatory, found on the Akropolis, 6
Oiniades, 197 n. 19
Oinochoe, 13, 73, 152, 156
Oinomaos, 159
Oinomaos Painter, 158
Oionokles (kalos), 109
Oionokles Painter, 109
Oionos, 183 n. 120
Okeanos, 159

Oltos, 44, 48–49, 53, 58, 167 n. 24
Olympia sculptures, 90, 93, 101, 103
Olynthos, plate found at, 156
Onesimos, 19, 77, 85
Onos, 133
Orchard Painter, 110
Orestes, 163
Ornaments, 10, 166 n. 14
Ornate Style of the Fourth Century, 156, 157–158
Orpheus and the Thracians, 125–126, 129–130
Orpheus Painter, 129–130
Oxford Grypomachy, Painter of, 158

PAIDIKOS (potter), 51
Painters, mural and panel, 5, 5a, 89, 127, 139, 154
Painters, signatures of. See signatures
Painting, 29–31; monumental, 1, 5, 8; mural, 1, 4, 6, 42, 56, 59, 93, 100; on marble stelai, 42; on terracotta slabs, 42; panel, 1, 4, 42, 56, 59, 93, 115, 139, 165 n. 2
Pamphaios (potter), 49, 50, 53
Pan Painter, 94–96, 97, 110, 129
Panaitios (kalos), 65, 76, 77, 84, 85, 86
Panaitios Painter, 6, 16, 45, 54, 65, 76–78, 81, 84, 85, 86, 159; circle of, 85, 86
Panathenaia, 145
Panathenaic vases, 11, 19, 22, 36; see also amphora, Panathenaic
Panels, wooden, from near Sikyon, 59, 165 n. 2
Paris Gigantomachy, Painter of, 87–88
Parrhasios of Ephesos, 139
Parthenon sculptures, 103, 115, 117, 122, 123, 126, 132, 191 n. 5
Pasiades, 17, 51
Patroklos, 134
Pausanias, 89, 101, 131, 197 nn. 20 and 22
Pausias of Sikyon, 154
Pedieus, 121
Peirithoos. See Perithous
Peisistratos, 1, 36, 44, 175 n. 23
Peisistratids, 36, 46
Peithinos, 52
Peleus, 101
Peleus Painter, 130
Pelike, 45, 94, 156
Pelops, 159
Penelope Painter, 3, 132

Penthesileia Painter, 69, 92, 94, 97–99, 100, 110, 128; school of, 100
Periklean buildings, 22; sculpture, 118, 122
Perithous, feast of, 102–103
Persephone, return of, 123–124, 132
Persephone Painter, 3, 123–124, 132
Persian debris, 65
Perspective, 90–91, 116, 135, 139, 140, 154, 158, 196 nn. 11 and 12; see also foreshortening, two-dimensional, third dimension, spatial relations
Pheidiades (kalos), 57
Pheidippos, 48, 50
Phiale, 11; see also bowl, libation
Phiale Painter, 122–123
Philiades (kalos), 55
Philoktetes, 134, 183 n. 120
Philon (kalos), 81
Phintias (potter), 56
Phintias, 6, 15, 17, 19, 45, 53, 56
Phrynichos, 166 n. 10
Pig Painter, 96
Pinax, Corinthian, 172 n. 120
Pindar, 2, 6, 49, 97
Pistoxenos (potter), 50
Pistoxenos (kalos), son of Aresandros, 121
Pistoxenos Painter, 54, 93, 99, 114
Plaoutine, N., 190 n. 154
Plaque, votive, 45, 52
Plate, 164
Plato, 6, 15, 140, 145, 166 n. 10, 167 nn. 32 and 33, 196 n. 10
Pliny, 42, 154, 196 nn. 4 and 5
Plutarch, 196 n. 7
Polion, 144–146
Pollias, father of Euthymides, 55, 178 n. 141
Pollias (sculptor), 178 n. 141
Polydektes Painter, 127
Polygnotos, 5, 18, 19, 97, 112, 117, 127–128; group of, 142, 143, 144; see also Lewis Painter, Nausikaa Painter
Polygnotos II. See Lewis Painter
Polygnotos of Thasos, 89, 94, 100, 115, 127, 131
Polyphrasmon (kalos), 84
Pompe ("Procession"), 161
Pordax (kalos), 46
Poseidon, 159
Pothos Painter, 146
Potteries, Athenian, 35, 42

Potters, 3, 5, 6, 11, 16, 17, 33, 48–49, 50, 52, 53, 73, 102, 163, 169 n. 69, 170 n. 73; at work, 23, 35, 170 n. 73; dedications by, 165 n. 6; see also under individual names
Praxiteles, 2, 155, 161
Praxiteles (kalos), 83
Priam, death of, 70–71
Proklos, 190 n. 171
Pronomos, Theban Musician, 22, 142, 151, 156, 197 nn. 18 and 23
Pronomos Painter, 142, 143, 150–151, 156
Prosagoreuo, group of alabastra inscribed, 51
Protagoras, 166 n. 10
Prothesis, 110
Providence Painter, 3, 74, 93, 182 n. 91; follower of, 109
Psiax, 3, 46–48, 49, 51
Psykter, 12, 45
Pythaios (kalos), 84
Python (potter), 50, 83
Pyxis, 93, 142, 152, 166 n. 19; see also kylichnis

Q PAINTER, 159
Quintus Smyrnaeus, 71

RAM'S HEAD, cup in form of, 111
Record reliefs. See "document" reliefs
Red ocher application, 28–29
Reed Painter, 153
Reichhold, K., 171 n. 97, 172 n. 120
Relief, details in, 32; objects in, 31
Relief vases. See Vases with reliefs
Relief Ware, Hellenistic, 164
Religious subjects, 165 n. 9; see also subjects
Replica, 87, 149
Retorted Painter, 158
Rhodopis (kale), 83
Richmond Painter, 127
Robinson, Maude, vi, 169 n. 69

SABOUROFF PAINTER, 112–113, 119; in manner of, 113–114
Sakonides, 179 n. 1
Santayana, G., 9
Sappho Painter, 75–76
Schoolboys, 107
Schumann, Theodor, 27, 170
Sculpture, Greek, scenes from, copied on vases, 117

Selinus, metope from, 54; Temple C of, 174 n. 9
Shading, 4, 115, 116, 139, 161
Shapes, 10–14, 45, 65, 93–94, 117, 156
Shuvalov Painter, 137, 196 n. 15
Signatures, 3, 6, 16–19, 21, 43, 66, 180 n. 10; double, 17; of painters (with egrapsen), 17, 18, 46, 48, 49, 50, 51, 52, 53, 54, 55, 56, 57, 66, 71, 77, 81, 83, 85, 97, 108, 112, 127, 144, 145, 149, 178 n. 130; of potters (with epoiesen), 17, 46, 49, 51, 52, 53, 54, 55, 56, 57, 58, 66, 71, 73, 76, 77, 81, 82, 83, 89, 99, 108, 111, 138, 146, 149, 152, 157; see also under individual names
Simonides, 2
Siphnian Treasury, reliefs from, 2, 22, 43
Skopas, 2, 155
Skyphos, 13, 94, 156
Skythes, 6, 52, 165 n. 8
Smikrion (kalos), 47
Smikros, 19, 56–57
Smikythos (kalos), 55
Smith, H. R. W., vi
Sokrates, 16
Sophanes (kalos), 131
Sosias (potter), 19, 57
Sosias Painter, 57
Sostratos (kalos), 56
Sotades (potter), 111
Sotades Painter, 19, 111–112, 171 n. 74
Spatial Relations, 2, 101, 126, 129, 139, 140, 142; see also foreshortening, perspective, third dimension, two-dimensional
Spellings, non-Attic, 6
Splanchnopt Painter, 100
Stacking, 28, 33
Stamnos, 17, 32, 45, 65, 94
Stand, 57, 85, 86, 150
Statue bases, in Athens, 43
Stencils, 10, 30
Stesagoras, 174 n. 21
Straggly Painter, 152
Street scenes, 128
Subjects, 5, 7–9, 165 n. 9
Suessula Painter, 143, 150, 151; style of, 142
Syleus Painter, 72
Syracuse Painter, 109

Syriskos (potter), 73
Syriskos Painter, 72–73, 189 n. 150

Talos Painter, 143, 150
Technique, 23–35, 63–64, 92–93, 116–117, 141, 155; white-ground, 113, 116; see also analysis, technical and stylistic
Telephos, 163
Telephos Painter, 107–108
Tex, J. den, 180 n. 10
Thaliarchos Painter, 51
Thamyris and the Muses, 147
Thanatos Painter, 121, 122
Theatrical subjects, 166 n. 9; see also subjects
Themistokles, 175 n. 33
Theognis, 167 n. 25
Theseus, 87, 159
Theseus Painter, 75
Thetis, 101
Third dimension, 2, 10, 36, 56, 63, 68, 90, 127, 129, 139, 163; see also foreshortening, perspective, spatial relations; two-dimensional
Thorvaldsen Group, 86
Throwing, in fashioning of vase, 24–25
Thucydides, 175 n. 32
Timagoras, 43
Tithonos Painter, 73–74
Tleson (potter), 49
Toilet box, 98, 166 n. 19; see also pyxis
Tomb of Lacedaemonians. See Kerameikos, Athenian
Tomb offerings, 113, 121, 122
Tomb paintings. Etruscan, 59
Triglyph Painter, 153
Triptolemos, 73
Triptolemos Painter (Douris), 18, 83, 184 n. 158
Troilos Painter, 73
Trophy Painter, 131
Turning, 25–26
Two-dimensional designs, 2, 5, 37, 56, 63, 129, 147, 163; see also foreshortening, perspective, spatial relations, third dimension
Tydeus, 131–132
Tymbos Painter, 114
Tyrannicides, 117, 179 n. 2
Tyszkiewicz Painter, 73

VASES, ATHENIAN, names of, 14; Dipylon, 28; fashioning of, 24–27; molded, 26, 111; plastic, 26, white-ground, 27, 31, 42, 75, 93, 123, 134, 141, 152–153; with reliefs, 155, 157, 162–164
Vienna Painter, 57
Vienna 116, Painter of, 159
Vienna 155, Painter of, 159
Vienna 202, Painter of, 159
Villa Giulia Painter, 104–105, 106, 124; school of, 106
Vitruvius, 90, 185 n. 3
Vouni Painter, 114

WASHING PAINTER, 136–137
Wedding Painter, 100
Well-groups, 175
Wells, vases dumped in, 45
Wheel work, 24–26

Wilhelm, A., 180 n. 10
Woman Painter, manner of, 153
Woolly Silens, Painter of the, 101–102
Worst Painter, 152

XENOKRATES, 174 n. 13
Xenon (kalos), 55, 135
Xenophantos (potter), 19
Xenophantos Painter, 157, 169 n. 60
Xenophon, 6, 32, 41, 167
Xenotimos, 19
Xenotimos Painter, 138

YALE LEKYTHOS, Painter of the, 93, 109
Yale Oinochoe, Painter of the, 109
Yale University Press, vi

ZEPHYROS PAINTER, 112
Zeuxis, 5, 139, 140, 154